美中區抗日戰爭史實維護會

THE RAPE OF BIOLOGICAL WARFARE

細菌戰大屠殺

The Rape of Biological Warfare
細菌戰大屠殺

Author
撰著

James Yin

尹集鈞

Editors & Translators   Anna Fan   Eugene Wei   Guo Cisong
編譯   范薇薇   魏樂   郭嗣嵩

James Yin
尹集鈞

The Members of the Japanese Biological Warfare Crimes Investigation
Committee: Gilbert Chang, Han Xiao, Sha Bilu ,Chen Zuliang ,
Victor Yung, Rock Cheuk, Pei Jiaqin, Oris Chiu ,James Eng, James Yin.
日軍細菌戰罪行調查小組委員會成員：
張培、韓曉、沙泌路、陳祖梁、容鴻、裴家勤、吳中信、
仇明倫、卓壽石、 尹集鈞.

Artistic Design: Karen Hon Yin
美術設計: 吳虹

Northpole Light Publishing House

San Francisco

This book is dedicated in mourn with deep grief of all the people and Allied Forces soldiers killed by Japanese biological warfare in Asia during 1932-1950

謹以此書悼念死難于日軍細菌攻擊下的亞洲善良父老和盟軍戰士（1932-1950）

勘 誤 表

頁 數	段 數	行 數	錯 誤	更 正
169	2	2	多字aten	去掉aten
179	4	2	帶民衆逃亡	帶菌民衆逃亡
180	1	3	profissor	professor
186	1	1	The Germ	The germ
186	最后1段	4	12th and	12th A. and
193	1	1	1940-1942	1941-1942
195	倒數3段	2	裏	里
195	倒數3段	3	二十人	二十人"
198			Name	County
206	13	1	Chapter co The Death	/
230	最后1段	1	細菌攻擊記録	/
231	2	2	moutains	mountains
231			日軍爲切斷中國東南戰役	日軍爲切斷中國東南戰綫
240	2	4	57	59
240	2	5	57	59
243			"ANNOTATIONS" P.332-P	"ANNOTATIONS" P.332-P.334
244	下圖		我在僞滿醫笠	我在僞滿醫科
244	下圖		Nanman Medicine	Nanman Dedical
267	最后1段	1	"大明報",	"大明報":
267	最后1段	2	新聞	所聞
270			plague were 25,089 death	plague were 25,089 people death
284	1	4	suggestsd	suggested
284	4	1	attacks.OF	attacks.
284	最后1段	2	Kwangtun	Kwantung
285	7	1	攻擊説	攻擊説
286	倒數3段	1	Tienwei Wn	Tienwei Wu
286	倒數2段	1	Arp.	Apr.
287			石光重	石光熏
290			北野正次	北野政次
291			篠田統	篠田統
292			Yoshimura東京帝大衛生學教授吉村的照片	移到P.326
311			篠甲統Subesu Shinoda	篠田統Sasada Osamu
感謝			沈珍寶夫妇	沈槇保夫婦

CONTENTS(目録)

"New York Times"

"紐約時報"

"Japan Confronting Gruesome
War Atrocity"(Extracts)

日本面對殘酷的戰爭罪行（摘録）

Introduction

前言

The New York Times

National Edition
Midwest: Southern Great Lakes,
cooler. Ohio Valley, continued warm.
Chance of severe thunderstorms late
in western Nebraska and western
Kansas. Weather map is on page A10.

Printed in Chicago   ONE DOLLAR

FRIDAY, MARCH 17, 1995

Copyright © 1995, The New York Times

Japan Confronting Gruesome War Atrocity

Unmasking Horror

By NICHOLAS D. KRISTOF

MORIOKA, Japan — He is a cheerful old farmer who jokes as he serves rice cakes made by his wife, and then he switches easily ... ... it is like to cut ... ... who is tied ...

A trickle of information about the program has turned into a stream and now a torrent. Half a century after the end of the war, a rush of books, documentaries and exhibitions are unlocking the past and helping arouse interest in Japan in the atrocities committed by some of Japan's most distinguished doctors.

Scholars and former members of the unit say that at least 3,000 people — by some accounts several times as many — were killed in the medical experiments; none survived. No one knows how many died in the "field testing."

It is becoming evident that the Japanese officers in charge of the

Japan's germ warfare research unit was near Harbin, China.

program hoped to use their weapons against the United States. They proposed using balloon bombs to carry disease to America, and they had a plan in the summer of 1945 to use kamikaze

A special report.

ing and after World War II: a vast project to develop weapons of biological warfare, including plague, ... and a dozen oth-... Japanese pilots to dump plague-infected fleas on San Diego.

The research was kept secret after the end of World War II in part because the United States Army granted immunity from war crimes prosecution to the doctors in exchange for their research data. Japanese and American documents show that the United States helped cover up the human experimentation. Instead of putting the ringleaders on trial it gave them stipends.

The accounts are wrenching to read even after so much time has passed: a Russian mother and daughter left in a gas chamber, for example, as doctors peered through thick glass and timed their convulsions, watching as the woman sprawled over her child in a futile effort to save her from the gas.

horrible. This ... work for the surgeons ... ly left an impression on me ... just ... war balloon cause it was my first time."

Finally, the old man, who insisted on anonymity, explained the reason for the vivisection: the prisoner, who was Chinese, had been deliberately infected with the plague, as part of a research project, the full horror of which is only now emerging, to develop plague bombs for use in World

War II. After infecting him, the researchers decided to cut him open to see what the disease does to a man's inside.

That research program was one of the great secrets of Japan dur-

It is becoming ... Japanese officers in c...

Continued on Page A4, Column 1

... Wartime Atrocity

JAPAN CONFRONTING GRUESOME WAR ATROCITY (Extracts)

"New York Times", March 17,1995

"A trickle of information about the program has turned into a stream and now a torrent. Half a century after the end of the war, a rush of books, documentaries and exhibitions are unlocking the past and helping arouse interest in Japan in the atrocities committed by some of Japan's most distinguished doctors."

"Scholars and former numbers of the unit say that at least 3,000 people –by some accounts several times as many-were killed in the medical experiments; none survived. No one knows how many died in the field testing."

"It is becoming evident that the Japanese officers in charge of the program hoped to use their weapons against the United States. They proposed using balloon bombs to carry disease to America, and they had a plan in the summer of 1945 to use kamikaze pilots to dump plague-infected fleas on San Diego."

"The accounts are wrenching to read even after so much time has passed: a Russian mother and her daughter left in a gas chamber, for example, as doctors peered through thick glass and timed their convulsions, watching as the woman sprawled over her child in a futile effort to save her from the gas."

(By Nicholas D. Kristof)

"紐約日報"評論

日本面對殘酷的戰爭罪行（摘録）

尼古拉·克雷斯托夫(一九九五年三月十七日)

"關于日本細菌戰工程的消息，過去祇有點滴的泄露，現在逐漸滔滔不絶地源源而出。戰爭結束了半個世紀，書籍、原始文件、實物展覽如潮水般涌出，打開了禁錮的鎖鏈，有助于在日本引起對這些最著名的醫生所犯的暴行的興趣。"

"學者和前"七三一部隊"的成員説至少有三千人—有些人説幾倍于此數—在人體實驗室中被毀掉，沒有生還的。"實地試驗"造成的死亡人數更無法計算。"

"現在已經明顯地證明，日本負責細菌戰制造的官員企圖用他們的武器對付美國，建議用氣球炸彈把細菌帶到美國。他們于一九四五年夏天制造了一項由"神風"駕駛員把感染鼠疫的跳蚤投擲于聖地亞哥城的計劃。"
在戰後，日本細菌戰的研究被保持秘密，部分原因是美國陸軍赦免這些醫生按戰犯追究，以其研究資料作爲交換。日本和美國的文件都明顯的隱瞞人體實驗。本應將這些禍首繩之以法，美國陸軍反倒給他們退休金。

"雖然時過甚久，這些記載仍使人不忍卒讀：一個俄國的母親和她的女兒被放在毒瓦斯室裏，日本醫生們從厚厚的玻璃外觀察她們痙攣的情形，看到那個母親爬到她孩子身上，妄圖從瓦斯氣下拯救幼小的生命。"

INTRODUCTION

Since the end of World War II, the Japanese biological warfare has been placed under a blanked of secrecy. Regarding the scope of the biological warfare, the Khabarovsk Trial in 1949 has shown that the Japanese Army had deployed special units to prepare and conduct germ wars. Fourty Three years later, in 1992, Peter Williams and David Wallace revisited the issue in their book "Unit 731: Japan's Secret Biological Warfare in World War II". They concluded that for "Unit 731" in the Japanese Imperial Army, the main purpose was to develop and use biological weapon during WW II. So just as shown by the Khabarovsk Trial, the authors have determined that biological warfare was the "intention" and "plan" and application by special units. Note that the word "preparation" was placed before "application", rendering "application" secondary in significance.

In 1994 celebrated prof. Sheldon H. Harris published the book "Factories of Death: Japanese Biological Warfare 1932-1945 and the American Cover-up". He covered the first biological assault, but still concluded that the Japanese biological warfare was the limited and localized activities of a few special units.

Between 1993 and 1994, the exhibitions held by the Citizens Committee on "Unit 731" was effective in affirming the four biological assaults launched by the Japanese. These are the ones in Nomanhan (1939), Ningbo (1940), Changde (1941) and Zhejiang-Jiangxi(1942).

In 1997 after further studies , Harris agreed that the scope of the biological warfare was much broader. When interviewed by Shaw Den of Sing Tao Daily , Harris made an adjustment and indicated that Japanese biological attacks had involved at least ten cities.

In the same year, following their earlier investigations in China, the coalition of lawyers to assist Chinese in their law suits revealed for the first time in Japan a map showing the Japanese offensives in 76 countries and cities in China. This discovery obsoleted the earlier misunderstanding that the scope of Japanese B.W. was just limited to "intention" and "preparation".

Recently more reports from further investigations have appeared. The Alliance for Preserving the Truth of Sion-Japanese War and the Japanese Biological Warfare Crimes Investigation Committee have also conducted several site visits.

Results of these investigations have proven that the Japanese B.W. had involved the entire Japanese Army. The basis for such a startling conclusion is as follows:

1. In 1944 among the 70 Divisions in the Japanese army, 60 were equipped with the special units for biological warfare-"Epidemic Prevention and Water Supply Unit"① In 1943, only 39 Divisions had these special units.② In 1941, 18 divisions had these special units.③

2. Live dissections and live experiments were practiced throughout the entire Japanese Army.

The cruel acts of live dissections were routine activities among Japanese army field hospital by 1944.

The Japanese military physician Kanisawa Herikuda who had performed live dissections on 14 Chinese admitted, "All the army physicians had conducted live dissections, numbering in tens of thousands". ④

According to the archives in the Japanese P.O.W. camps (after 1945) in Taiyuan and in Fushun, 49 Japanese military professionals and testified to the crimes of direct participation of live dissections between 1945 and 1955. These individuals worked in various Japanese army hospitals, including army physicians in the Red Cross hospital

前 言

二戰結束後，日軍細菌戰一直被神秘所籠罩。對于細菌戰的規模，一九四九年"伯力審判"裁定爲"建立特種部隊來準備和進行細菌戰"。一九九二年，即"伯力審判"後四十三年，彼得·威廉斯、大衛·瓦雷斯在其《七三一部分： 第二次世界大戰中的日本細菌戰》一書中認爲"日本帝國陸軍七三一部隊的故事，是在第二次世界大戰中，唯一爲人所知的主要企圖把制造的細菌武器配發在戰爭中使用；與"伯力審判"一樣，將日軍細菌戰定性爲特種部隊所進行的"企圖"和"準備和使用"。（請注意，"準備"在前，"使用"在後，使用已是次要的了。）

一九九四年著名的美國加州北山大學哈立斯教授，對日軍細菌戰進行大量研究後所出版的專著，書名爲《殺人工廠》，雖然例舉了日軍的幾次細菌攻擊，但仍認定日軍細菌祇限于"殺人工廠"屬于少數特種部隊的局部行爲。

一九九三年至一九九五年有影響的"日本七三一展"，確認日軍進行四次細菌作戰，即諾門罕（1939）、寧波（1940）、常德（1941）和浙贛綫（1942）。

一九九七年哈立斯進一步研究後判定日軍細菌戰的規模擴大了。他在接受《星島日報》記者邵丹的訪問時，修訂説：日軍細菌攻擊"至少十幾個城市"。

同年，東京律師援華控訴圖成員在中國調查後，首次在日本披露一張日軍對華76個縣市進行細菌攻擊的地圖，從而推翻了日軍細菌戰規模祇限于"企圖"、"準備"的論點。

而今，更多的調查報告陸續出現，美國"抗日史實維護會"和美國"日軍細菌戰罪行調查小組委員會"也多次進行實地調查。查證的結果，能夠斷定日軍細菌戰規模已擴大到日本全部陸軍。

作此驚人判斷的主要依據是：

一、 一九四四年日本陸軍七十個作戰師團中，配備有細菌作戰的特種部隊—防疫給水部的，有六十六個師團。①而一九四三年是三十九個師團配備有這種特種部隊，②一九三八年則是十八個師團有這一部隊。③

二、活體解剖和活體試驗推廣到全軍

活體解剖的殘酷行徑，一九四四年已成爲全日本陸軍軍醫的慣行作業。曾以活活將14個中國人解剖致死的日軍軍醫湯淺謙承認，"非常多的軍醫，護士和衛生兵都參加過活體解剖手術，也許是幾萬人。"④

根據"太原戰俘管理所"和"撫順戰俘管理所"的檔案，已查知有四十九人于一九四五年至一九五五年間供認直接參與過活體解剖罪行，這些供認人服務于各地的日本陸軍醫院，甚至供職于"紅十字醫院"的軍醫，也從事這一罪惡勾當。

活體試驗範圍，則早已越過特種部隊的電網，泛濫到各日軍部隊。山東省濟南市日軍第十二軍"中國戰俘營"— 日稱"新華院"，活體試驗致死的人數不下一千。⑤山西省大同市口泉的"平旺礦工醫院"（屬日軍第一軍），一九四六年在接收時，發現有六千多具不滿周歲的中國嬰兒尸體藏于該院地下密室。⑥

三、細菌生產能力的擴大，遠遠超過特種部隊的需要。一九四四年日軍除了在哈爾濱平房"七三一本部"完成新的細菌生產綫外，又在中朝過境山區開建另一個"平房"基地。

一九四五年四月份，單平房就有四千五百臺跳蚤繁殖機在二十四小時運轉。有近三百萬老鼠在强化飼養，爲完成石井生產20億個鼠疫跳蚤的命令而忙碌。至同年八月九日平房奉命炸毀時，已儲備四百公斤的乾化細菌（日軍平房炸毀人增田知真語），不論二十億鼠疫跳蚤或四百公斤乾化細菌，都足夠消滅整個人類。

四、細菌武器的使用，已跳過戰術攻擊，進入戰略攻擊，成爲日本陸軍重要的戰略之一。

如果把一九四零年至一九四五年間日軍進行的細菌攻擊點連接起來，制成一份攻擊地圖，將可以使人看到日軍已經把細菌攻擊作爲重要的戰略在應用。

例如對黄河河套，山西省西部等的多次鼠疫攻擊（如下圖），範圍擴及一十三個縣，構成沿黄河走向的細菌死亡帶，以防阻中共軍隊的第八路軍東進：

正是戰略攻防的要求，日軍細菌攻擊次數已大幅上升至161次，攻擊一百九十個縣市，對一些戰略要則反復進行多次細菌攻擊，如對常德，一九四一年、一九四二年兩次鼠疫空投外，又播放霍亂。如對浙江省的麗水，一九四零年一九四四年共進行五次細菌投放,志在完全消滅重點城鎮的民衆。

本書就沿着一九三零年日本開始細菌戰研究到一九四五年大規模細菌進攻的全過程，進行深入的調查研究,來理清日軍在二戰時期細菌戰罪行的深度,還原被掩蓋長達半個多世紀的秘密。

The scope of live experiments has been known for a long time to have gone beyond the special units and had reached all Japanese troops. In the earlier Chinese P.O.W. camp under the Japanese 12th Army in Jinan city, Shandong province, the number that had died from live dissections was at least a thousand.⑤In 1946 during the takeover of the Pinhuang Miners Hospital in Koutsuen, Datong, Shanxi (Belong to Japanese, 1st Army), more than 6 thousand dead bodies of Chinese babies, all less than a year old, were found in the secret rooms in the basement.⑥

3. The expansion of the bacteriological assaults was way beyond the initial plans of the special units in 1944 besides completing the germ production line at Pinfang, Harbin by "Unit 731", the Japanese also building another concentration camp near the border of China and Korea.

In April 1945 in Pinfang, there were 4,500 machines running 24 hrs a day for the breeding of fleas. There were 3,000,000 rats undergoing fortified feeding. These were kept busy to meet order of General Ishii in the production of 2,000,000,000 fleas for bubonic plague. On August 9 of the same year, when Pingfan was ordered to be destroyed by explosives, there was already 400 kg of freeze-dried germ, each one was more than enough to wipe out the entire human race!

4. The use of biological weapons had already exceeded the stage of selected experimented attacks and had entered the stage of strategic assaults, and had become an important method of destruction in the Japanese army.

If one links the sites of biological attacks launched by the Japanese army during WWII(1942 and 1944) to construct a map showing their distribution, one can see that the Japanese army had adopted biological assaults for operational use in important battle strategies.

For example, the Yellow River Region (Hetao),west Shanxi: Numerous plaque B.W.attacks . The scope reached 13 counties, creating death from germ infection along the river, and impeded the eastward movement of Mao's communist army.

To meet these strategic needs, the frequency of Japanese biological attacks was greatly increased to a total of 161 times including 190 counties in China and Burma . In some major strategic locations, the germ attacks were repeated numbers times. For example, in Changde, in addition to the aerial dropping of plague germs in 1941and 1942, cholera germs was also dispersed in 1942. Between 1940 and 1944, plague germs were dropped Lishui, Zhejiang province at least five times.

The map of Japanese B.W. attacks for
impeded the eastward movement of Moa's army
日軍爲防堵中共軍隊東進的細菌攻擊圖

Japanese occupied areas
日占區

Japan's germ attacked area
日軍細菌攻擊區

The base of CPC
中共根據地

Japanese germ attacked on
1941 Hegu
1942 Hegu, Wuyuan, Nanxian, Xinxian,
　　　Desheng, Baotou, Sutaimiao, Fugu,
　　　Hexi, Boade, Wuling, Dengkou,
Dongshen,

日軍攻擊記録：

1941年 河曲（鼠疫）
1942年 河曲、嵐縣、興縣、得勝、包頭、
蘇臺廟、府谷、五原、河西、保德、五臨、
磴口、東勝

Notes:
① For details, please refer to " The map of arrangement of Japanese B.W. units" in Chapter I.
② "Unit 731 Exhibition", Japan.
③ Ishii's own words in 1938.
④ Confessed by Kanɪsawa Herikuda on Nov. 20, 1954. The Central Archives of China, Beiging.
⑤ "The Japanese B.W. 2'nd unit in China" , "Central Daily News", Korea, July 21, 1989.
⑥ Chanying "Past Impression", P.268-269,No.1, China Social Publishing House, 1998.

注譯
①　、　詳見本書第一章,"一九四四年日軍細菌戰部隊分布圖"。
②　、　日本"七三一部隊展"。
③　、　石井四郎談話,一九三八年。
④　、　湯淺謙供詞,一九五四年十一月二十日
⑤　、　韓國"中央日報"一九八九年七月二十一日"日軍在中國的第二支細菌戰部隊"。
⑥　、　成鷹"老印象、鬼子兵制造的慘案"第一輯、第268-269頁,中國社會出版社,1998年版。

CHAPTER 1
THE ROUTE TO CRIMES

第一章
罪惡之路

1930

Ishii Shiro came back from Europe he completed the investegations of biololgical weapons.

Water filtration truck designed by Ishii.

Ishii Shiro
石井四郎

Water filtration truck
過濾供水車

General Nagata, Ishii's supporter
永田鐵山（日本陸軍省軍務局長）

一九三零年

石井四郎在永田鐵山支持下，完成歐洲細菌武器的考察歸來使石井自1925年開始研究細菌戰的工作向前推動了一大步。石井發明軍用濾水車。

1932

The Japanese Medical School of Army Surgeons where the research of biological weapons starts.

After "Sep. 18 Event" of 1931, Japanese Kwantung Army occupied Northeast of China and established "Unit Togo" in Beiyinhe, Wuchang county, Heilongjiang province for biological warfare researchs, managed by Ishii, Kiyoshi Ota is the assistant.

Live human experiments was conducted also in Sankeshu (Bingjiang railway station)

The Japanese Medical School of Army Surgeons
日本陸軍軍醫學校

Culture of Bacteria
細菌培養

Epidemic Prevention Section
防疫研究室

4

These Two Foreign skulls is a part of human bones discovered under the ground of The Japanses Medical School of Army Surgeons (Tokyo) in July, 1989.

這是一九八九年七月在東京原陸軍軍醫學校地下發現的大批外國人骨中的兩具頭骨。

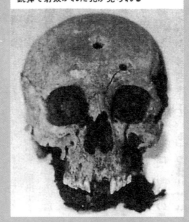

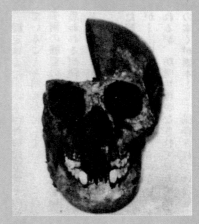

旧陸軍軍医学校跡地で発掘された頭蓋骨
L字形に切り取られたり、
銃弾で射抜かれた孔が見られる

The site of "Unit Togo"

"東鄉部隊" 遺地

石井在一九三二年給東京上司報告稱："在您的幫助下，我們已在細菌研究上獲得很大進展，開始實驗階段業已成熟，敬希把我們的人員派往滿州國去開發新的武器。"

Ishii reported to his superious in Tokyo in 1931 that "due to your great help we have allready achieved a greatd deal in our bactelia research. It's time We start to experiment. We appeal to be send to Manchukuo to develop new weapons". (Dong Shenyu "The Unit 731 0f Japanese Kwantung Army")

一九三二年

日本陸軍軍醫學校開始研究細菌戰。

"九一八事件" 後，日本關東軍占領中國東北，在黑龍江省五常縣的背陰河設立 "東鄉部隊"，用活人試驗進行細菌戰研究。

主持人，石井四郎。

同期，石井又在哈爾濱的三棵樹濱江車站一個地下室進行活體試驗。

The site of "Unit Togo"
"東鄉部隊" 遺地

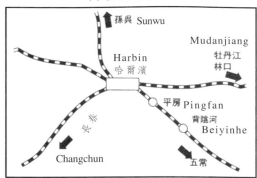

背陰河位置

The Beiyinhe located in So. of Harbin.

背陰河位置

The arrangement
of "Unit Togo"
東鄉部隊配置

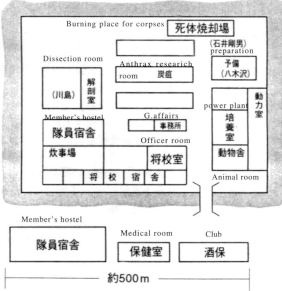

Provided by:
Yukiko Yamabe
寫真提供：山邊悠喜子

Normally, there has 500-600 prisoners held, just a half of the capacity of one thousand persons

　這裏的監獄通常關押五百至六百人，祇占其設計關押容量一千人的一半。

The site of "Unit Togo"
"東鄉部隊" 舊址

★1 In 1993, G. Endo Kazuo's the assistant chief of staff of Kwantung Army wrote the following in his diary after the inspection of Beijinhe:

"Thursday, Nov.16. sunny day, performing inspection with Colonel Anta, Lt. Colonel Tachibana at the experiment ground,...... used two communists for the experiment.

Victims of experiment were locked up in tight railings, and giving the injections of a variety of germ......".

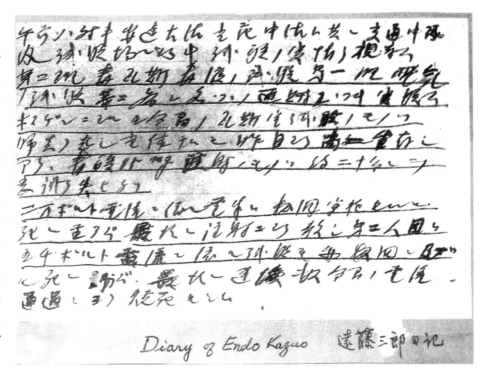

Diary of Endo Kazuo 遠藤三郎日記

("General's Last Wards the dairy of Endo Kazuo ", Mainichi Shinbun , 1985.)

一九二二年，關東軍副參謀長遠藤三郎到背陰河視察後在日記上寫道：
"十一月十六日，星期四，晴朗。午前八時半，同安達大佐、立花中佐一起到實驗場視察試驗情況......分別各用兩名[共匪]進行試驗......
被試驗者一個一個嚴密地關在柵欄裏，把各種病菌移植入活人體內......"
（日，遠藤三郎 "將軍之遺言　遠藤三郎日記"，每日新聞，一九八五年）。

★2 Karasawa Tomio (Major) remembered in Khabarovsk Trial, he said: " In the winter of 1939...... Ishii teld me that he had experimented on cholera and plague on Machurias and discovered that plague was more effective as a B.W. weapon during 1933-1934."
(Doc.9306, "Statement of Major Karasawa Tomio". P.10. Record Group 331, The National Archives.
柄澤十三夫審訊記録 "DOC、9306，第10次
柄澤十三夫在蘇聯 "伯力審判" 時指出：
"一九三九年冬......，石井告訴我，在1933-1934年間他曾在滿州的馬賊身上做霍亂和鼠疫實驗，結果發現作爲細菌武器鼠疫很有效"。

★3 Some Chinses made an insurrection from Beiyinhe's prison in Sep.30,1937,most be killed ,12 prisoners escaped successful, exposed the clandestines of experiments. So, Ishil declared" armoury blew up " and then closed the base immediately.

一九三四年九月三十日被押在背陰河監獄裏的中國人發起越獄，數十人被殺，十二人成功逃亡。背陰河秘密被揭露後，石井對外謊稱 "武庫爆炸"，緊急關閉了該基地。

Wu Zemin he lived in Beiyinhe village and gave some helping for prisoners runaway.

幫助越獄者逃脱的背陰河村民吳澤民

1936

The Department of Kwantung Army Epidemic Prevevtion and the Kwantung Army Military Animals Epidemic Prevention Plant set up.

Tokyo decided building up a new B.W. center in Pingfan, Heilongjiang covering 120 squar Kmetres.
Later, The Department of kwantung Army Epidemic Prevention changed to: The Department of Kwantung Army Epidemic Prevention and Water Supply, alias "Unit 731". The Kwantung Army Military Animals Epidemic Prevention Plant changed to The Department of Kwantung Army Military Animals Epidemic Prevention, alias "Unit 100".

< The Documents of Kwantung Army's demand >

關　東　軍　文　件

The demand of establishing the Department of Kwantung Army Epidemic Prevention

關東軍防疫部

The demand of establishing the Kwantung Army Military Animals Epidemic Prevention Plant.

關東軍軍獸防疫嚴

一九三六年

　　日軍關東軍成立"關東軍防疫部"和"關東軍軍獸防疫廠"

　　東京決定在平房建立一個面面積達120平方公里的細菌戰中心。

　　後來，"關東軍防疫部"，改稱"關東軍防疫給水部"或"七三一部隊"，"關東軍軍獸防疫廠"改稱"關東軍軍獸防疫部"或"一〇〇部隊"。

The facilities of "Unit 731" under construction. The picture was taken by the aviation & photography corps of "Unit 731"
正在建築中的"731部隊"由"731部隊"航空攝影班所攝.

No. 1539 Order, given by The Headquarter of Kwantung Army to establish special millitary area in Pingfan.
　　關東軍司令部關于設立平房特別軍事區域的第1539號訓令。

The sign of "Millitary Area"
地標牌

The "pathogen factory" of "Unit 100", located in the suburbs of Changchun.

日軍 "100部隊" 在長春市郊孟家屯所設的細菌工廠殘迹

"Unit 100" base occupied 20 sguar kms, it's known that the laboratories produced annually 100kgs of anthrax bacterium, 500 kgs of nose baceteria and 1,000 kgs glanderes bacteria. Japanese prof. Ashidi pointed out that the horse epidemic around the Janshe Temple was made by "Unit 100", he said:

"These horse anthrax epidemic broke with tremendous force, few thousands horses were death in short time, Japanese accused it's made by S.U., but it's real spreaded by Japanese special unit".

"100部隊" 基地占地 20 平方公裏, 1941 年到 1942 年, 部隊每年大約生産了 1,000 公斤炭疽菌, 500 公斤鼻疽菌。日籍醫學教授盧田指出, 北安至黑河間建設寺發生的馬疫病是出于 "100部隊" 之手, 他説: "此次發生馬炭疽病很嚴重, 時間不長却死掉馬匹數千。日本人當時造謠説是蘇聯施放的細菌, 實際上是日軍特種部隊所作爲"。

The water supply in the
battle of Changzhou in
Northern China on Sep.
20 1937 after discharged
germ.

　1937年九月二十日在
華北滄州戰役對水源施毒
後日軍的供水情形

1938

Established the germ warfare troop "Unit 1855" in Beijing.

Founded the Department of Epidemic Prevention and water Supply in 18 divisions. (according to Ishii's tongues).

The "logs" seize and transportion system was set up for support live experiments.

Germ attacked on chinese sixe areas.

Research center of "Unit 1855" at Beijing (I'st section)
華北（北平）北支甲第
"1855" 部隊第一課（檢驗課）
及病毒戰劑研究室設在原
北平協和醫學院

Japanese writer Mireko Nichino issued has report "The Verification of Unit 1855, Beijing" in "The Forum of Against Aggression and Safeguard Peace", Harbin, 1995 . She pointed out:

"According to the Imoto Diary in Autumn 1939, unit 1855 expended $210,000 to set up biological weapons research eguipments and tookover The Rockeffelles Plan (Beijing Xiehe hospital with connected [Kigo Plan])

日本女作家西野留美子于一九九五年在哈爾濱"反對侵略維護和平座談會"上發表"北京甲一八五五部隊的驗證"一文說：

"據井本日記記載，一八五五部隊于昭和十四年（1939）秋，耗資21萬日元，置辦細菌武器研究設施等，現已完成九成，并說正在接管洛克菲勒計劃（北京協和醫院）與[木號計劃]建立了聯系。"

一九三八年

北京"一八五五部隊"成立

日軍在18個陸軍師團設立細菌戰部隊（石井自語）

爲提供活人作活體試驗和活體解剖的捕送系統建立

對延安等地發動6次細菌攻擊

Tomoyoshi Naguda confessed in Nov. 1. 1954:

"I arrived at unit 1855 for bacterium quarantine training in July 1943, when we are visited 'Unit Nishimura's' (belong to'Unit 1855') culture room, the officer let me know about the 5pcs. cholera culture bacteria eguipments said: Right here, has been an innumerable cholera germ enough to kill all the people of the world, if we are use it".

日本戰俘長田友吉于一九五四年十一月一日供：

1943年7月我到北京1855部隊參加細菌檢疫訓練，在該部西村部隊細菌培養室，室內有五臺30cm×50cm×30cm的鋁制霍亂培養器，值班軍官解釋說："這裏面培養着難以計數的霍亂菌，有了這些霍亂菌，可以一次把全世界的人類殺死。"

Beijing "Unit 1855"(Culture of bactreia room)

北京"1855"部隊細菌培養所

Bacteriological Weapon Research
Center of "Unit 1855" at Beijing
(3'rd section)
華北（北平）北支甲第 "１８５５
部隊" 第三課
（細菌武器研究所），設在前北平
静生生物調查所。

"In1944, We transport prisoners three times to the 3'rd section of 'Unit 1855' at the Feng Tai camp (6 people, 5 people and 6 people respectively). Two military surgeons came from the headquater of the 'Unit 1855', gave injection of germ for the six people. These people died overnight and were sent to the 2'nd section for dissections."
(By kiichi Hirakause, member of "Unit 1855")

"一八五五部隊" 士兵平川喜一證實指出:
　　"當時豐臺有俘虜收容所,從那裏用汽車將俘虜裝到北京。一九四四年，我所知連續帶來了三次（6人、
　　5人 6人）直接帶到了第三課。第一次帶來6個人後，當天（也可能是第二天）從軍部來了兩名軍醫一起
　　進入房間裏，穿着白大褂，給俘虜注射細菌。過一夜，俘虜都死了,死後的解剖在第二課進行."（日本 "戰
　　争的研究" 第二期 P.49，1993）

Special Agency in Harbin to sieze and tronsfer victim to "Unit 731" for live experiment.
哈爾濱憲兵隊（"園木" 捕送系統）

Yataka Mitsao (former M.P. Captain) revisited the building of Special Agency in July,1995, he pointed out: " has 15 room down the basement for prison cell, 20 persons ea. room."
　　原憲兵隊長三尾豐1995年七月重返哈爾濱憲兵隊時指出: "在地下室有15間囚室，每室可關
　　20人。"

A lot of "logs" under Japanese escorting to
Pingfan.
大批"圓木"在日兵押送下

No.1 Combat Order issued
by Hirano Military Police
Corps(the second part of the translation).
平野憲兵隊第一
號作戰命令（譯文之二）

No.1 Combat Order issued
by Hirano Military Police
Corps for "logs" transfer
(the I'st part of the translation).
平野憲兵隊第一
號作戰命令（譯文之一）

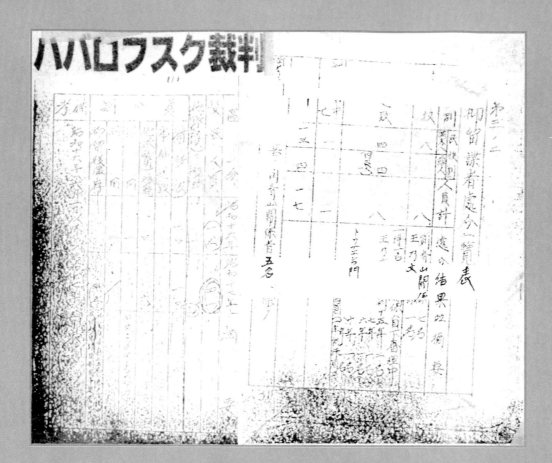

The materials of seize and transportion in filing cabinet.
現存的捕捉和傳送檔案

Fang Zhenyu, the witness who saw "Unit 731" sending Chinese. under escort to prisons by train.
"七三一部隊"用火車押運中國人的見證人方振玉

From 13 law cases of "Special Transifer" of Japanese/ Manchukuo's files found out that has had 1,203 chinese deliveried to "Unit 731".
在東北清理日滿遺留未毀的檔案中，查出13例"特別輸送"案，計"輸送"1,203人至"七三一部隊"。

"Logs" in "Unit 731"
被 捕 的 "圓 木"

A Chinese boy , the victim of germ
tests.
細菌試驗的受害者 －－ 中國男孩

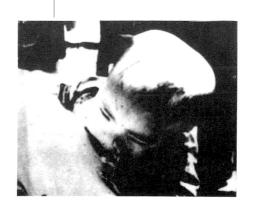

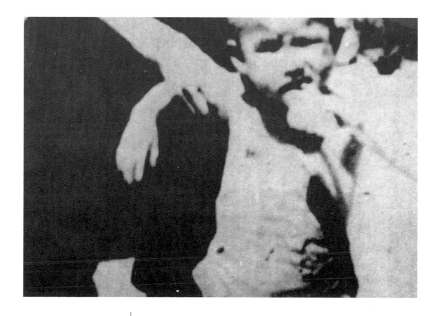

A Chinese child suffered from germ experiment
中國男孩也是 "圓木"

1939

Established the "Unit 1644" in Nanjing and the "Unit 8604" in Guangzhou (Canton).

Half of "Unit 731" mumbers joined in the Nomanhan battle using germ warfare. Japanese were defeated, but Ishii received a certificate of merit.

There were germ warfare attacks an seven citeis include Xian, Chongqing.

南京 "一六四四部隊" 主樓

"In the mainbuilding, I'st foor has the research room of cholera, typhoid and plague, 2'nd floor for raise rats and breed fleas, 3'rd floor for experiment, 4th floor was the prisons, take 20-30 prisoners into custody for test and some times over 100 prisoner there, included women and children. Every body came in, no one came out alive. even the soldiers transfered to this unit, were not get back to Japan alive."

(By Asano Fumisan, reporter of "Asuhi News")

日本 "朝日新聞" 記者朝野富三在南京調查後報導：

"在主樓的第一層爲霍亂、傷寒和鼠疫研究室，二層爲飼養老鼠和繁殖跳蚤，三層爲人體試驗室，四層監禁受試者的地方。平時 20－30 人，人多時超過 100 人，其中還有婦女和兒童，受試者一旦進入就不可能活着回去。就是一進該部的日本士兵，也沒有一個活着回來的。"

Building No.7# of "Unit 1644"
"一六四四部隊" 七號樓

Inside section of Bulding No.7,
F.3 for vivisection
活體解剖室在七號樓第三層

一九三九年

南京"一六四四部隊"、"廣州八六〇四部隊"建立.

日蘇諾門罕衝突中, 日軍使用細菌戰, 石井獲獎. 細菌攻擊西安等地 (計七次攻擊).

The animal breeding lab. of "Unit 1644"

第 "一六四四部隊" 動物培植室

Evidence from Mazmodo's illustration: Human experiment in Nanjing" Unit 1644" and a cage for the captured.

用繪圖説明松本博的見證, 南京 "1644部隊" 的人體實驗和監禁犯人的籠子。

Japanese Army "Unit 8604" in Guangzhou.(Canton)

廣州華南"8604部隊"舊址

"Unit News ", Hongkong, reported about that Kasukawa Tani interview Mutsuo Inoue, he is the member of "Unit 8604 " in 1943-1945, Guangzhou.

Inoue was the helper of vivisection of Keiu Hashimo to (section leader of pathology), they made live dissect four or five chinese spies (may be Chinses gurrilla), average 4-5 persons per day.

香港"聯合報"一九九五年十月六日報導日本糟川良谷于同年七月二十日訪問廣州"八六〇四部隊"成員井上睦雄的記錄。井上是該部隊病理班班長橋本敬佑的解剖助手,一九四三年進入"八六〇四部隊"。被解剖的人體有中國間諜(可能是抗日游擊隊員),每天解剖四五具。

第一防疫給水班行動圖

The map of Ishii Shiro unit action
line in Namanhan
諾門罕第一防疫給水班行動圖

Gunji Yoko "The Real situation, Unit B.
W. of Ishii" (Norimo Syaten, Japan)
郡司 陽子『真相・石井細菌戦部隊』(德間書店)

（1940年5月23日、朝日新聞）

Ishill Shiro achieved a certificate of merit of
Nomanhan battle from the Tokyo
石井四郎在諾門罕細菌作戰有功獲獎

Ishii's unit participated in the July 12, 1939 Nomanhan battle. Ishii was in this photo (upper center).

1939年7月12日石井部隊出現于諾門罕戰役中，上面中央是石井四郎。

七三一部隊在"諾門汗"之役使用細菌戰証言

Testimony of Unit 731's part in Nomanhan battle (by "Unit 731" member A)

The main compound of "Unit 731"(Model made by the "Japanese
[Unit 731] Exhibit Committee".)

"731 部隊"本部（取材于"日本731部隊"展覽）

The Map of Pingfan Arrangement (1944)

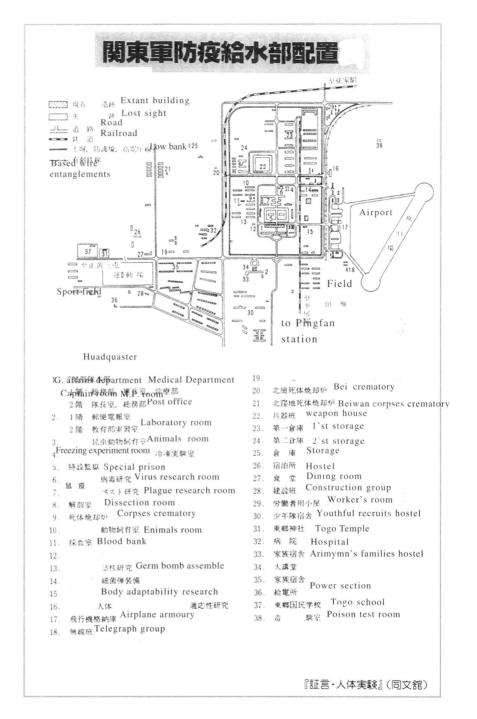

"Testimony, live experiment" ("Toubun kan", Japan)

The authorized size of "Unit 731" (1945) <set up by Syoji Kindo>
"731部隊" 編制表 (近藤昭二制作)

部隊編制是以1945年當時情况爲基礎，1945年
以前存在的編制也加以補充後制作而成的。

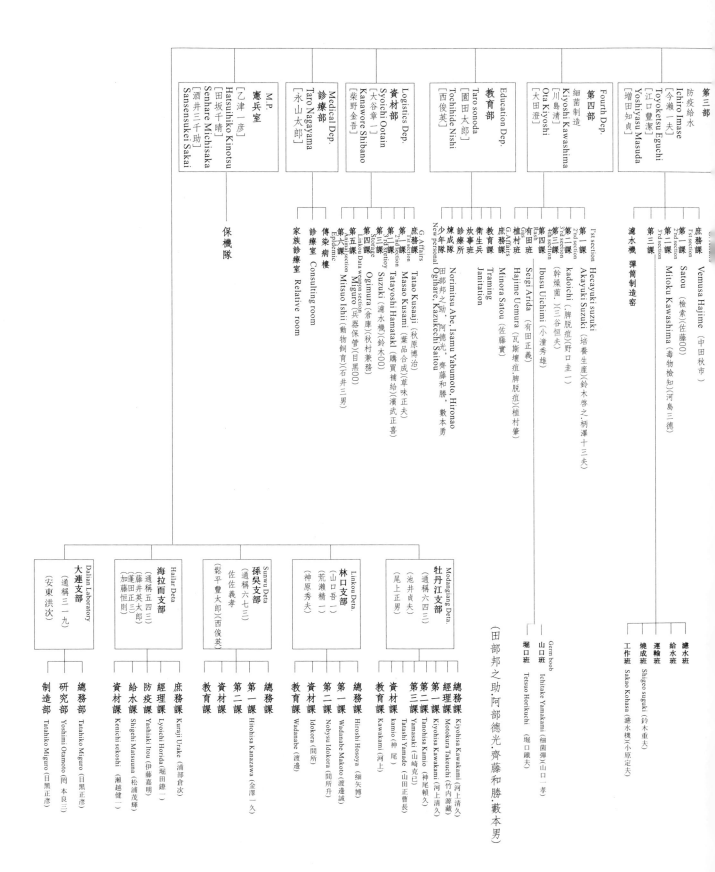

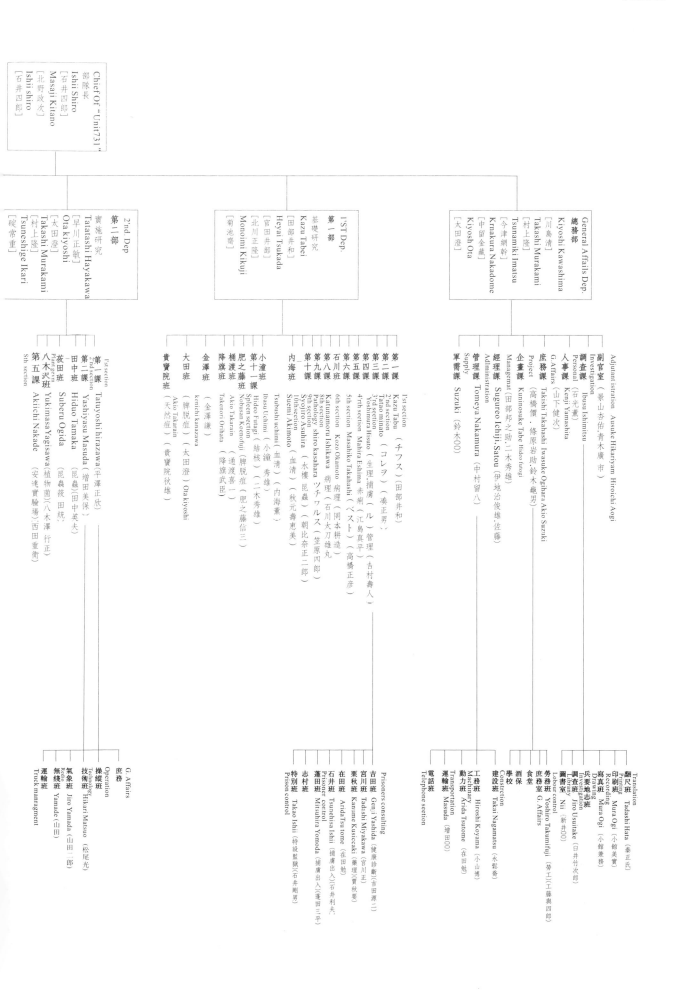

The first building of "Unit 731."
"731 部隊" 本部第一棟樓

The 3'rd Department's building
第三部大樓

The remains of "Unit 731." These are the rooms used for the storage and production of bacteria.
日軍 "七三一部隊" 儲藏細菌的處所遺迹

Basement
地下室

Inside of experiment room
試驗室內部

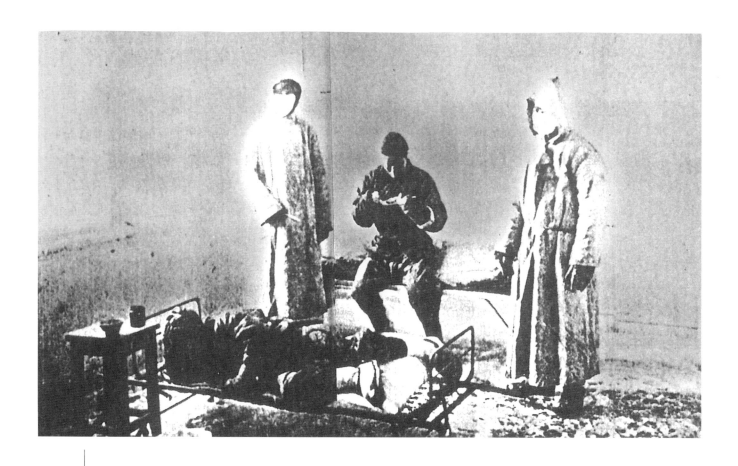

"Unit 731" in researching the spread of disease placed healthy and infected individuals together for observation.
日軍 "七三一部隊" 正進行細菌感染實驗，讓染病者和正常人共居一室，以觀察他們互相感染的情形。

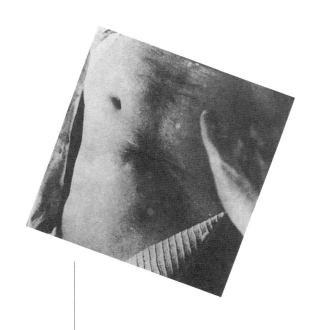

A survivor's body
幸存人身上的傷痕

Dead was at the door awaiting him
死亡已站在他的門口

A picture of marudas or "logs". Note that besides the Chinese, there are also European marudas.

　　這批即將面臨悲慘命運的"圓木"（日文稱"丸太"）絕大多數是中國民眾，也有部分歐美民眾。

The dead body of the victim of gas tests.

毒氣試驗受害者的尸體

Victim Hsiao Gene

幸存人蕭靜

The report of cold observed on babies by prof. Hisato Yashimura (a member of "Unit 731"), published in "Japanese Physiology".

"七三一部隊" 成員吉村壽人在 "日本生物學" 發表的他從嬰兒所作的活體凍傷報告

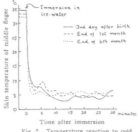

Age (years)

Nos. of subj.

Fig. 1. Ages and reactivity to cold.

about 20 Chines
years. The res
averaged on grou
and changes of
with progress of
as is seen in fig
reactivity was fo
25 to 29 years, an
younger or older
erally decreased
cept that in chil
than in puberty.
aspect of change
age was similar
phyisological fun
    Though detai
be attained on ch
of age, some obs
ried out on a bab
2, the reaction w
the 3rd day afte

Fig. 2. Temperature reaction to cold observed on a baby.

Table 1. Sexual difference of reaction index estimated on Orochons

A scene of frostbite experiment. The experiment is a Mongolian teenager

凍傷實驗，被實驗者是一蒙古人少年

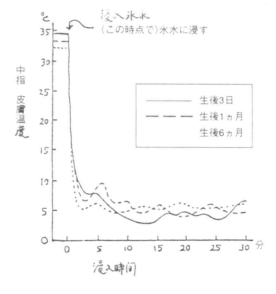

A picture of marudas or "logs".

這批即將面臨悲慘命運的 "圓木"

The report of live human experiment by Ishikawa
"七三一部隊" 成員石丸太刀雄所著之活體試驗報告

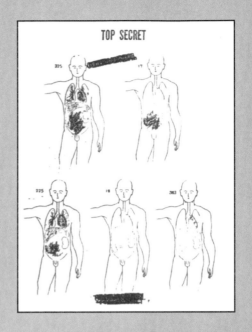

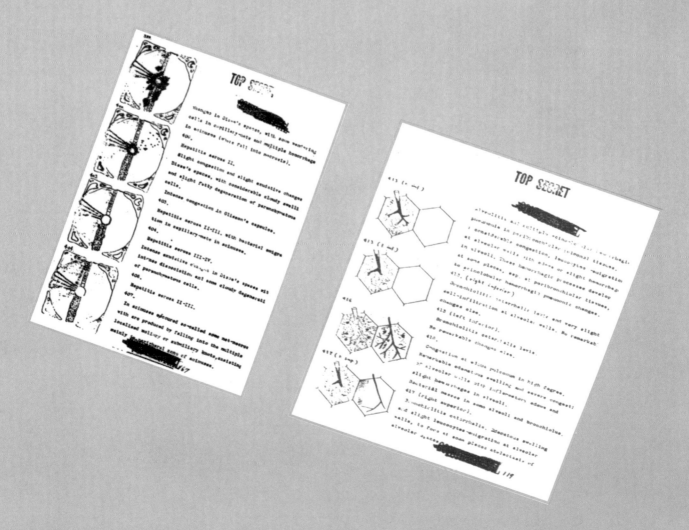

This is an old bookstore in Tokyo where a report about experiments with tetanus was found. The author is Naeo Ikeda. The report records the sequence of events until death after tetanus was innoculated into the feet of the victims.

在東京神田區的舊書店－－有關破傷風的一篇研究報告在此被發現。作者池田苗雄中校，病歷包括
從菌種種入被實驗者的脚跟開始，一直到病人死亡。

The result of spread anthrax bacteria by air

空中散布炭疽試驗

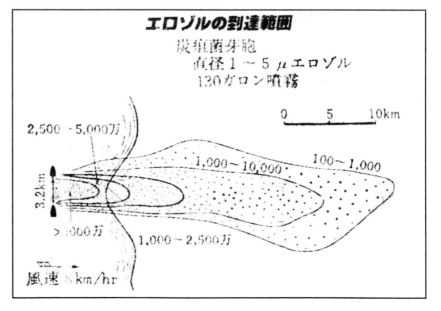

Large prison of "Unit 731"

"七三一部隊"的巨大監獄

The four keys dug up on the site of a special prison.

在特別監獄遺址挖出的四把鑰匙

In the Headquarter buildings they had an underground passage leading to the special prison through which a lot of Chinese were sent under escort as victims of tests.

"七三一部隊"本部大樓地下設有通往特別監獄的地下通道，利用這條地下通道押進試驗對象的中國人。

Special prison
中央廊下　特設監獄

Prison door
獄門

The remains of the special prison
特設監獄原址

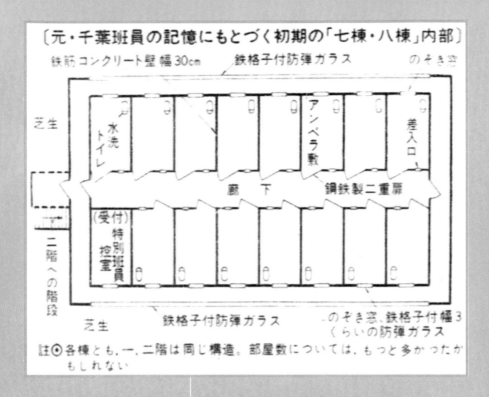

〔元・千葉班員の記憶にもとづく初期の「七棟・八棟」内部〕

鉄筋コンクリート壁 幅30cm　　鉄格子付防弾ガラス　　のぞき窓

芝生

水洗トイレ

アンペラ敷

差入口

廊　下　　　鋼鉄製二重扉

二階への階段

(受付) 特別班員控室

芝生　　鉄格子付防弾ガラス　　のぞき窓、鉄格子付幅3
くらいの防弾ガラス

註⊙各棟とも、一、二階は同じ構造。部屋数については、もっと多かったかもしれない

the sketch map of the internal structure of a special prison
特別監獄內部構造示意圖

About the number of the prisoners in "Unit 731", the member of this unit Noboru Yamashita ("A" section I'st sguad leader) confessed in 1954: "Our sguad made live test on 10-20 persons every day, over 400 men used pour germ down the throat, over 250 men by injection....., 5-6 were women......
With the germ of plague, typhoid ,diphtheria, these victims should be died after experiment 3-7 days."

　　關于平房監禁的人數字，七三一部隊"A"隊一分隊長山下井于一九五四年口供："一九四三年五月派到七三一部隊。一九四四年八月任分隊長.我們隊每天用１０−２０人進行試驗，用灌的方法（口灌細菌）有四百多人，進行皮下注射的有250多人……，被試驗人中，有五六個是婦女…….我們隊用的多為鼠疫菌、傷寒菌、白喉菌.這些人被試驗後，有三天死的，有七天死的……。"

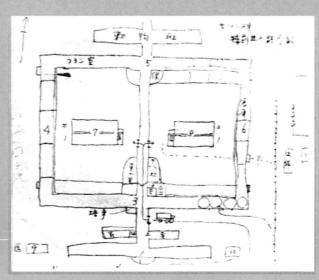

One of the former members of the special detachment drew the sketch map of the special prison penitently when visiting Pingfan district in 1986
　　原"七三一部隊"特別班隊員在１９８６年訪問平房時，以懺悔的心情繪制了這張特別監獄示意圖。

Some results of CW and BW
human experiments
活體試驗受害人

The prisoners of "Unit 731"
731 部隊做實驗的中國人

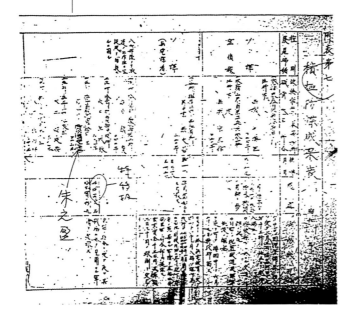

Victim Zhu Yuanyi
受害人朱元盈（檔案）

The file of Zhu Yuanyi in Pingfan
被"七三一部隊"殺害之朱元盈的檔案

Zhu's wife
朱之妻

Feng Qingchang's father
killed by "Unit 731".
馮慶章的父親死于平房

Due to the over abundant, piles of dissected
human victims were left rotting in caves.
經過實驗後的屍體，有些拋弃坑洞，任由腐爛

research room
細菌彈研究室

These remains discovered in Pingfan.
平房 731 部隊遺址發現的部分受害者遺骨

Field training
野外訓練

Training place
(Standing up: Major Kazu Tabei)
訓練地(站立者爲田部井和少校)

A scene of "Unit 731" field test; on the corner of
left rear standing "Maruda"(logs)
"七三一部隊" 野外實驗情景，後方左角前邊站
的是'圓木'。

44

To find a most effective way to sperad germ through water, air, and food,
these Japanese scientists in China perform experiments
在中國的日本科學家們爲了要把那些可怕的病菌在水中、空氣中或食物
中發展成爲做最有效的感染媒介,常常做野外實驗。

Training place
訓練地

Training
訓練

Field exercise of "Unit 731", ar-
row inducation a small container
for plague; on the right the two in
white clad in winter uniform of
biological warfare.

"七三一部隊"細菌戰野外演
習，箭頭所指是裝鼠疫的小型容
器，右邊著白衣的兩個人，穿的是
細菌戰冬季服。

Boats of "Unit 731"
"七三一部隊"船隊

The heater on the motor used in the winter
"七三一部隊"冬季在野外活動時，使
用的機動車保溫加熱器。

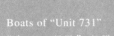

Training of attacking
細菌戰訓練

46

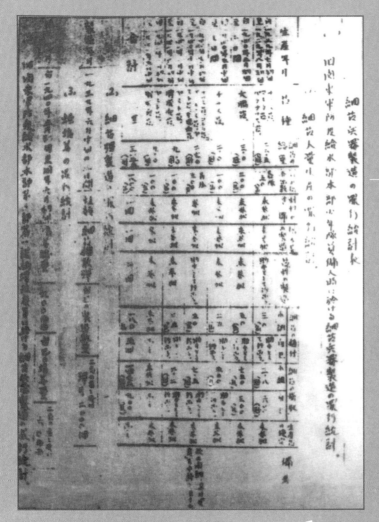

The figures of the bacterial productive capacity of "Unit 731".
日軍七三一部隊的細菌生產能力統計表

On the marching
防審帽、防害靴をつけて構内進すむ
七三一部隊に配属された將校達。
"七三一部隊の教育訓練の様がとく現
われている寫真の一つ" と元隊員た
ちはいら。

Shooting
第七三一部隊の射撃訓練光景。細菌戰
實施の際、敵軍と交戰しつつ撤退するの
ざこの訓練の眼目であったとら。

The prepare working
before attack.
攻撃前的準備

47

The training place　　訓練地

Ishii on horse back reviewing "Unit 731"
石井四郎騎馬檢閱 "七二一部隊"

"Unit 731" members assembled at the playground
"七三一部隊" 人員在操場集合

Yamaguchi Detachment's
under ground storeroom.
山口班地下貯藏室遺址

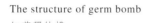

One germ bomb was to
be excavated out from
Pingfan
在平房被挖出的細菌彈

The structure of germ bomb
細菌彈結構

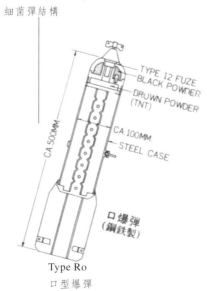

TYPE 12 FUZE
BLACK POWDER
DROWN POWDER
(TNT)

CA. 500MM.

CA. 100MM.
STEEL CASE

口爆彈
(鋼鉄製)

Type Ro
口型爆彈

石井陶瓷細菌炸彈

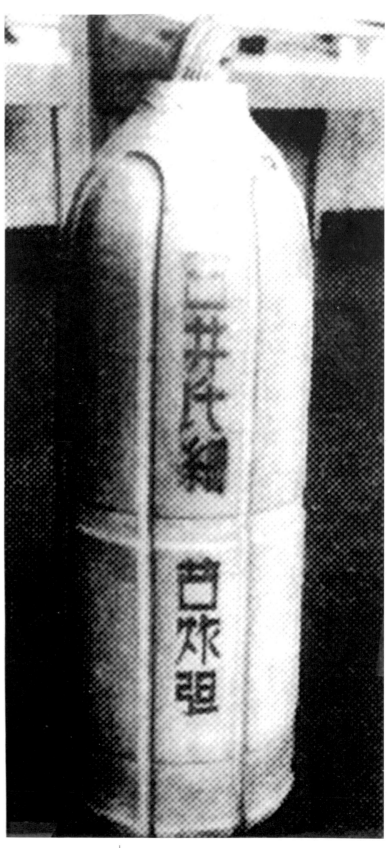

A Ceramic germ bomb, containing plague,
anthrax, cholera, etc, an invention by Ishii.
石井陶瓷細菌炸彈

Types of germ bomb

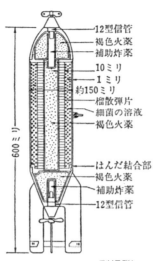

- 12型信管
- 褐色火薬
- 補助炸薬
- 10ミリ
- 1ミリ
- 約150ミリ
- 榴散弾片
- 細菌の溶液
- 褐色火薬
- はんだ結合部
- 褐色火薬
- 補助炸薬
- 12型信管
- 600ミリ

▲八型爆弾

八型爆弾　Type Ha

●形状および構造—爆弾の特性:
　円筒型、頭部は卵型、尾翼は鋼鉄性。部屋は二つ。炸薬は中心部と両端。他は鋼鉄性小球と細菌の溶液を充填。小球の数は1500個(1個 2.8グラム)、細菌溶液700cc。

●作動: 着地時に爆発。細菌溶液といっしょに爆弾の破片と小球を飛散。

●有効性: 破片と小球は高く舞いあがらない。殺傷効果は高い。小球の60〜70％に菌が付着。

●欠点:
1. 細菌溶液の流出
2. 細菌の生存率が低い。爆発が強すぎるため
3. 弾道が不安定
4. 製作がむずかしい
5. 取り扱い困難

●結論: 攻撃には有効であろう

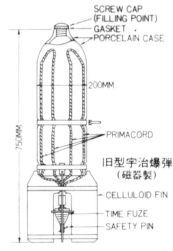

- 12型衝撃信管
- 噴霧口
- 12型衝撃信管
- 約180ミリ
- TNT炸薬
- 導火線
- 圧搾空気室 2リットル
- 遅延信管
- 時限装置
- 約1020ミリ

▲ウ型爆弾　Type U

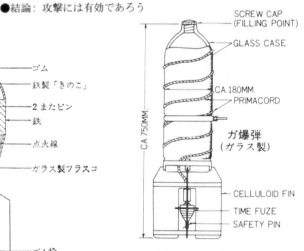

訓練用爆弾を改造したもの
重量1キログラム

- ゴム
- 鉄製「きのこ」
- 2またピン
- 鉄
- 点火線
- ガラス製フラスコ
- 空気
- 空間
- 本台 ガラス緩衝用
- ゴム栓
- 鋼鉄製垂直安定板
- 穴が4つ

▲海軍7号爆弾　Navy No.7

- SCREW CAP (FILLING POINT)
- GLASS CASE
- CA.180MM.
- PRIMACORD
- ガ爆弾 (ガラス製)
- CA 750MM.
- CELLULOID FIN
- TIME FUZE
- SAFETY PIN

ガ型爆弾　Type Ga

- SCREW CAP (FILLING POINT)
- GASKET
- PORCELAIN CASE
- 200MM
- PRIMACORD
- 旧型宇治爆弾 (磁器製)
- CELLULOID FIN
- TIME FUZE
- SAFETY PIN
- 750MM

ノを付着させた榴霰弾を四散させるためのもの。この三種類に大別される。

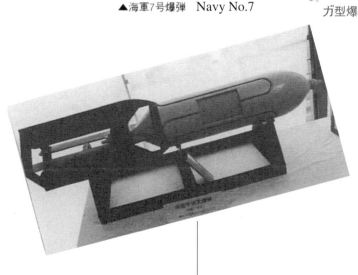

Anthrax germ bomb
宇治50型爆破弾

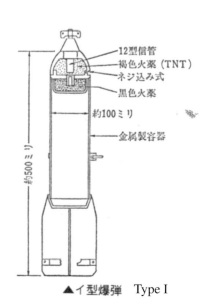

- 12型信管
- 褐色火薬(TNT)
- ネジ込み式
- 黒色火薬
- 約100ミリ
- 金属製容器
- 約500ミリ

▲イ型爆弾　Type I

The factory of germ bomb
細菌彈工廠一角

The former site of the factory producing shell cases of germ bombs of clay run by "Unit 731" in the district of Yangmajiazi (now in Harbin Longjiang Rubber Plant).
　　位于揚馬架子的原七三一部隊土陶細菌彈殼制造廠舊址(今哈爾濱龍江橡膠廠內)。

The kiln for baking shell cases of germ bombs of clay.
焙燒土陶細菌彈殼的窯體。

The germ bomb shells
細菌彈殼

54

Invented by Ishii's group, these are pieces of a bacteria bomb found behind the "Square Building" after the retreat of "Unit 731".

　"七三一部隊"撤離後，在主樓後面發現的石井陶瓷細菌炸彈碎裂片。

Under ground armoury for germ bombs

細菌彈地下貯藏室。

The kind of airplane
used by the Japanese to
drop pellets of bacteria
or contaminated fleas.
這是用來空投細菌
和跳蚤的日本飛機之
一。

The aircrafts of the "Unit 731"
"731 部隊"的飛機群

An airfield of the "Unit 731"
"731 部隊的飛機場

rat breeding cells
老鼠飼養室

Inside of the rat breeding cell
老鼠飼養室內部

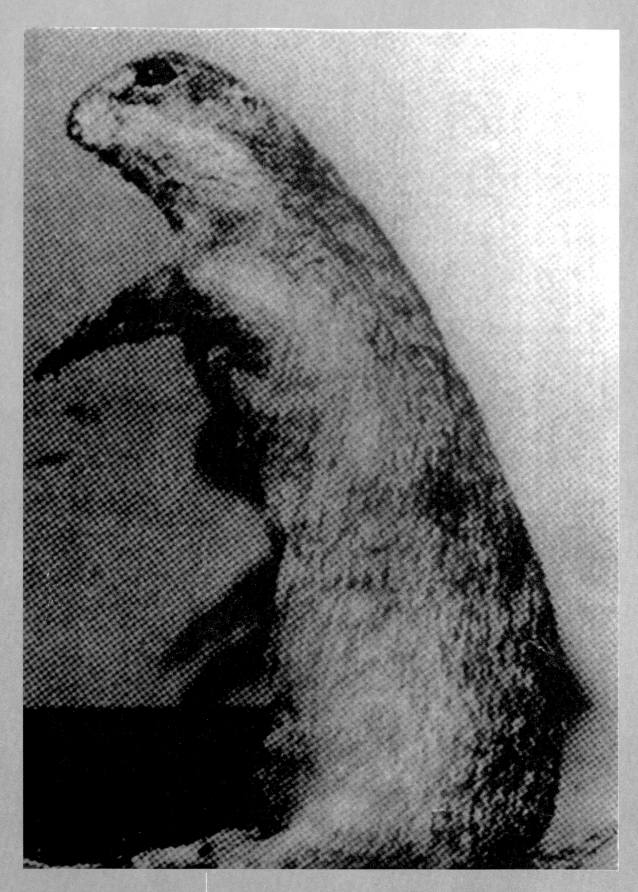

Yellow rats used by "Unit 731" to reproduce
plague contaminated fleas.
被 "731 部隊" 用來繁殖鼠疫跳蚤的黄鼠，

Gunshi Youko, the raiser of rats
黃鼠飼養員郡司陽子

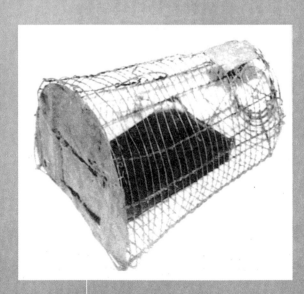

The exterior view of the restored
ground yellow rats raising house.
復原的黃鼠飼養室外景

The mousetrap used by "Unit 731"
"７３１部隊"使用的捕鼠籠

In order to make research on germ infecting media. "Unit 731"
set up an insect research detachment.

爲了研究細菌傳媒介物."七三一部隊" 設立了昆蟲研究班.

The former site of the insect building
of Taknaka Detachment

昆蟲舍舊址

The seal used by "Unit 731"

"七三一部隊" 使用的圖書章

The interior view of the audito-
rium of "Unit 731".

"七三一部隊" 大禮堂內景

The special store of "Unit 731"

"七三一部隊" 商店（酒保）

The armband of labour leader of "Unit 731"
日軍七三一部隊所屬勞工隊長袖章

The members of "Unit 731" in a
street of Harbin.
外出的 "七三一部隊" 隊員在哈
爾濱的大街上（進城必須便裝）

professor's room
專家室

61

The relics of "Detachment 673" in Sunwu.
孫吳第六七三支隊的遺物

Sunwu Deta.
孫吳支隊跡

The site of "Detachment 643"
第六四三支隊本部遺址

The site of "Detachment 543" in Hailar.
海拉爾第五四三支隊遺址

The site of "Detachment 162" in Linkou.
林口第一六二支隊遺址。

Dalian Laboratory of "Unit 731"
大連研究所

The Ji-Lin Branch of "Unit 731". This is the key stone through which "Unit 731" made contact the outer world.
吉林街分室，"731部隊"藉此處與外界聯絡

Attacks on Zhejiang in 1940:

Japanese attacked Zhejiang province with germ warfare as following:

Sep.: Taiahou (Linhai),Wenzhou, Lishui and Yushan (Jiangxi province), cholera and plague;

Oct.: Ningbo (2 times), Zhuji, Quzhou, plague;

Nov.: Jinhua, Quzhou, plague;

Dec.: Shanyu, Tangxi, Jinhua, Cixi, Longquan, Qingyuan, plague;

Japanese made these assaults ordered by The Chief of Staff of Japanese Army in June 6,1940. According to the "Imoto Dairy" (the daily of Imoto, the operational section chief of C.S.J.A.) recorded:

The germ detachment advanced in to Chekiang (formerly the Chinese Central Airforce School, Hangzhou, China) in July 1940.

"Unit Canoyashi" started from Harbin at July 26, assemble with next day. Defined the attacking targets: Ningbo, Jinhua...carry out six times attacks from Sep.18 to Oct.7, 1940.

Ishii ordered to produce:

Fleas of plague 5 Kg.

Concentrated liquids of plague and typhoid 270 kg.

Naoji Uezono (A youthful recruit of "Unit 731") remembered that:

"Unit 731" received "Bin #659" order from by Kwantung Army. The members of expeditionary detachment rode ten railway coaches at 5:00 p.m. July 26. Fourty armymen of germ warfare were in one coache. The other nine coaches eguipped with germ armaments, aircrafts, and 70 Kg concentrated liquid of typhoid.

Canoyashi and Tatao Sonoda was the commamders of this transportation.

Ishii made a suggestion in Nov. 1940, asked attack and occupy Ningbo for inspect the effectivenese of the plague dispersed in disorder, but refused by Nanjing Commander.

Until to next year, has be approved Ishii plan and occupied Ningbo in Apr.1941, and then Ishii sent 11 professors to the epidemic area. (Moa Yiquan"A lot of comfirmtions of Japanese B.W.", "The Dangdai Daily", Feb.12, 1950)

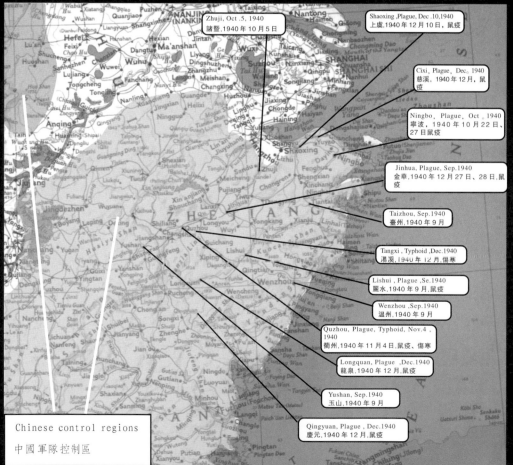

Zhuji, Oct .5, 1940
諸暨,1940年10月5日

Shaoxing ,Plague, Dec .10,1940
上虞,1940年12月10日，鼠疫

Cixi, Plague, Dec. 1940
慈溪，1940年12月，鼠疫

Ningbo, Plague, Oct .1940
寧波，1940年10月22日、27日鼠疫

Jinhua, Plague, Sep.1940
金華,1940年12月27日、28日,鼠疫

Taizhou, Sep.1940
臺州,1940年9月

Tangxi, Typhoid ,Dec.1940
湯溪,1940年12月,傷寒

Lishui , Plague , Se.1940
麗水,1940年9月,鼠疫

Wenzhou ,Sep.1940
溫州,1940年9月

Quzhou, Plague, Typhoid, Nov.4 , 1940
衢州,1940年11月4日,鼠疫、傷寒

Longquan, Plague ,Dec.1940
龍泉,1940年12月,鼠疫

Yushan, Sep.1940
玉山,1940年9月

Qingyuan, Plague , Dec.1940
慶元,1940年12月,鼠疫

Chinese control regions
中國軍隊控制區

The map of germ attacked on Zhejiang, 1940
一九四〇年細菌攻擊浙江圖

The germ warfare attacking base in Chekiang, China,
formerly the Chinese Central Airforce School.
杭州筧橋機場（原中央航空學校）浙東細菌戰基地

一九四〇年日軍以浙江爲重點細菌攻擊目標，計：

九月對臺州、溫州、麗水和玉山（江西省）的傷寒、霍亂、鼠疫撒播；

十月對寧波、衢州、諸暨，鼠疫；

十一月對金華，鼠疫；

十二月對上虞、湯溪、金華、慈奚、龍泉、慶元，鼠疫和傷寒。

攻擊命令于一九四〇年六月五日由日本陸軍參謀本部下達，據本部作戰課長井本雄男中佐當天的業務日記（簡稱"井本日記"）記載：

細菌部隊七月進駐杭州筧橋航空學校，七月二十六日，"奈良部隊"由哈爾濱出發，八月五日與南京"榮"字第一六四四部隊會合，翌日到達杭州筧橋基地。九月十日，確定寧波、衢州、金華爲攻擊目標。九月十八日至十月七日，進行六次細菌攻擊，輸送細菌二十三次。

石井在接受命令後返回哈爾濱，下令生産出跳蚤五公斤，鼠疫及傷寒的濃縮菌液二百七十公斤。

曾參加"七三一部隊"的少年隊員石橋直方清楚地記述如下：

"七三一部隊"于一九四〇年七月二十五日接到關東軍司令部（關作命）丙字第659號命令，石井下令于七月二十六日晚五時從本部登上專用列車。列車由十節車廂組成，一節客車廂乘座四十名細菌戰軍人，其餘裝載細菌武器、飛機，有幾個標有"給水器具箱"方型木箱裏，裝有七十公斤傷寒濃縮液。

這些器材的運輸指揮是飯田奈良少佐和園田忠男中尉。

八月六日晚抵杭州。

九月十八日至十月七日間的六次攻擊中發現鼠疫效果較好，故十月二十二日、十月二十七日，用飛機在寧波進行兩次鼠疫跳蚤的撒放，很快引起鼠疫流行，被石井稱爲成功的攻擊。（李力"浙贛綫細菌戰"）。

爲進一步檢驗鼠疫攻擊效果，石井于十一月末提出由陸軍攻占寧波，遭南京派遣軍拒絕，至次年四月批準石井要求，于四月十九日占領寧波，五月初，十一名石井的研究人員到達疫區，進行驗證。（毛一全"一連串的事實證明日寇作細菌戰"，"當代日報"，一九五〇年二月十二日）。

Survivor of Ningbo's plague,
Mr.Chien Gueifa.

寧波鼠疫幸存人　錢貴法

Dong-siao-zi Temple in the south-gate of the city wall,
was used as an isolate-station for plague patients. The
Jia-bu isolate-hospital was station here. Mr Chien
Gueifa was detained here.

　作爲鼠疫隔離設施被使用的舊縣城南門的董孝子
廟。疫區被燒毀之後，甲部隔離醫院搬遷至此，錢貴
法先生就曾被隔離于此。

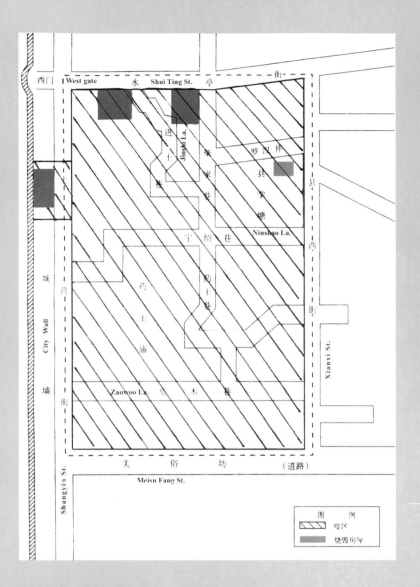

Plague's fleas fell on Chaija lane of
Quzhou in Oct .4, 1940.
　衢城柴家巷——日軍飛機撒播
細菌區之一（1940.10.4）

The map of plague epidemic area of the
Quzhou City (1940)
1940 年衢州縣縣城鼠疫發生地區圖

Cheng Xiuzhi, she explains the
isolated ward where her sister
was dead of the plague.(96.11)
　程秀芝女士正在介紹因鼠
疫病故的姐姐被隔離的房屋。

Survivor Suang chungyuan said: "Japanese aircrafts sowed a lot of wheats, some
persons has had died after few days.I have escaped away,stayed in the boat of
Qu River a long time...... "
　衢州鼠疫攻擊下的幸存人黃運椿述說："一九四〇年日機在這裏撒下許多麥
粒，不久不少人就得黑死病死了。我躲到衢江的船上，呆了很長的時間……"

69

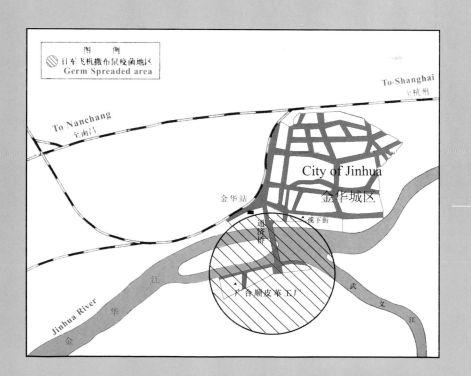

The map of plague epidemic areas of Yiwu city, 1941-1942
義烏市區鼠疫流行圖（1941－1942）

（注）虚线内是主要的鼠疫发生地
（道路名称为现在的名称）

Plague Epidemic Area

北 N.

Railway Station
义乌站

Shanliden
小云里号

Lingshia
岭下

North Gate
旧北门
北街
工人西路 旧东门
其前街
至金华
新马路
To Jinhua
旧南门
South Gate

图 例
日军飞机撒布鼠疫菌地区
Germ Spreaded area

To-Shanghai
至杭州

To Nanchang
至南昌

City of Jinhua
金华城区

金华站

通济桥
溪下街

大吕顺皮革工厂

Jinhua River
金华江
武义江

The map of Japanese aircraft spreaded plague on Jinhua in 1940
日軍飛機在金華撒布鼠疫菌示意圖

1941

Established a new Germ Experiment Base in Anta which is larger than five previous bases (Hailar 1938, Jiamus 1939, Taolaishao 1940, Donglin 1940, Chengzigou 1941).

Launched germ warfare attacks on Changde etc. 22 counties.

Anta
安達野外試驗場

The site of Anta proving Ground
安達實驗場遺址

A conservative estimate would give human casualteis of at least several hundred just in Pingfan and Anta anthrax and B. prodigious tests. Field testing undoubtedly increased the toll by thousands. (Harris "Factories of Death")

平房和安達兩地炭疽和細菌試驗傷亡人數，保守估計至少有幾百人，毫無疑問，野外試驗傷亡人數要達數千人。（哈里斯"死亡工廠"）

The distribution sketch map of the persons to be experimented on in Anta Proving Ground.
安達特別實驗場被試驗對象配置示意圖

"Unit 731 Exhibition", Tokyo
東京"七三一部隊展"

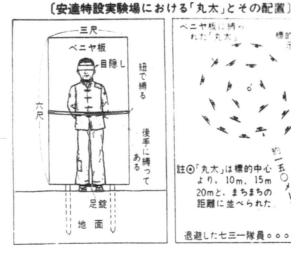
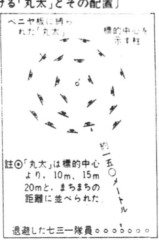

一九四一年

建立新的細菌攻擊實驗場——安達實驗場，在安達之前設立的實驗場有：

海拉爾實驗場（一九三八年）；佳木斯實驗場（一九三九年）；城子溝實驗場（一九四一年）；

陶賴紹實驗場（一九四〇年）；東寧實驗場（一九四〇年）。

此外，在肇東的滿溝，呼倫貝爾草原，東部山區還設有臨時實驗場。

日軍對常德等地發動二十二次細菌攻擊。

The Live Body Test at Taolaishao

The "Unit 731" performed three live body tests of anthrax bomb in September 1941 at the Taolaishao Proving Ground.

Thirty Chinese victims were bounded to the pillars in the center of the experiment field. Members of the "Unit 731" retreated to 800 meters outside of the target.

Watataro Kamido and Tanuimoto, members of the "Unit 731", reported the wind direction, speed, and temperature to Major Tsuneo Mitsutani.

An airplane dropped the bombs contained the anthrax germ at the height of 500 meters. Japanese soldiers equipped with protecting cloths went to the experiment field and took the victims into the prisoner's van. The soldiers also collected the shell splinters.

The next day, two more tests were performed.

The result of the tests:

Testimony of "Unit 731" Engaging in Biological warfare at Taolaishao
七三一部隊在黑龍江省陶德昭進行細菌實驗證言

Han Xingyan, the witness of field tests made by "Unit 731."
"七三一部隊" 野外試驗的見證人韓行岩。

1. The victims contagious by the anthrax died in a few days.

2. The germ on the shell splinters generated new germ despite the high temperature of explosion.

Seiichi Hasoaki, Michio Nakamura, Takiichi Eda all participated in these tests.

(The above were quoted from "The Crime History of the Unit 731" by Mr.HanXiao, p.124-133, Heilongjiang Publishing House,1991)

一次活人實驗在陶賴紹實驗場

一九四一年九月，"七三一部隊"在陶賴紹實驗場進行了三次炭疽炸彈對活人（中國人）的實際攻擊實驗。

第一次，三十名中國人用"特別囚車"由"七三一部隊"的特別監獄運到，綁在實驗場的木柱上，"七三一部隊"成員則退至 800 公尺外觀察。

實驗開始前，上田彌太郎（"七三一部隊"第四部）和利本向三谷恆夫少佐（第四部第三班班長）報告風向、風速、氣溫等數據後發出了實驗訊號。

一架飛機在靶場上空五百公尺高度向人靶投下裝有炭疽菌的炸彈，爆炸後有一批穿着防護服的士兵進入靶場，把靶人拖回囚車，收集散落彈的細菌原片。

第二天，這種實驗又進行兩次。

實驗結果：

1）被炭疽感染的靶人陸續死亡；

2）原彈片上的炭疽菌，通過了爆炸時的高溫，生長成新的菌株。

參加這次實驗的還有：細昭清一、中村道夫、江田武一。

（摘自韓曉"口軍七二一部隊罪惡史"P124-133，黑龍江人民出版社，1991）

Chengzigou, the site of the ancient city in Liao and Jin Dynasties, near Pingfan district, was once used by "Unit 731" when they did their germ tests.
"七三一部隊"曾利用平房附近的城子溝遼金古城遺址進行細菌實驗。

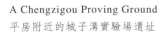

A Chengzigou Proving Ground
平房附近的城子溝實驗場遺址

People in Changde, their relatives were killed of plague germ warfare. (96.12)

在細菌戰引起的鼠疫中親屬慘遭殺害的常德人們。

Nie JiaLin, he witnessed that the plane dropping for germ warfare, Ye Rongkai, in the rear is a historian,

細菌戰的飛機空投物的目擊者聶家林,身後是當地的歷史學者葉榮開.

The local authorities in Changde, they express their anger against germ warfare of Japanese military.

表明常德市民對日本軍細菌戰的忿怒的當地行政人員（左側），右側是檢查技師汪正宇先生，他對1941年11月的空投物以克式量染色法進行染色之後，用顯微鏡作了檢查。

Occusations of B.W. in Changde（常德的控訴）

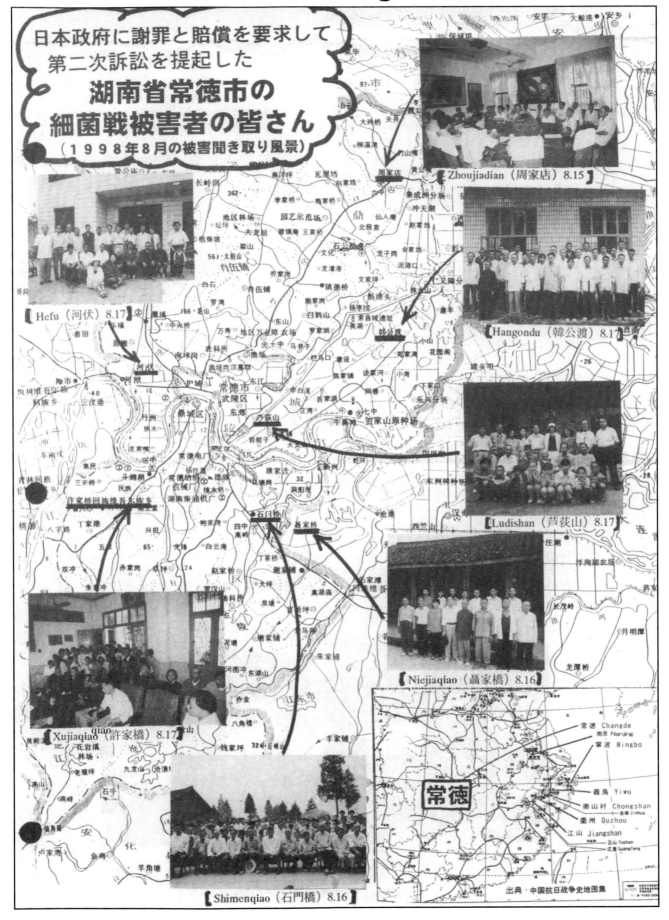

日本政府に謝罪と賠償を要求して
第二次訴訟を提起した
**湖南省常徳市の
細菌戦被害者の皆さん**
（1998年8月の被害聞き取り風景）

【Zhoujiadian（周家店）8.15】

【Hefu（河伏）8.17】

【Hangondu（韓公渡）8.17】

【Ludishan（芦荻山）8.17】

【Xujiaqiao（許家橋）8.17】

【Niejiaqiao（聶家橋）8.16】

【Shimenqiao（石門橋）8.16】

出典・中国抗日戦争史地図集

People in Shimen Bridge, who testify injuries of Japanese germ warfare.(97.4)

對細菌戰引起的鼠疫灾情作證的石門橋的人們

Li Yuxian, her father LI Yousheng, was infected with the plague in castle wall town in Changde. After he returned Tao Yuan, he was died. Then his germ infected her mother, two younger brother, elder and aunt. They were dead, too.(97.4)

李玉仙女士，她的父親李佑生在常德縣城感染了鼠疫，回到桃源後去世。她的母親，姐姐，二個弟弟和伯母從她父親那裏感染了鼠疫，也因此過逝。

　　一九四一年十一月四日由"七三一部隊"航空隊的增田美保駕駛員九七式轟炸機，從南昌飛往常德，投下鼠疫的跳蚤36公斤（見"井本日記"）。

　　十一月十二日常德關廟街的十二歲女童蔡桃見發病送至廣德醫院校診，經付院長譚學華指定汪正宇進行血檢。并在次日蔡桃興死後進行解剖，驗證結論是"敗血癥鼠疫"。

　　鼠疫迅速泛濫，五月傳到蘆秋山鄉的伍家坪村，六百多口人死亡201人，德山鄉楓樹崗村同期死亡247人。六月傳到許家橋民族村，有54人致死。七月傳到南坪鄉白馬村，九户人家死二十九人，九月傳到東郊鄉易家灣村。

　　日機在一九四二年第二次向常德投擲鼠疫，一九四二年當年參加常德防疫工作的湖南衛生防疫隊長劉禄德曾親眼目睹日機投下的跳蚤擲體和細菌跳蚤。（常德侵華日軍七三一部隊細菌戰受害者接待處，劉雅玲"常德細菌戰始末"第二十六頁）

　　常德鼠疫死亡人數，至一九九八年調查完畢爲10，400人，其中軍人3，000人，還有部分鄉村未及調查，鼠疫蔓延至常德周圍十個縣、三十六個鄉、一百五十六個村。

In Caigoaweng Village, all people were died by plague, only one alived his name is Cai Winlong.

常德蔡家溝村，全村371人，除蔡文龍在外打工幸存，其餘370人全部死絕。

Survivor Cai Winlong with his family

幸存者蔡文龍 及其家人

The people of Changde against the Japan's B.W.

常德群众抗议日军细菌战

Plague extended to 1941 in Quzhou
衢州鼠疫蔓延至一九四一年

The list of died by Japanese plague from Apr.1 to Apr. 4,
1941, reported by "Quzhou Daily" (Oct.7.1941).
《衢州日報》（1941.4.7）第二版公布的四月一至四
日鼠疫死亡者名單

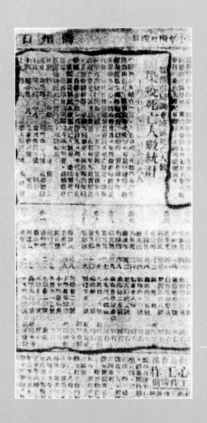

The list of Quzhou city's people they are killed by plague in
March, 1941, Reportes: "Qughou Daity"
《衢州日報》（1941）的三月份鼠疫死亡者名單

Plague attacking place, Linshua La., Qugzhou
1941

衙城寧紹會館（寧紹巷）臨時留驗所

Yang Haifeng killed by Japanese plague attaking on Quzhou
in March 1941

一九四一年三月死于日軍細菌攻擊的衢州人楊惠鳳

Isolation ward of plague at Xiao Ximen, Quzhou, Mach 10, 1941

小西門龍王廟（臨時隔離病室外貌）（1941.3.10）

1942

Set up "Unit 9420" at Singapore.

Unleashed sixty nine times germ attacked (Two times on Burma .)

Singapore B.W. Command Office
在新加坡的南方軍防疫給水部

一九四二年

新加坡"九四二〇部隊"建成。

發動六十九次細菌攻擊戰,(其中緬甸兩次),五月在中緬地區的昆明-保山,實施霍亂散放,致死的人數達21萬。七八月在浙贛綫進行鼠疫、霍亂、和炭疽菌大面積攻擊,也至少造成幾萬人死亡(詳見第二章)。

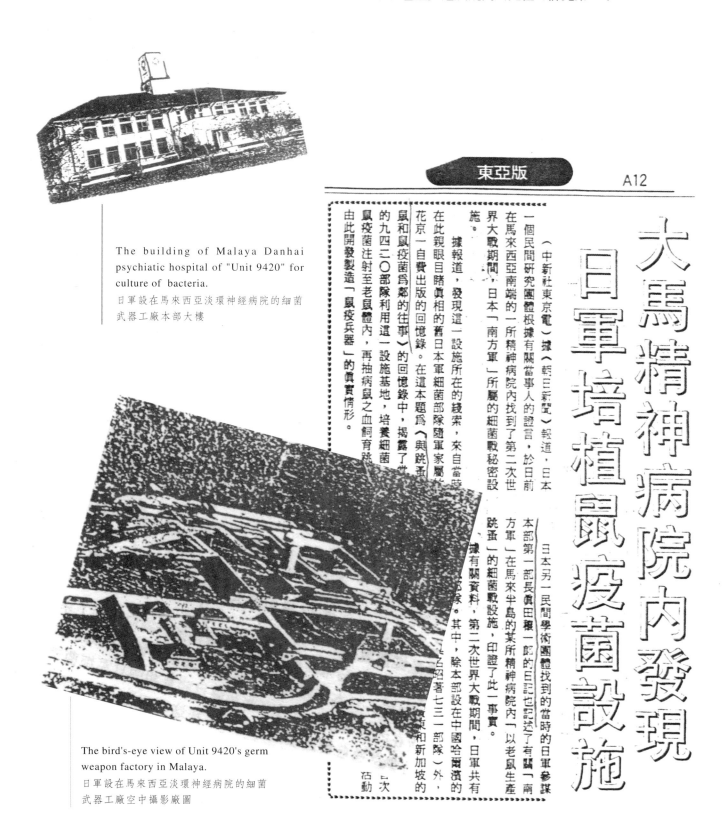

The building of Malaya Danhai psychiatic hospital of "Unit 9420" for culture of bacteria.

日軍設在馬來西亞淡環神經病院的細菌武器工廠本部大樓

The bird's-eye view of Unit 9420's germ weapon factory in Malaya.

日軍設在馬來西亞淡環神經病院的細菌武器工廠空中攝影廠圖

東亞版　　　　　A12

大馬精神病院內發現
日軍培植鼠疫菌設施

(中新社東京電)據《朝日新聞》報道,日本一個民間研究團體根據有關當事人的證言,於日前在馬來西亞南端的一所精神病院內找到了第二次世界大戰期間,日本"南方軍"所屬的細菌戰秘密設施。

日本另一民間學術團體找到的當時的日軍參謀本部第一部長真田穰一郎的日記也記述了有關"南方軍"在馬來半島的某所精神病院內"以老鼠生產跳蚤"的細菌戰設施,印證了此一事實。

據報道,發現這一設施所在的綫索,來自當時在此親眼目睹真相的舊日本軍細菌部隊隨軍家屬花京一自費出版的回憶錄。在這本題爲《與跳蚤鼠和鼠疫菌爲鄰的往事》的回憶錄中,揭露了當年的九四二〇部隊利用這一設施基地,培養細菌鼠疫菌注射至老鼠體內,再抽病鼠之血飼育跳蚤,由此開發製造「鼠疫兵器」的真實情形。

......有關資料,第二次世界大戰期間,日軍共有......隊。其中,除本部設在中國哈爾濱的......著名七三一部隊之外,......東和新加坡的......次

......在動

84

　　一九四一年十一月，日軍發動太平洋戰爭，并侵略香港等地，大批香港難民被遣返回廣東。一九四二年初廣東省政府原懲教場改為難民收容所，日軍"八六零四部隊"用細菌將成萬難民殺掉。

Photo of refugeree camp taken in 1942. These refugees fled from Hong Kong to Canton Province after the Japanese began invading Southeast Asia. and then killed them by germ of "Unit 8604", has had over ten thousands people were death there.

Inside of refugee camp, a lot of
people escaped from Hongkong.

廣東難民所一角

The map of B.W. attacks in 1942

一九四二年日軍細菌攻擊圖

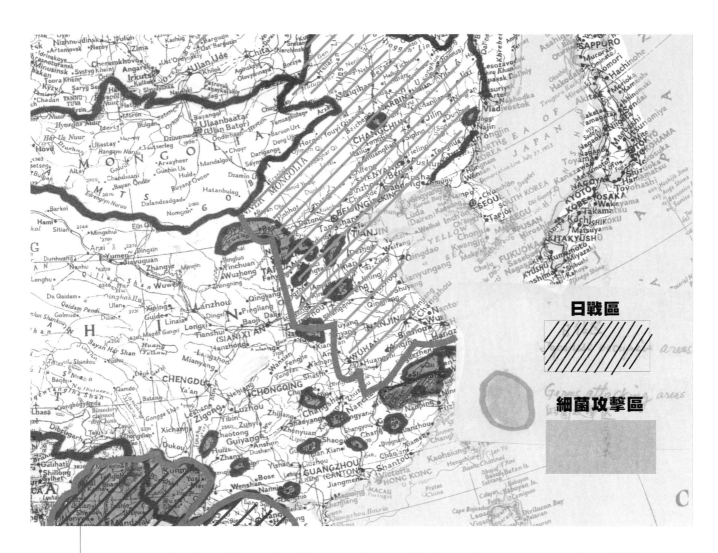

日戰區

細菌攻擊區

Japans historian Seiko Mori made brilliant exposition at "The Forum & Against Aggression and Safeguard Peace," Harbin 1995, he pointed out:

"Germ attacked on Quzhou again ......,has 3,000 persons were death by Japanese spreaded germ when they are pull out from Qughou by grand land , some germ as plague, dysentery, typhoid , cholera etc . so as to inflection diseases epidemic , has broken out around the Quzhou.
According to the figur, has had 17 whole family to died by plague... ...its expanded to Changshan, Youlong, Jiangshan, and continued to next four years......"

　　日軍史學家森正孝在一九九五年哈爾濱 "反對侵略維護和平座談會" 論證：
"衢州再次受到侵略之害，死者三千.日軍從衢州撤退時，再次散布細菌.這
次從陸上散布鼠疫、赤痢、傷寒、霍亂等菌，致使衢州一帶再次流行傳染病，
鼠疫的蔓延尤其顯著......
據這三年統計,在衢州全家死于鼠疫的有十七戶......鼠疫擴及常山、游龍、江山
等縣，在此後連續發病四年".

< Assault on Kunming Boashon(对昆明，保山的霍乱攻击）>

Chang's neighbourhood compound in Baoshan county, the l'st target of cholera attaked village in May-July 1942, wiped out a half of the population were death (37 pepole). After 58 yrs. Changs has still hanging the buddhist dectrime in comemoration of deceased persons.

保山金鷄村最先發生霍亂的張體成大屋，在一九四二年五月至七月，有一半居民死于日軍之霍亂攻擊，計死亡三十七口。

事過一個多甲子，張體成大院內仍懸佛救超渡當年冤死亡魂。

When remembered the rape of cholera, his tear has been shed over.
survivor Don Youyung, Boashan county, 78yrs. old.

幸存人 董有榮 78歲
不覺泪涕而下

"I was Infected by the cholera, survived by the crude opiums . However, my family lost 13 members including my parents."

我染上了霍亂後，靠打針和吃烟土療救，我家則死了十三口：

蘇轉金	董有滿及妻
蘇鳳榮	蘇老扁
蘇鳳通	蘇鄭民
蘇老麥	趙文民
董新民的父親母親	（董新民是董有用榮叔）

< The Calamity of Chongshan Village >

Among all the germ warfare attacks in Zhejiang province by the Japanese in 1942, Chongshan village in Yiwu County suffered the most.

Chongshan village is located in the Southern part of Yiwu County along the Zhejiang-Jiangxi Railway. The Village suffered two germ warfare attacks in 1942.

The first attack was in September 1942. Japanese airplanes spreaded the plague germ over the village . A young peasant name " Tiger" was the first one found sick. He was taken to a traditional doctor,Mr.Wang Daosheng's clinic for treatment. Tiger died very soon before identifying the cause . Subsequently, the Wangs were dead too . Many people in the village died if unknown causes.

On October 11,1942, Japanese special unit advanced into the village . Claiming "epidemic prevention", they forced everyone out of the village into Linshan Temple and burned more than 200 houses. Japanese claimed to do physical examination one by one . Actually, they were investigating the results of the plague attack. Three days later,The Japanese performed life dissect and experiment of these people. No one survived.

The report of plague killed 300 persons of Chongsham village by the Chief of District in Nov.15, 1942

代電 [illegible]十五日

義烏縣縣長鈞鑒[illegible]江灣一帶於本年九月廿九日(即廢曆八月二十日)起發生鼠疫蔓延甚劇現在疫勢猶撅有增無減統計死亡不下三百餘人較諸去年城區尤為嚴重職為防止疫病蔓延起見業經令飭鄉長王芝生王文格等迅速組織防疫委員会並举办病人隔離注射防疫針暨对死者妥善埋葬外理合電陳鈞座鉴核迅賜轉電專署省府派員蒞区治療並予撥款救濟以極民命臨電不勝迫切待命之至佛堂区区署区長周樹萱叩

　　幸存者王榮良，當年祇有 15 歲。一家 9 口人，父母、4 個弟弟、叔父、嬸母和他，先後都染上鼠疫。母親最先得病，不斷地說胡話，總喊口渴要喝水。接着父親也病倒了，連續發高燒。父母明知不會好，怕傳染給孩子們，便有氣無力地對榮良説："良啊，你爹媽恐怕活不長了，還是把我們抬到荒坡上，搭個草棚讓我們呆在那吧，不然的話，我們全家都會受連帶而死。你們抬去後，不要去管我們。如果我們能活下來，過兩天再把我們抬回家。"榮良深刻理解父母的好意，同時也知道這鼠疫病的厲害，于是含着泪按照父母的話辦了。結果沒過一天，母親就先死在荒草搖曳的山坡上。這時弟弟已死在家裏。又過一天，父親也死在荒野上，他身後竟留下一條長長的爬印，看樣子他是在臨死前想最後看一眼親人啊。可是我們誰也沒敢去看望和照顧老人，他終于未能爬到家。父母、弟弟和叔父、嬸母一個個地暴死，王榮良傷心地哭喊着，萬惡的日本鬼子怎麼這麼狠心使我小榮良變成孤兒！

Suwivor

Wang Rong liang (王榮良)

Japanese B.W. unit in Zhejiang attacking by Japanese “Asahi News” paper June 3, 1942

（日刊）　（明治十二年三月十七日第三種郵便物認可）　昭和十七年六月三日　朝日新聞

朝日新聞

京阪
工[…]

産業立地ならびに人口配置の適[…]綱を閣議で決定、爾來企畫院第[…]東亞國土計畫の策定も着々進捗[…]濟建設が行はれるにつれ國內の[…]を放置する時は國土計畫の策定[…]惡影響をおよぼすおそれがある[…]において工業規制地域及び工業[…]から企畫院總裁談の形式でその[…]および人口が過度に集[…]る地方、名古屋地方、[…]下關、北九州五市を中[…]し一部の例外的場合を除き工[…]

空襲防衛に[…]

本日の閣議において決定を見た工[…]にもとづき內地において工業およ[…]內地においてさし當り急速に生產[…]力擴充を必要とする業種につき工[…]的なる進展に資せんとするもので[…]ある

[…]はもちろんであつて[…]究立案中なるが四大[…]

尊し・ペスト撲滅隊

今次の浙東作戦で防疫給水班に新しくペスト撲滅隊が組織され挺身第一線部隊とともに乗り込んで涙ぐましい活躍をつゞけてゐることは既報の通りであるが、大陸のこのごろの炎暑にもかゝはらず全身ゴムの作業服に包んでペスト撲滅に挺身する隊員の辛苦は筆舌につくしがたい、病魔は重慶軍に見放されて置去りにされた敵兵にまで神のやうな救ひの手をさしのべる皇軍の貴い姿でこの手あつい看護のもとに瀕死の重床から一命をとりとめて感泣する重慶兵の数も多いとのことである（浙東戦線義烏にて白瀬特派員撮影）

大

発 朝日新聞
大阪市北区中之島
電話交換代表番号
振替貯金口座

名譽の戰死者

遠藤海軍大佐

[…]校を卒業後潛水艦乘組[…]艦、那智の副長を歷任[…]縣豐橋市小向町出身で

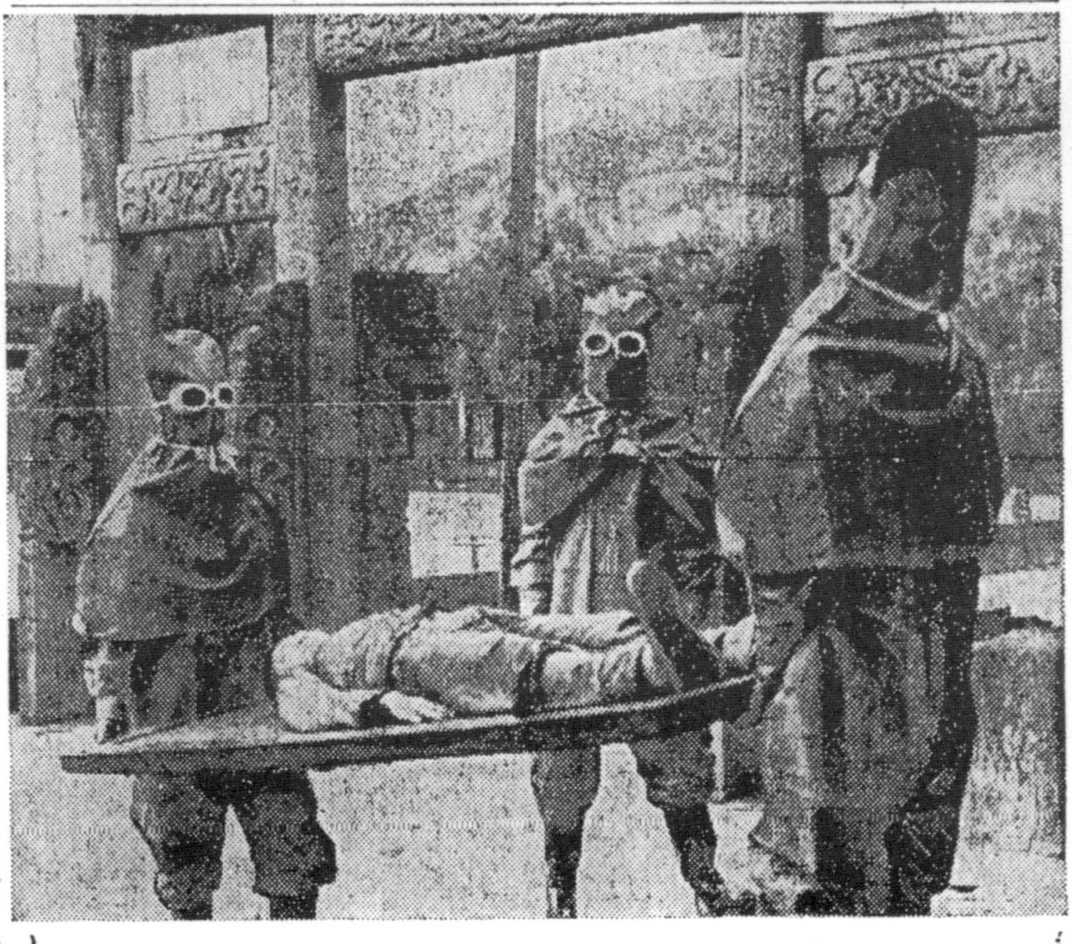

The Japanese Army soldiers were burning down residential houses in plague epidemic area where the "Unit 731"had waged germ warfare earlier.

在 731 部隊細菌戰後，疫病流行，日軍在疫區燒毀民宅，準備進駐。

Linshan Temple,
the dissection place.

林山寺,日軍臨時解剖室

A lot of people were died and lay in the ground to turn over in them graves
崇山村頭日本人制造鼠疫時留下的累累荒墳

Denounce meeting
控訴會

Terrain accusing
現場指控

Some survivors of plague of Chongshan village(1995)
崇山村的現存部份鼠疫之劫的幸存人（1995）

1943

Launched germ warfare attacks 16 times in China.

Extended B.W units to all Japanese divisions. Shifting the B.W. toward the U.S. divisions:

a) Spreaded germ all over places in Burma.

b) Performed life body experiments on 500 American POWs in Shanghai.Transported . 1,174 American POWs from Philippine to Mukden for life experiments.

c) Allocated B.W. units in nine Japanese divisions in Burma and nine D. in Pacific region training by"Unit 731".

d) The Japanese navy successfully tested the "Mark VII" bacteria bombs in the Gulf of Tonkin.

Col.Tomosada Masuda in Burma

緬甸日軍細菌戰指揮官增田知貞

U.S invesrigator Lt. Col. Murray Sanders, he was I'st attached to Tomosade Masuda.

負責首次調查增田知貞的莫瑞 ·桑德斯中校

一九四三年

對中國進行 16 次細菌攻

擴大對陸軍師團的細菌部隊配備，攻重點逐漸移向美軍：

a）緬甸全境的細菌散播

b）繼對上海500美俘作活試後又從菲律賓押送千餘美俘到沈陽活試

c）駐緬甸的日本陸軍 9 個師團全部配備細菌部隊。在太平洋戰區的師團中有 9 個 師團由 "七三一部隊" 訓練為細菌作戰部隊。

d）日本海軍在北部灣試爆細菌彈 "馬克七號" 成功。

The members of Japanese germ troops were throwing germ into a small lake.

日軍細菌部隊人員往水泡裏投撒細菌。

< Burma , the New Focal Point of germ warfare >

The Japanese launched large-scale germ warfare in Burma using"glass germ bombs"
The glass bombs were principal manufactured by the Osaka Chemical Research Institute. During the first three months in 1944, there were over 30,000 glass bombs shipped to China according to the report of the "Nanjing Evening Journal" .
Peter Williams and David Wallace , British writers, mentioned the glass bombs in their book: "There are similarity between the glass bottles and glass bacillus bombs."(P.140)
In early 1944, the American Chemical Warfare Division called a top-secret meeting of all intelligence agencies alerting that the Japanese were distributing by air the "Christmas Balls" in the China-Burma border.(p.146)
The " Crimes of the Unit 731" published by the Heilongjiang Culture and History Archive describes the glass bacillus bombs as follows:
"The bombs were made of glass tubes and would break upon hitting the ground. Their size were 10cm in length and 5 cm in diameter. Members of the "Unit 731" put plague germs into the tubes and stored underground".
The "Channel Times"of Singapore reported in September 19 , 1991 as follows:
The former Ambassador of Singapore in India , Mr. Othman, recalled his work for the Japanese "Unit Haneyama"(Unit 9420) during the war (1942-1944). He transported the fleas from rats (after narcotic)by pliers into the glass bottles. These glass bottles were shipped to Thailand......
Dr. Leonard Short came to Burma in 1942 and conducted the research and intelligence collecting of Japanese medical activity in Burma. His report describes as follows:
"The Japanese has intentionally employed germ and disease against the British and Allied Forces......"
Tomosada Masuda told Lt. Colonel Murray Sanders, U.S. investigator, that he and Kiyoshi Hayakawa were in Burma in 1943.
The 15th Division of Japanese Army, the most experienced B.W. division (carried out the Zhijiang-Jiangxi Line B.W. attacks in 1942) was stationed in Burma in 1943.

< 緬甸，新的細菌攻擊重點 >

日軍在緬甸大面積散布細菌，其主武器是玻璃裝的細菌彈。

細菌彈由"七三一部隊"設計，而主要是由日本大阪化學研究所和新加坡"9420 部隊"生產，一九四四年三月"南京晚報"報導，自一九四四年初到同年三月已由日本運載三萬個玻璃炸彈到達中國"。

英國作家，彼得.威廉斯，大衛.瓦雷斯在"七三一部隊"一書中的"盟軍情報知多少"一章內兩次述及玻璃細菌彈：

"與細菌彈有關的已經討論過的玻璃瓶子，同另一個玻璃杆細菌炸彈的報告相符合"（P.140）

"一九四四年初，美化學戰組織在緊迫中召集有關情報機構舉行一高度的秘密會議，警告與會者，日本人在中緬邊界，已經有了規律的方式，空投聖誕節球容器（這可能是賀字玻璃細菌炸彈）（P.146）

這種玻璃細菌彈之一的玻璃杆彈，其概況已由黑龍江省文史資料委員會在"日軍 731 部隊罪惡史"第 299 頁加以說明：

"它是由坡璃制成，管狀十公分長，直徑 5 公分，落地即碎，731 人員把研制的鼠疫菌等裝進去，加以密封，存于地庫"

新加坡"海峽時報"一九九一年九月十九日報導了前新加坡駐印度大使奧斯曼回憶說："一九四二年他在新加坡日軍羽山部隊（即[九四二O部隊][血清研究所])駐地打工，從麻醉的老鼠身上用鉗子取下跳蚤和使其感染鼠疫，再將它取下來放入玻璃瓶運往泰國。"

一九四二年派往緬甸負責收集日軍醫學和技術情報的雷諾特·蕭爾特醫生，對緬甸的細菌戰所作的概括：

"日軍蓄意以疾病來攻擊英軍和盟軍。"

日軍派往緬甸進行細菌戰指揮官，原南京"1644 部隊"部隊長增田知貞，于戰後在美軍桑德斯中校審訊時，承認自己于 1943 年至 1944 年在緬甸專注于"疾病"的控制。

同時期又將駐扎于中國南京附近的，在1942年對浙贛綫進行地面細菌攻擊的部隊日軍第十五師團一個專業支隊派往緬甸。

The map of arrangement of B.W.units
in Japan's Armys & Divissions(1944)
日本陸軍軍和師團配備細菌戰部隊分布圖

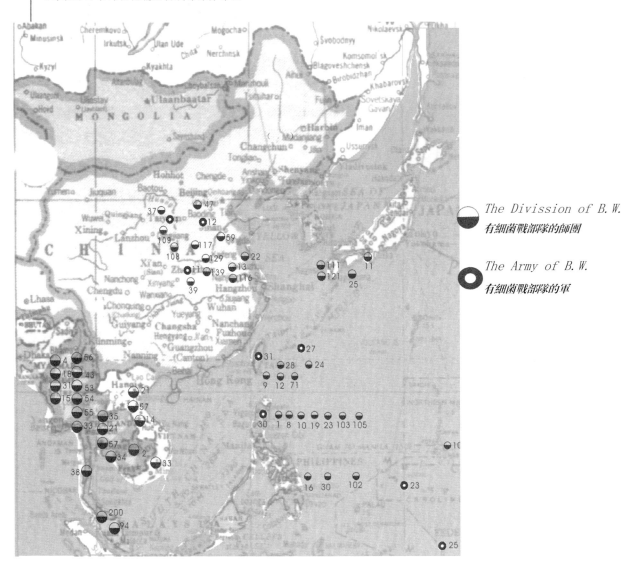

The Division of B.W.
有細菌戰部隊的師團

The Army of B.W.
有細菌戰部隊的軍

1944

Launched Grem warfare attacks 14 times in china.

Based on the results of life body experiments on American POWs in Shanghai and Mukden, Tokyo concluded that the germ cultivated on the Chinese live body could be used to attack the U.S. divisions. The development of plague bombs and germ balloons had some progress. While the Japanese forces getting inferior to the U.S. forces , the Germany forces were retreating on all fronts. Japanese generals intended to reverse the inferior situation by deploying the B.W.

Since 1943, the Japanese suffered heavy casualties at Pacific battle , lost thousands airplanes and hundreds vessels. Thus the transportation of germ weapons were hindered.

A reliable source revealed that G. Ishii had planed to spread the plague-infected fleas on the runway of Saipon airstrip before the landing of U.S forces. Ishii sent 17 "Unit 731" members on a vessel to the Saipon Island. The vessel was sunk by U.S. submarine and survived one member.

Regarding the balloon bomb tests, there were 900 to 1000 non-germ balloons Arrived in the American continent, 300 were discovered.

Arrangement of the B.W. Special Units

日軍細菌戰特種部隊分怖圖 （1944）

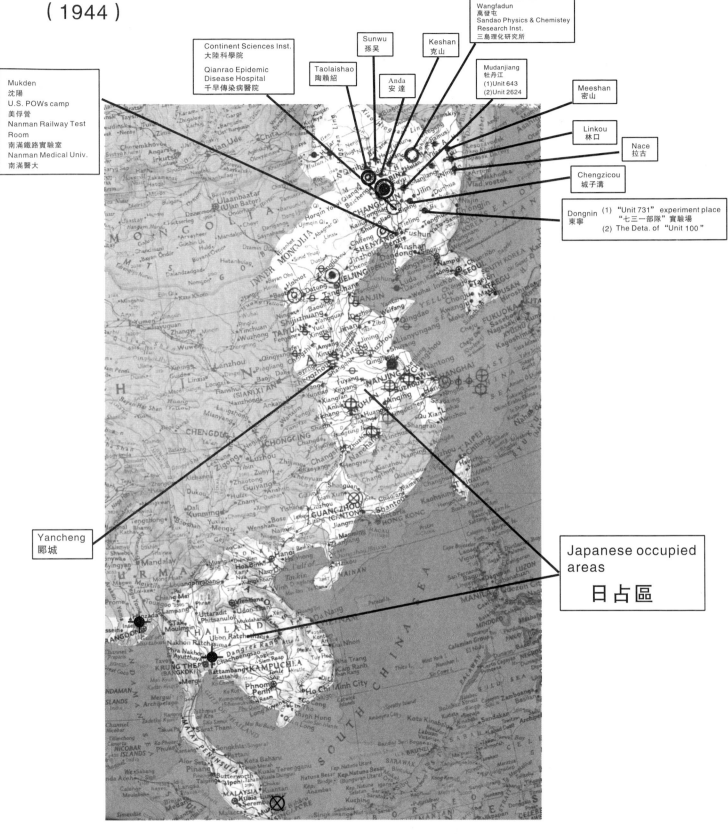

Mukden
沈陽
U.S. POWs camp
美俘營
Nanman Railway Test Room
南滿鐵路實驗室
Nanman Medical Univ.
南滿醫大

Continent Sciences Inst.
大陸科學院

Qianrao Epidemic Disease Hospital
千旱傳染病醫院

Taolaishao
陶賴紹

Sunwu
孫吳

Anda
安達

Keshan
克山

Wangfadun
萬發屯
Sandao Physics & Chemistey Research Inst.
三島理化研究所

Mudanjiang
牡丹江
(1)Unit 643
(2)Unit 2624

Meeshan
密山

Linkou
林口

Nace
拉古

Chengzicou
城子溝

Dongnin (1) "Unit 731" experiment place
東寧   "七三一部隊" 實驗場
      (2) The Deta. of "Unit 100"

Yancheng
鄲城

Japanese occupied areas
日占區

◉ "Unit731" （"七三一部隊"）
◎ "Unit 100" （"一00部隊"）
✦ Experiment base （實驗場）
✚ Detachment of "Unit 731" （"七三一" 支隊）
◎ Research Inst. （細菌研究機構）
◉ "Unit 1855" （"一八五五部隊"）
⊕ Detach. of "Unit 1855" （"一八五五" 支隊）
φ Antirote team （上海防腐隊）

⊕ Transfer station （上海轉運站）
⊕ Training center （上海訓練中心）
⊗ "Unit 8604" （"八六0四部隊"）
⊗ "Unit 9420" （"九四二0部隊"）
⬤ Detach. of "Unit 9420" （"九四二0部隊" 支隊）
⬤ "Unit 1644" （"一六四四部隊"）
⊖ Detach. of "Unit 1644" （"一六四四部隊" 支隊）

According to :

731 Exhibition July 1993–Dec.1994,Japan
Most informations came from the confessions of Japanese POWs.
資料來源:
1）"731部隊展"，一九九三年七月至于一九九四年十二月，日本。
2）中國戰場細菌戰部隊的布置，主要依據于日軍戰俘的供詞。

105

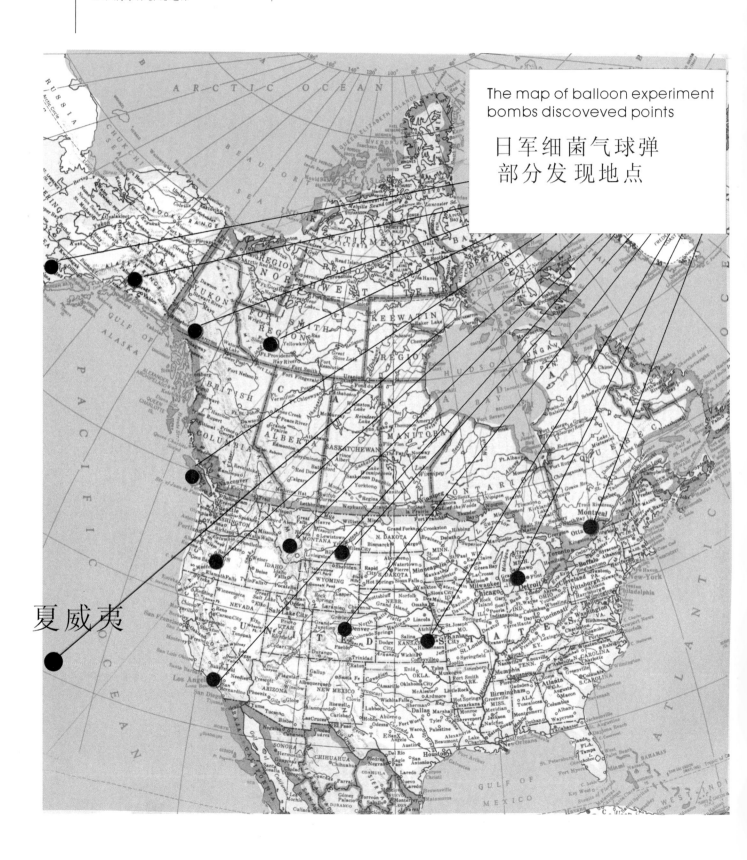

The map of balloon experiment
bombs discoveved points

日军细菌气球弹
部分发现地点

夏威夷

the germ bomb's balloon
气球细菌炸弹结构

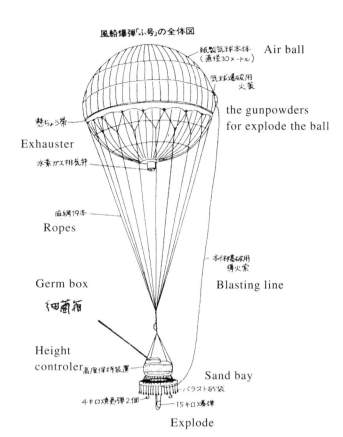

風船爆弾「ふ号」の全体図

紙製気球本体
（直径10メートル） — Air ball

気球爆破用火薬

懸ちょう帯 — the gunpowders for explode the ball

Exhauster
水素ガス排気弁

麻綱19本 — Ropes

本体爆破用導火索 — Blasting line

Germ box
细菌箱

Height controler 高度保持装置

バラスト砂袋 — Sand bay

4キロ焼夷弾2個
15キロ爆弾

Explode

Japan's proposed using germ balloons against America

一九四四年

對中國實施 14 次細菌攻.

經過對上海、沈陽美俘的細菌試驗，未發現人種對血清免疫力有不同區別後，東京認為十多年來在中國人身成功所作活試所培養出來的強悍細菌，也可以攻擊美軍。同時期，在鼠疫細菌彈和氫氣球細菌彈的改進上也獲得進展，用細菌攻擊美軍和美國本土的準備已趨成熟。而日美實力對比，已明顯出美方居于優勢，加上歐洲戰場德軍已由列寧格勒退到東德，從英法海峽退至萊茵河畔，一些日軍高級將領有意寄托于細菌攻擊來扭轉戰局。

但是，日軍自一九四三年下半年接邊在馬紹爾、馬列裏亞納、塞班和菲律賓戰役中受到重創，損失飛機近萬架，軍艦百餘艘，喪失了對海空的制權，使細菌的越洋供應發生困難。

六月十五日美軍登陸塞班前，石井決定把塞班機場的跑道噴射鼠疫感染的跳蚤，并由"七三一部隊"選派 17 名隊員組成敢死隊，人員由船支運往塞班途中為美潛艇擊沉，僅一人生還（吳天威："日本對美國的細菌攻擊"）

細菌氣球彈的試驗，已有九百至一千個沒有載細菌的氣球到達北美，其中被美方發現的有三百個，然而，由于害怕美方的細菌報復而動搖了飄襲美國的決心。

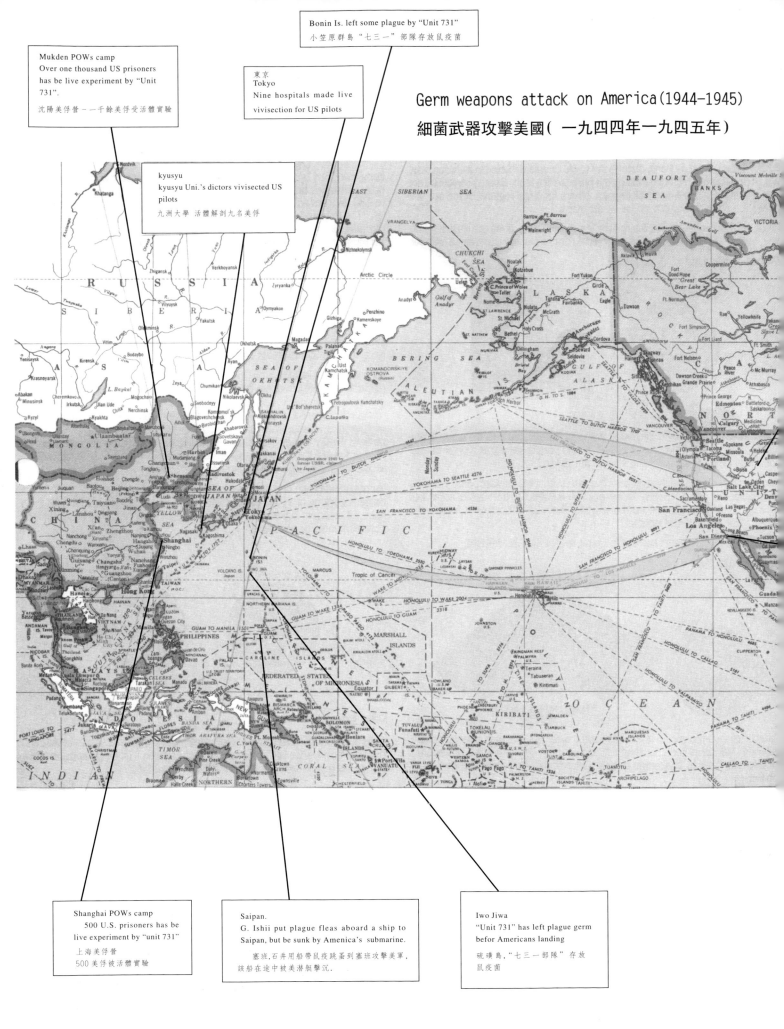

Mukden POWs camp
Over one thousand US prisoners
has be live experiment by "Unit
731".

沈陽美俘營--一千餘美俘受活體實驗

Bonin Is. left some plague by "Unit 731"
小笠原群島 "七三一" 部隊存放鼠疫菌

東京
Tokyo
Nine hospitals made live
vivisection for US pilots

Germ weapons attack on America(1944-1945)
細菌武器攻擊美國(一九四四年一九四五年)

kyusyu
kyusyu Uni.'s dictors vivisected US
pilots

九洲大學 活體解剖九名美俘

Shanghai POWs camp
　500 U.S. prisoners has be
live experiment by "unit 731"

上海美俘營
500美俘被活體實驗

Saipan.
G. Ishii put plague fleas aboard a ship to
Saipan, but be sunk by Amenica's submarine.

　塞班.石井用船帶鼠疫跳蚤到塞班攻擊美軍,
該船在途中被美潛艇擊沉.

Iwo Jiwa
"Unit 731" has left plague germ
befor Americans landing

硫磺島, "七三一部隊" 存放
鼠疫菌

108

1945

The war situation has been take a sudden turn and then developed rapidly. Tokyo ordeded The command of general mobiligation, all B.W. Units into a last-ditch fight position, but it's too late.

Plague attack on San Diago" Cherry Blossom Night Plan" has not come true.

Japanese surrendered "Unit731" with other B.W . units made a through distruction to perished the evidences of crimes

---

Balloon bombs 900 Pcs. or 1,000 pcs. arrived U.S
氣球炸彈,九百至一千枚投向美國.

一九四五年

戰局急轉直下，日本動員全部細菌部隊與全日本陸海軍作殊死戰，但為時已晚。鼠疫攻擊聖地亞哥的"櫻花之夜"計劃未能實現。

"八一五"日本投降前，"七三一部隊"作緊急破壞，消滅罪證。

San Diegs "Cherry Blossom Night"

In June 1945," The task fource would leave Japan for U.S. military harbor at San Diego on Sep.22. Twenty members of the attacking team will take by submarine to the point 500 K.M from the har bor, where they would be flown by airplane to the back of harbor. After landing they, whose bodies had been infected with bacteria, would spread the plague germ around......"
(Morimasa Takashi "Unit 731 and B.W.")

聖地亞哥
日軍"櫻花之夜"襲擊計劃

一九四五年六月"七三一部隊"組成20人的細菌突擊隊，小幡石雄爲隊長"，九月二十二日從日本出發，目的地是聖地亞哥軍港。二十一名特攻隊員乘潛水艇接近距軍港500公里處，改乘艦載機着陸于軍港背後，攻擊隊員手執鼠疫跳蚤，自身也成爲感染源，向四周散布鼠疫菌……。細菌工廠實行二十四小時連軸轉體制，并且研制了毒性比平常細菌大十倍的變异菌種……。(森正孝"七三一部隊與細菌戰")

All buildings and equipments of Pingfan base destroyed completely by
artillersys fire and engineer's explod in Aug. 10-14,1945、 killed four
hundred "logs"、 shot Chinese interpreter Lee Chuten with 500
labourers......
Successive demolitions and did away with a witness, it's just for without
leaving a single trace of crimes.

七三一的毀滅

"七三一部隊"在一九四五年"八一五"宣布投降前的八月十日至八月十四日間，用步兵炮和工兵爆破，炸毀平房全部設
施，殺死四百監禁供活試、活剖的中國人（也有少數白種人）和五百勞工，搶殺中國翻譯李初庠。
爆炸、滅口就是為了罪行的絕跡。

PingFan after explored
平房被炸之後

The destroyed central of Square Buildings
被炸毁的四方楼中心

活體解剖室一角
Dissect room No. #1

The remains of the anatomy lab.

Air team
航空隊

The remains of the
virus lab. of Kasahara.
笠原班病毒研究室殘迹.

Pingfan in ruins.

平房成廢墟

Pingfan in ruins.
平房成廢墟

Weapon storage
武器庫

兵器班迹
Weapon Section

The remains of the
weapon detachment
兵器班殘遺

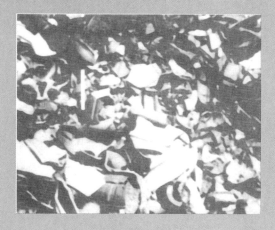

Yamaguchi group's bacteriological bomb research institute.
山口班細菌彈研究室

The laboratory in which "frostbite experiments" took place on human subjects.
吉村班冷凍實驗室舊址

Inseet building
被燒毀的田中班昆蟲舍

The burned-down flea breeding lab of Tanaka Section.
被燒毀的田中班跳蚤培植室

The enclosing wall of
Tanaka
田中班

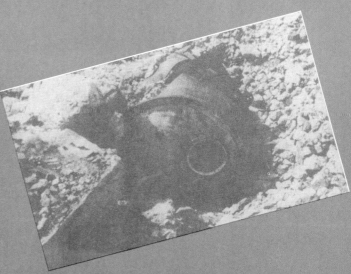

The site of a special prison
特別監獄遺址（一）

The site of a special prison
特別監獄遺址（二）

The remains of a special
prison underground labo-
ratory
特別監獄的地下實驗室殘迹

The site of a special
prison
特別監獄遺址
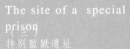

Producing special bacteriological
weapons which looked like sticks &
fountain pens.
筆型或棍型的細菌武器制造工廠遺迹

The remains of the
interior of the strain
storeroom.

菌種貯藏室內部殘迹

The remains of the germ lab

細菌研究室殘迹

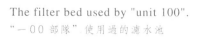

The filter bed used by "unit 100".

"一〇〇部隊" 使用過的濾水池

"七三一部隊" 逃亡路綫
The Route of "Unit 731" Runaway

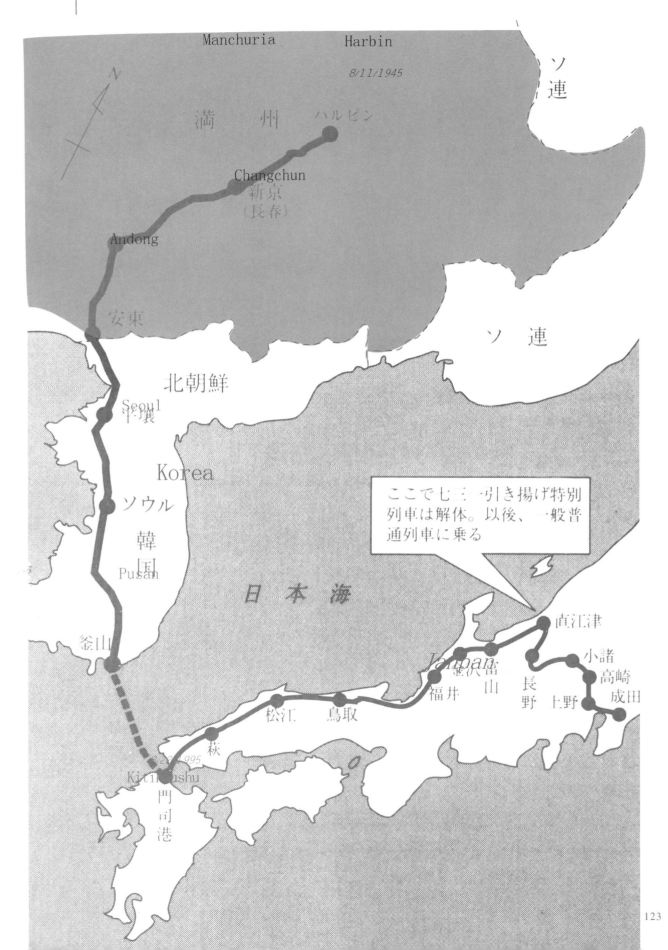

Noma Shrine in Kanazawa, in which
the members of "Unit 731 " were
hiding affer the war ended.
金瀘，野間神社，二戰結束後，七三一
部隊人員的藏身處。

CHAPTER II
THREE MAJOR GERM ASSAULTS

第二章
三次重大的細菌攻擊

Section   1
The Cholera Assaults on Kunming-Boashan

When Yotsuke Matsuka, the Foreign Affairs Minister visited Germany seven months prior to Pearl Harbor attack, Adolph Hitler once again urged Japan to activate its military actions against the British and American Forces in South Pacific to coordinate with the movement of the German army in Europe .This was based upon the Tri-party Agreement signed among Germany, Japan, and Italy on Sep.27,1940.

Hitler has dreamed of a German-Japanese military union in the Middle East.

Thus Matsuka signed a peace pact with Russia in Apr. 1942 not to attack one another in order to relieve itself of any danger in the back door while Japan concentrated its efforts in South Pacific.

On Oct. 18, 1941, in order to fulfill its promise to Hitler, Japan allowed the formation of military cabinet headed by the war minister Hideki Tojo.

On the eve of Dec.7.1941, Japanese simultaneously staged air, naval, and land surprise attacks at Pearl Harbor, Wake Island, the Island of Guam, Hong Kong, Philippenes, and Thailand. In Pearl Harbor Japan sacrificed 27 war planes against the sinking of five and seriously damaging of three American battleships while destroying 250 American fighter planes. The U.S. military command on Wake Island surrendered on Dec 23rd. Two days later the British Commander-in -Chief in Hong Kong along with 100,000 British troops raised white flage to Japan. A few days later Japan occupied Manila on Jan.2,1942,...... By

Apr. of 1942, after 70,000 U.S. troops in Bataan (Philippines) were disarmed by the Japanese, no more major battles await the Japnese military takeover of South Picific. Then the land forces of Japan pushed forth westward from Indo-China into Burma in 1942.

In the meantime, according to Hilter's command notice No.41 (Apr.5, 1942), the German troops started to attack S.U. planning to meet with the Japanese forces in Asia Minor.

The Japanese military high command made up a very
 ambitious plan of action called:
"Ki Go Direction Plan" which
 included six major targets:

1 . K u n m i n g (Y u m a n province, China)

2. Lishui, Yushan, Quzhou. Guilin, Nanning.

3. Samda

4. DH. AD. KA

5. Australian air bases.

第一節
昆明、保山的霍亂攻擊

一　九四一年十二月日本偷襲珍珠港前的七個月，希特勒在日本外相松岡洋佑訪德時，根據"德意日三國同盟條約"（一九四〇年九月二十七日簽訂于柏林），再次督促日本發動對美英的太平洋南進攻勢，配合德軍的東進，然後德日兩軍完成在中東的會師。

松岡遂于次年四月與日本在中國東北滿洲相對峙的蘇聯訂立"日蘇互不侵犯條約"，解除其南進時的後顧之憂。

一九四一年十月十八日，日本政府為實現與德謀約，由陸相東條英機組成決戰內閣，十一月七日日軍分別在太平洋的珍珠港、威克島、香港、菲律賓和泰國、馬來亞半島同時展開突然襲擊。

日軍的襲擊頻頻得手，美軍在珍珠港海軍主力被毀，日機以二十七架的損失，獲得美主力艦五艘的沉沒、三艦重創和美機二百五十架的毀滅。威克島美軍于十二月二十三日投降，兩天後英國駐港司令和十萬英軍舉起白旗。接着日軍又于一九四二年一月二日占領馬尼拉，二月十五日新加坡英國海軍在主力艦"威爾士王子"、"却

敵"號被炸沉而沒有後援情況下，十四萬英軍投降于日軍山下奉文將軍摩下。到一九四二年四月，日軍南進計劃已完全實現，七萬美軍在巴丹解除武器後南太平洋戰區已無大戰。日軍主力遂由印度支那揮師西進緬甸，從那裏進攻中國的雲南和印度。同時期的德軍，由希特勒下達"第四十一號元首訓令"（四月五日），限令攻入蘇南的高加索，以便最終與由南亞西進的日軍勝利實施戰略合圍。

東京參謀本部據此制定出龐大的細菌攻擊計劃，該計劃名曰"木號指導計劃"。計劃確定攻擊的六個地方為：A、昆明（中國的雲南省省會）；B、麗水、玉山、衢州、桂林、南寧（均為美機起降的沿太平洋一線的航空基地）；C、SAMDA；D、DH、AD、KA；E、澳大利亞空軍基地；F、加魯加塔CALCUTTA，（又譯加爾各塔、印度東部美英軍基地）。①

細菌進攻由日軍南方軍（司令部駐新加坡）的"波字九四二〇部隊"負責進行。該部隊成立于日軍攻陷新加坡兩個月後的一九四二年四月十五日，離日軍參謀本部要求細菌進擊雲南昆明的時間（五月初）非常接近，顯然準備不足。于是，由東京調令其他軍區的細菌部隊前往緬甸和雲南前綫。

Honolulu Star-Bulletin 1st EXTRA

WAR!

SAN FRANCISCO, Dec. 7.—President Roosevelt announced this morning that Japanese planes had attacked Manila and Pearl Harbor.

OAHU BOMBED BY JAPANESE PLANES

SIX KNOWN DEAD, 21 INJURED, AT EMERGENCY HOSPITAL

Attack Made On Island's Defense Areas

Hundreds See City Bombed

最先向美國公衆報告珍珠港事件的是《檀香山星訊報》發出的號外。報紙上的大字標題為："戰爭！瓦胡島遭日軍飛機轟炸"。

Join force Plan of German with Japanese(1942)
日德會師計劃（一九四二年）

6. Calcutta (India)①

The B.W. attack of the Japanese South Army, was executed by "Unit 9420". This special unit was established soon after Japan took over Singapore in Apr. 15, 1942, very close to the bacteria attack date of early May for Kunming-Boashan, "Unit 9420" was obviously not yet equipped for this action, so that other B.W. forces had to be transported to Burma-China border.

The 2'nd Archives Bureau in Nanjing has comfirmed from reliable records that there were two special units of Japanese B.W. group that were sent in Apr.1942:

1. From Guangzhou (Canton), Special "Nami xx Unit".

2. From Nanjing special unit "Aki 7371" of 15 th D.②, led by Captain Akiba③

We have evidence indicating that the primary unit of B.W., "Unit 731" from Harbin (Manchuria) also played a major role in this action in 1942. The expert on two of the diseases cholera and typhoid, Major Kiyoshi Hayakawa had already been transferred from Harbin to Singapore by this time, and Tomosada Masuda, the assistant of G. Ishii was came from Nanjing④.

It was further discovered that everyone of those more than ten divisions which belonged to Japanese South Army were fully equipped to do B.W.. Among these the 56th D. did indeed spread the diseases-carrying germ along China-Burma border during Apr.1942.

One of the "supplemental" soldier of the "Unit 113" in 56th D. by name of Minori Shinano admitted that:

"......,using B.W. in the battlefield, my most frequent experience was during 1942. For example,

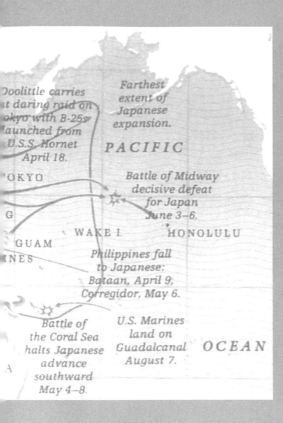

在中國南京"第二檔案館"已查明有兩支細菌部隊分別由日軍華南軍司令部（廣州）和華中軍司令部（南京）派往南亞支援：

廣州派出的"波（　）部隊"②

南京派出的"15D.部隊"所屬，以部隊長秋葉大尉所率的"祭七三七一部隊"。③

日軍細菌戰的主力——哈爾濱的"七三一部隊"也肯定在這一細菌攻擊中出任要角，該部隊的細菌戰專家石井的助手增田知貞也趕往緬甸。早川清這時已由"七三一部隊"調赴新加坡。④

南方軍所轄的十多個師團，全部配備齊細菌作戰部隊，已查明第五十六師團于一九四二年四月在中緬邊境施放過細菌。

日軍第五十六師團第一一三聯隊補充兵品野實，在一九九一年出版的《中日拉孟決戰揭秘——异國的鬼》（群衆出版社）中承認："在戰場上，使用的細菌最多的是一九四二年；當時下命讓久垣兵長去炸毀臘戌的水源地。而實際是讓他去施放細菌。"

同年五月該細菌部隊前進至雲南保山前綫的松山與中國軍隊在怒江

The city of Boashan before assaults
劫前保山

devices with large quantity of "germ bomb" containing cholera disease. on that day more than 10,000 people were instantly killed with the survivors running to the hills and mountains and other nearby counties, leaving Boashan a ghost town overnight.The people who originally lived in the countryside were poor farmers, when they saw the city dwellers all running away aften 78% of the houses and buildings in Boashan were destroyed, many of them went into the city to gather the leftover food and dry goods. For example, one famer from Jinji country named Ai Shan went into the city and carried home a role of nice looking cloth material, hope to make some new clothes for his family. But Ai was in contact with the germ on the way and started to vomit as well as to have diarrhoea. He soon died and transmitted the disease to his family.

Since the May 4th Japanese bombardment has destroyed 78% all the city and more than fulfilled its military purposes at Boashan, there was no more reason for its airforce to bomb the city again. Thus, those there more major bombing missions of Boashan on May 5th, 6th and May 8th obvious were no meant to kill more people by explosives or by burning. These renewed bombing missions appeared to be used to the refugees from Boashan to other areas. This action forcefully accelerated the spreading rate of the diseases.

Yayi Type Maggets bomb
宇治型蛆蟲彈

This Japanese tactics was repeated again such as in the South-Western region of Shandong province in Fall of 1943. In the Fall of 1943 the Japan's troops first initiated the infection of Chinese farmers with cholera, then broke the river dams and sent water and sent their troops to attack the already infected areas to force the spread of that disease to much wider areas.

In 1999 the "Japanese Biological Warfare Crimes Investigation Committee" from the U.S. visited Boashan and interviewed a Mr. Lin Yuyue who was out of the teacher at Wen Chang Gong Elementary School, You Wang Village, Shi Dian County, a survivor of that horrible experience. The witnesses included Mr Lin and his follow teachers Su Zhizeng, Zheng Yongkang, and a Mr. Zhang. They all saw a bomb that was not completely shattered. The bomb was like one meter long about 20 some centimeters in

The shall shrapnels
of germ boom.
細菌彈彈片

diameter. Inside that bomb contained yellowish waxy substance and many live flies struggling to get out to fly away. Mr.Lin repeated himself under guestioning by the investigation team members. From the gestures and language and details in his story, the appeared to have told the truth. Due to the number of years from 1942 to 1999, Mr. Lin was unable to accurately describe the shape and size of the bomb he saw, But when he was prsesented with a picture showing eight different types of germ bombs, he immediately identified the one type of bomb called "Maggets Bomb".

Another suivivor Mr. Huang Zhengkang also saw one of these "Maggets Bomb". His aunt, sister and his younger cousin all died of the same disease.

According to one of the members of the "Unit 731" Ueno in his written confession dated May 8,1951:

"When we were dropping Maggets Bombs around Kunming region, one of the Japanese bombers of the Unit 731 was shot down. The pilot ,Captain Yanaginose was killed in action". (Ueno attended the funeral).

The cholera disease started in Jin Ji village on May 7, 1942, just three days after the 1'st bomb was dropped. The 1'st victim in Jin Ji village, was Zhang Duan, the mother was Zhang Xiyuan. She died both vomitting and having diarrhoea at the same time. At 1'st due to sibling quarrels on other matters, Zhang Xiyuan accused someone putting poison in their food. Then another young man

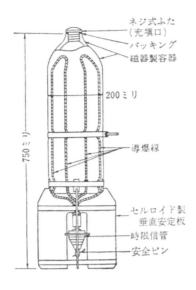

The constructions of Yagi
Type "Marggets" bomb
宇治型蛆蟲彈

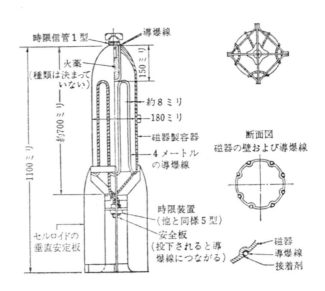

Yagi 50 Type "Marggets" bomb
宇治50型蛆蟲彈

軍細菌罪行調查小組委員會"的調查人員訪問林毓越，林反復陳述了上述事實。

　　由于年代太久，林毓越對細菌彈的尺寸在開始面對調查時，記憶不清。當調查人員向他展示一張畫有八種不同的日軍細菌彈的圖片時，林一下子就指出其中的一種，這一種就是"蛆蟲彈"。

　　由旺鄉的黃正康也看到同形炸彈，當時一些人好奇也去圍看，不久許多人都患霍亂死亡，黃的姐姐、姑媽、表弟也同時死去。"蛆蟲彈"投下後，保山城附近隨即發生霍亂。

　　對保山進行霍亂攻擊的同時，日機也在昆明至保山公路沿綫投下細菌彈，據"七三一"部隊成員上野一九五一年五月八日的口供："在昆明方面使用細菌彈時，七三一的飛機被擊落，駕駛員柳瀨大尉戰死"（上野曾參加柳瀨的葬禮）。

　　霍亂病最初發生于一九四二年五月七日，保山縣金鷄鄉金鷄村的張錫元之母張段氏，她是第一個上吐下瀉致死的，張錫元因兄弟不合，曾責怪有人下毒。張體成家大院一個剛從保山城揀回一塊鹽巴的張昭，患同樣病症暴死。漢莊街的蔣庭瑞也死于同病，才知道發生了"瘟疫"。

　　這時候，霍亂病也在保山城四郊的村寨相繼發生。五月中旬在各鄉發展，五月十三日，雲南省急派衛生實驗處處長繆安成率十二人趕到保山進行臨時防治。由于醫藥缺乏，醫務人員不足，對染病民眾完全沒有治療，僅在保山三十萬人的疫區注射霍亂防疫針一萬零二百人次，用漂白粉對水井消毒八百五十次，藥物用盡被迫停止，故沒有控制住疫情。霍亂遂迅速向四下擴散，形成發病高潮。

　　同時期，保山以南四十一英裏的施甸縣和保山以東通向昆明的永平縣也發生霍亂。

　　以保山地區含保山城、施甸縣和永平縣為中心的霍亂向四下蔓延，又大體上是順難民流亡的人流方向由西向東。六月在保山至昆明的中間站距保山一百三十英裏之大理（原稱南津）造成新的霍亂潮，然後遍及雲南一百一十八市中的六十六個縣，至同年七月霍亂病始轉低落。

　　這一時期死于霍亂病的人數以保山最多，基于史記載的資料有：《保山縣志》："炸（指出1942年5月4日）後數日，保山城鄉到處發生霍亂傳染病，猖獗一時。染病者，上吐下瀉，朝發夕死。持續數月，全縣約死五、六萬人之多"。⑤

　　保山縣縣長孟立人于一九四六年三月十五日所呈報之《滇西抗戰時期保山損失慘狀并懇請救濟》一文中，述及"及經五 四慘炸，霍亂遂大為流傳，到處發生，朝不保夕，相繼死亡，傳染之屬，竟至死後無人抬埋者，所在皆是。據當時統計，死亡在五、六萬人之多"。⑥

　　《保山市志》"五月十二日開始，霍亂在城鄉大流行，沿滇緬公路繼續蔓延，尤以板橋、金鷄……八個鄉鎮最為嚴重。……潰軍、駐軍、難僑也多數被傳染，無藥醫治，慘死者不計其數，死尸遺弃路邊溝壑，無人料理。據不完全統計，此次霍亂大流行，死亡六萬餘人"。⑦

The map of cholera attacked on Kunming, Baoshan
昆明、保山霍亂攻擊圖

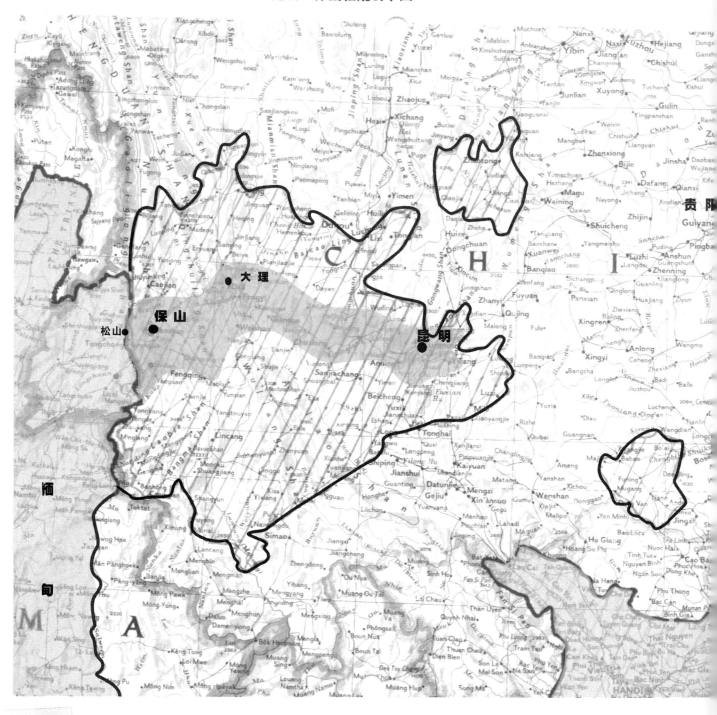

 Under the heel of cholea 霍亂蔓延區

 Japanese occupied area 日軍占領區

 Serious cholea area 霍亂嚴重病區

Survivor Chang Ticheng, 75 yrs. Old, he condemned the Japan's cholera attack: "My family has 8 relativies death took place cholera epidemic, they are name as following as: Uncle Chang Zhao, Grandfather Chang Chunmao, Brother Chang Tigang, Aunt Meng ,Shuixiu, Sister in-law, Yung Alian Grandmother Yung Atai, Aunt Chang Shun, Aunt Chang Liufeng."

張體成，七十五歲
"日本霍亂後，使我家死亡的有：叔張昭、祖父張春茂、兄張體剛、叔嬸孟水秀、二嫂楊阿蓮、叔祖母楊阿太、姑張順、張劉鳳。"

Survivor Ma Jilin, 78 years old, his father Ma shaoan died from cholera attacking.

控訴人：馬驥麟　78歲

"一九四二年五月四日，日機來炸保山，我家逃往甫津。五月十日逃上彌松山，停留二月。李根源動員大家返回保山城。不久，我父馬紹安患霍亂，沒有醫生，吃"十滴水"二瓶，又放"小痧"，無救，死于楊柳鄉。"

"我爹死于霍亂後，同學陸玲嬌也病死，逃來的華僑也有些人死于霍亂後，我房前給"中國銀行"打雜的青年亦死。"

in the larger court yard next door named Zhang Zhao who took a chunk of rock salt back from the city soon died of the same symptoms. Right after that on a neighboring street, Han Zhuang street, a man named Jiang Tingrei died in similar conditions. Everyone in the village then realized that a contagious disease was now exploding among them. When cholera was happening and spreading very quickly, Yunnan Provincial Health Center immediately sent the chief health officer Mr. Miu Ancheng with 12 people in his team race to Boashan in Mid-May to do temporary prevention work.

Due to the lack of medical supplies, lack of sufficient trained health officers and staff, in Boashan region only 10,000 people were actually immunized out of 300,000 population. Only 850 wells received bleach for dis-injection. When the chemical was used up they were forced to stop. Thus, the disease was not at all under control. The same disease cholera quickly happening in Shi Dian County 41 miles south to Boashan and to Yong Ping County East of Boashan toward Kunming. By June the same disease had fully spread to 66 counties out of 118 in Yunan Province. It did not wind down until the end of July.

According to historical documents we found, Boashan County suffered the worst among all the counties in Yunan Province.

Boashan County Official record: "A few days after the bombardment, the cholera disease because rampant all over Boashan city and its suburbs. It lasted several months, with total death toll around 55,000 people" ⑤. On March 15, 1946, the county chief Mr. Meng Liren submitted a report to the Province Off ice reguesting for financial assistance.

The report was entitled: "Western Yunnan Lives and Property Loss During WW Ⅱ " part of it went as follows:

"...... After the May 4th bombardment, the cholera disease spread throughout our Boashan county like a wild fire. In some cases the entire family or families all died within days that there was no one there to bury the dead. According to official tally at the time, about 55,000 people died in our county." ⑥

Boashan City official record said: "Starting approximately May 12,1942, cholera spread quickly along highway in countryside, especially seriours among Ban Chieao, Jin Ji...... township and villages,...... the retreating soldiers, garrision soldiers, and rufugees also were infectcd in large numbers. There was largely no medicine to treat the majority of them. Many died bodies were left in road side ditchs for a long time without anyone to cover or burn them. Our official record shows more than 60,000 dead." ⑦

In an old record by the Dual Provincial Inspector (Yuman and Gueizhou provinces) Mr. Li Genyuan on June 7, 1942 in a telegram asking for financial assistance, he said:

"...... A few days after the beastial attacks by the Japanese bombers, cholera disease became rampant around Boashan region. Up to this day the dead body count around the immediate area is more than 60,000" ⑧. This was before the "high tide" of the disease in that region.

The National Rescue Commission under the Yunan of the Republic of China issued a report in

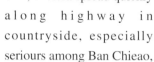

Surviror Dong yousong, 78 Yys. Old, he said: " I suffered cholera in 1942, but safed from death by some opiums. My family has had 13 persons were died same time."
控訴人：董有榮　78 歲
　　"我染上霍亂後，靠打痧和吃烟土獲救。我家則死了十三口：蘇轉金、蘇鳳榮、蘇鳳盈、蘇鄭氏、蘇老麥、趙文明、董有滿及妻、蘇老扁、董新明的父親和母親（董新明是董有榮之叔）。"

　　國民政府舊檔案所載雲貴監察使李根源在一九四二年六月七日發出的"文昌府文徵．保山慘變乞賑通電"："獸機肆虐之後數日，城鄉各處發現霍亂，迄今日環山周圍平壩，死者已五、六千人" [8]。這是保山霍亂病發高潮前期的死亡人數。中華民國行政院善後救濟總署滇西辦事處一九四六年"滇西災區救濟工作報告及業務計劃"指出："保山于民國三十一年（即一九四二年）霍亂致死六萬人"。[9]

　　保山．魏蘭馨當年作歌，歌詞：

　　"五月偕六月，瘟疫特猖狂，殺人六萬名，數目驚天蒼。……" [10]

　　歷史學家方學瑜所著《抗日戰爭滇西戰事篇》述及保山縣之霍亂致死人數說："事後統計死亡五、六萬人"。[11]

　　"由緬甸逃來的難民和軍人還沒有計入，鄉下死于霍亂的人比城裏還嚴重。" [12]

　　一九四一年底保山縣人口未有統計。一九三六年（日軍入侵前六年）人口統計數為三十六萬人，一九四二年底統計為二十八萬三千人。日本投降後一九四五年統計數為二十五萬六千人。[13] 未查出日軍入侵之前保山縣發生嚴重影響人口變遷的因素。一九四二年五月日機轟炸保山城，除炸死城區居民一萬人 [14] 和支前民工死亡三千五百人外，全縣總人口劇減六萬五千人。[15] 其中流動人口既未計入，也影響不大。如緬甸逃來的華僑使人口增加，（依五月四日日機炸保山時，劉言昌縣長向省長報告中提及華僑被炸死七百人推算應有華僑滯留保山縣約五六千人，全保山境內應有三萬人左右）。日機轟炸和霍亂流行又使當地民眾和華僑向東逃亡而使人口減少。逃亡的人中間，祇有較為富裕的人家才能逃往昆明，一般城鄉居民眾多逃往保山城不遠的山區。如這次調查中，五十六戶逃亡人家，祇有保山縣的富裕戶、原任過國府官吏的馬紹安逃往大理，金鷄鄉的楊子林逃出保山，渡過瀾滄江，張春和一家一度逃往怒江邊的芹菜塘，計三戶十六口人。

count around Boashan had not included the refugees and retreating soldiers from Burma".[11] [12]

Six years prior to the Japanese attack of Boashan in 1936, the county census was around 360,000. At the end of 1942 the census was 283,000. After the surrender of Japan in 1945 the census went down to only 256,000[13].

Since 10,000 were instantly killed in the May bombing of Boashan[14], and about 3,500 civilian laborers died in the frontiers, the sudden decrease from 360,000. (If we assume that there was no increase in six years) down to 283,000 meant that 65,000 were not accounted for[14]. Of these the new borns minus the natural deaths were not included.

Therefore, the 65,000 number due to the spread of the cholera disease in a solid number. This was about 1/6 reduction of Boashan county.

If one looks at figuere of 9 towns and villages surrounding Boashan city, one might find that the 65,000 number might be on the conservation side:

Out of these nine townships and villages we inspected on site, only Jin Ji village was one of the "eight villages and Townships" that suffered "the most". Therefore, the 1/6 reduction in population from 360,000 to 283,000 due to the

Mr. Chang B.S. To weep at the throught of his family's sorrows.
張本善爲死難家人而淚下

Wu Litin's uncles Wu Yongjing,Wu yongyu and Wu Yongguang all killed by cholera in 1942.
控訴人：武李庭　80歲
死于霍亂的叔叔有：
　　武有金（當時四十歲）
　　武有玉（三十歲）
　　武有光之弟武阿發，四十多歲，由緬甸逃回來的，幸存未死人武有全，"打痧"得活。

140

一的有三個村，占三分之一的有四個村，占四分之一的有兩個村，全部超過全縣所占的六分之一的死亡率。

由于調查所到的鄉村，祇有金鷄是一九四二年保山霍亂死亡率最高的八個"重災鄉鎮"之一。（八個"重災鄉鎮"為：板橋、北上、北中、束哨、金鷄、永順、永和、五綫），應具有代表性。因此全保山縣有六分之一的人死于霍亂，實屬可信。

保山以外的霍亂病亡人數，也有部分記載：

施甸縣據《施甸縣志》記載："霍亂暴發蔓延至本縣的三岔河、瓦房村、仁和橋、沙溝、何家村、華興村、四大莊、姚關、萬興、太平、菜子一帶廣為流行。染病人多為上吐下瀉、脫水休克、朝發夕死，死亡萬餘人。"[16]

龍陵縣據陳祖梁的調查，龍陵的臘猛、董別、老街子、碧寨、大龍、鬆山村、阿石寨、平安鄉和猛糯九個村寨，死于霍亂的有一千多人。其中如松山村的施煥娣一家十一口，霍亂死亡六口；馬鹿塘李三家七口，病亡六口，鄭東周家五個兒子，死了四個。[17]

作家李家茂所作"霍亂為何蔓延滇西"，親述他一九四二年從保山經大理到昆明的實地見聞，文稿中述及"下關（即大理）死兩三千人，永平死一千多人。"[18]

依此計算，雲南省除保山縣死亡六萬多，施甸縣死亡一萬多外的六十四個傳染霍亂的縣份，平均死亡人數應在兩千以上。

此外，霍亂也讓不少不計入當地戶口的駐軍和緬甸逃回來的數萬華僑染病致死。據幸存人武李庭的老人回憶其死亡的親戚中，有一個叫武阿發是其堂兄武有光之弟，剛從緬甸逃往回家鄉，不到二十天就染上了霍亂病死亡。

另一個被采訪的原駐守保山的國軍第五十三軍第六百九十一團"三十七小炮連"的士兵張吉劉、八十七歲，回憶說："霍亂也部分傳染到軍隊裏來。記得在新界坡埋了許多兵，都是死于霍亂的。"

關于駐軍被霍亂菌傳染病的情況，也鑒于當時駐軍司令官之一的宋希濂將軍，他在其《遠征軍在滇西的敎訓和反攻》一文中述及"那時軍隊全部都注射了防疫針，感染情況不嚴重"[19]，雖然不嚴重，卻已感染是實。

一九四二年五月——七月駐防保山國軍檔案，不少部隊均向上報告士兵有甚多染疾，如：第十一集團軍"一九四二年五月五日至六月一日惠通橋、騰衛、龍陵地區間戰役戰鬥詳報"中稱："我軍平時官兵敎育時間短促，且疾病患者衆多……"。[20]

保山以東各縣，發病日期已記載的如下：

"I have contracted cholera with my brother Ma Enyan, Sister Ma Ahuan. I am very lucky lived to now, but they are all died."By Ma Damai, 63 Yrs old, 1998.

"我也染上霍亂，下吐下瀉，沒有藥吃，就吃石灰水，吃得人吐白沫，在地下滾，才沒有死。我的弟妹都病死了，弟弟馬恩源、妹妹馬阿歡。"馬德美（63歲）控訴。

cholera disease in Boashan, Yunnan was a conservation figure.

Out side of Boashan county, we have found record in some of the counties of Yunnan that also suffered from the Japanese B.W. of 1942:

Town or village	Total population	Dead by Disease	%Reduction
1. JinJi village	900	300	33%
2. Liao Guan Village	750	250	~33%
3. Hai Tang Village	600	300	50%
4. Xiang shang Township	800	200	25%
5. Ssndriver Village	900	300	33%
6. Wu's #2 village	105	28	25%
7. Wu's #3 village	<90	27	33%
8. Hong Miao village	600	300	50%
9. Xi Zhuang village	400	200	50%

Shi Dian county (county record):

More than 10,000 died of cholera disease in the summer of 1941, villages that were hit the hardest includes: San Chahe, Wa Fang, Ren Heqian, Shagou, He Jia village, Hua xing, Si Dazhuang, Yao Guan, Wanxing, Tai Ping, Ye Zi, etc.[16] [17]

Long Lin county:

More than 1,000 people died in side of Long Lin Highway station, according to Mr.Chen Zuliang. Villages suffered the most are: La Meng, Dong Bie, Lau Jie Zi, Bu Zhai, Da long, Song Shan village, Ah shi zhai, Ping An village and Meng Leng, etc.

Mr. Li Jiamao wrote: "The cholera spread throughout western Yunnan?" Mr. Li told about his personal experience while traveling from Boashan through to Dali to Kunming. He said: "Xia Guan, i.e. Dali, had suffered about 2,500 deaths, Yong Ping county suffered about 1,500 deaths".[18]

If we were to take an average of these two and extend to the other 64 counteis of Yunnan we have not found any record available, at 2,000 deaths average per county we'd have an estimate of about 128,000 from 64 counties other than Boashan and Shidian counties.

According to the words of a few surviving Chinese soldiers many soldiers and officers in the Chinese army did contract the disease.

In certain units there were a few deaths due to the disease.

According to eye witnesses on the highway from Boashan to Kunming, in Yongping, Yangbi, and Dali counties, bodies found near the bus stations in May, 1942 were as many as "more than 10" in Yongping, "more than 30" in Dali on the road side. Dali is about 125 miles from Boashan. We can now conclude that the total numbers of deaths in Yunnan province due to Japanese cholera might have exceeded 210,000.

It might be not able to comment that according to all the ancient history of Boashan county which had been known as Yongchang, Tengyue or Longlin in the old times, a contagious disease such as cholera was never mentioned in its

Chang Xinda, 91Yrs. Old, he cried himself blind in cholera accident of his family.

控訴人：張西達 91 歲

"日軍的霍亂癍，害死我的好多親人：小炳祖姑太、兄弟張爲火、張明德及妻李氏，祇留下一個孩子，由我拉扯，好苦啊！我流了多少淚，眼都哭瞎了。"

施甸縣保山以南六十三公裏，一九四二年五月六日發現第一個病例。永平縣、保山以東一百公裏、保山至昆明路中，一九四二年五月六日發現霍亂。李家茂着《霍亂為何蔓延滇西》一文，介紹他當年過境保山、永平一綫時目擊該日看到永平縣汽車站一帶霍亂死尸："路旁的尸體至少不下十具"。大理縣和漾鼻縣（大理距離保山二百公裏），五月九日從昆明向西前往滇西的雲南省衛生實驗處處長繆安成，在抵大理車站時發現霍亂已經造成三十餘人死亡，而漾鼻縣車站因霍亂關閉。

永平、漾鼻、大理，均在保昆公路上，五月九日在上述三縣之鄉村，霍亂還未流行，據當時逃亡于大理縣楊柳鄉的馬驥麟對調查人員陳述說："我和我父親馬紹安是五月中旬逃到大理山裏的，他是那裏死于霍亂的第一個人，時間已經是七月份了。"

劍川縣發病是七月，昭通縣已是七月下旬，根據上述霍亂攻擊致死人數應超過二十一萬人，而歷史學家方國瑜先生則認為"滇西數十縣為此症（指霍亂）而死者數十萬"。

保山地方史志最早追溯到東漢楊終撰寫的保山地方志"哀牢傳"，魏晉年間的"永昌郡傳"（保山故稱永昌、騰越、龍陵），清朝的保山史志有"永昌府志"、"騰越州志"、"騰越廳志"、"騰越鄉土志"；中華民國撰修的有"龍陵縣志稿"、"保山縣志稿"、"永昌府文稿"。這些諸多史志，在紀錄疾病方面，于一九四二年前均未提及霍亂。雲南省的"衛生志"以及雲南省的衛生檔案室，也沒有一九四二年前在滇西發生霍亂病的記錄。

一九四二年五月至七月大肆流行的霍亂病，有人認為可能是大批逃亡歸國的緬甸華僑帶入的病毒所蔓延。

為此疑點回查緬甸華僑由緬北逃入保山之前的逃亡路綫，查清須經德宏州之中緬邊境口岸瑞麗、畹町、芒市、再東渡怒江才到達保山轄區。在怒江以西，即華僑難民逃亡必經的整個德宏州，一九四二年五月日軍入侵前并未發現過霍亂病例，這就推翻了華僑帶入病毒的論點。

日軍對昆明、保山的霍亂攻擊後，霍亂在昆明及其以西的廣闊地區，形成一個疫病的死亡帶，使缺乏防疫能力的中國軍隊被迫推遲在這一區域的反攻大結集，讓日軍得以抽軍于其它戰場。這種相對平靜的情勢延續到一九四四年，達一年多之久。

顯然東京參謀本部擬定的"木"細菌攻擊昆明、保山的計劃，完成了戰略目的。

"The death-rate in the 1942 cholera epidemic was very high, have 5 persons were died in my family". By Chang Jichao

控訴人：張斷超

"霍亂的死亡率很高，我家裏就死去五人，伯伯張俊（當時24歲）、嬸嬸張胡氏、二公張文忠（張應昌之父）、二叔張阿長、二伯張伯，我母也被染上霍亂，立即打痧獲救。"

history of several thousand years.

Some skeptics had mentional the possibility that some of the Chinese in Burma could have carried the disease across Nu river to Boashan.

Upon our inspection, however, we have found no cases of this disease west of Nu river all the way to Burma prior te May 4th 1942, the day the Japanese airforce bombed Boashan, case closed.

In conclusion, as a direct result of this B.W. strategy by Japan, the entire region west of Kunming became a "diseased region" which caused delay of Chinese counter attack by at least one year in this region such that Japan was able to pull its forces out of this area for other battle fronts in South Asia. Thus the highest command of Japanese South Forces had successfully executed and fulfilled its goal in the "Ki Go" B.W. attack plan.

No record about cholera or acute gastroenteritis in history of Baoshon area.

諸多的保山史志中均無霍亂的記載

Notes:

①. "Imoto Diary" Dec.4.1940

②. "Unit Nami", belong to "Unit Nami 8604". According to "The establishment material of Japanese Army", captured by 11th A. of Chinese Army in 1942.

The testimony of Tatao Sonoda (a member of "Unit 731") "Unit 8604 has some staff sent to the South Army of Singapore".

③. "Imoto Diary" Aug.24, 1942.

The commande office of 15th D. located in Nanjing, China, this division launched an all-out offensive on Zhejiang–Jiangxi Line since May, 1942 to Sep.1942, for spreaded bacteria.

④. Kiyoshi Hayakawa, assistant of Ishii, he attened the Nomanhan battle in 1939.

⑤. "The History of Boashan county" No.5#

⑥. "The History Material of Boashan", "The hiof the War of Resistance Against Japan" NO.2# P.313

⑦. "The History of Boashan City", P.575

⑧. Li Genyuan "The wipe of Yinchang. Boashan's Massacre" No. 30–2.

⑨. "The Western Yunnan Rescue Report and Action Plan", "The History Material of Boashan." P.393

⑩. Writer, words of song colleted by Chen Zuliang.

⑪. "The Culture Material of Yunnan" No.19. P.168

⑫. The conversation of Lin Yayue with investigator of JBWCIC, May 24,1999.

⑬. "The History of Boashan City" P.84–P.85

⑭. Ibid ⑨ P.320

⑮. Ibid ⑨ P.284

⑯. Ibid ⑥

⑰. "The History of Shi Dian County" P.496–P.497

⑱. "The History of the War of Resistance Against Japan" P.84–P.85

注釋:

①、一九九三年六月，對外開放的日本防衛廳防衛研究所圖書館，存列了原日軍陸軍中央干部的四部業務日記中的"井本日記"。

②、一九四二年在保山之怒江前綫對日軍作戰的國軍第十一集團軍怒江戰役戰利品統計表。民國三十一年（即一九四二年），表上陳列繳獲的日軍文件中，有一項注明爲"波（ ）部隊本部編成表"一份，另外一項注明"波（ ）部隊本部雇員表"一份。這兩項文件有四個疑點：

第一，波（ ），爲什么不填入號碼？顯然屬"絶密"。

第二，"雇員"，指該部隊是技術部門才是"雇員"，既是技術部門又何來"絶密"？

第三，查遍國軍情報資料，緬甸一綫日軍番號之代號中，均未發現有"波"字出現，有的是：

"龍"字代表日軍第五十六師團；"勇"字代表日軍第二師團；"安"字代表日軍第五十三師團；"菊"字代表日軍第十八師團；"狼"代表日軍第四十九師團；"祭"字代表日軍第十五師團；指出"波"字部隊，不是屬于陸軍在緬甸的師團部隊。而在日軍廣州的"華南軍"司令部下屬有"波字八六〇四部隊"。原日軍于一九三八年進軍廣州時，以第二十一軍爲主力，該軍即冠以"波"字爲代號，占領廣州成立華南日軍司令部后，不再使用"波"字，只因細菌戰屬絶密，所以該司令部所轄的細菌戰部隊——"防疫給水部"保留"波八六〇四部隊"的稱號。

據731部隊成員園□米勇的證言所述：8604部隊與南方軍防疫給水部之間有過人員調動，也旁證了保山前綫出現"波"字部隊是確實的。（見"侵華日軍細菌戰紀實"中文版，北京燕山出版社第428頁）

③、"15 D."，即日軍第十三軍之第十五師團。一九四二年五月日軍正組織好向中國的浙贛綫進行細菌戰。該戰役自五月十五日由第十五師團開始從浙江省杭州西進，八月十九日夜由江西廣豐撤離至同年九月結束戰役回歸杭州。該師團的細菌戰任務由東京參謀本部預制。"井本日記"一九四二年八月二十八日記載中，有一段關于第十五師團施行細菌的記録："長尾參謀，以上'木'號的實施現狀爲題寫了報告，其中有這樣的内容：(1)廣信PX（A）毒化跳蚤；PX（B）毒化跳蚤液注射給鼠，將鼠放跑；廣豐PX……待撤退后再進行細菌攻撃15 D.（即第十五師團）"。

第十五師團派出的"祭七三七一部隊"，一九四二年五月進駐地址是中緬邊境的八莫，（距雲南省保山前綫九十五英哩）。當時由駐中緬戰場中國軍隊繳獲的日軍第"56R"文件，"作命甲第一四七部"之部隊編成表中，也證實有第十五師團支隊在中緬邊境的存在，指出編入一百五十人。

④ 早川清就是一九三九年日軍在内蒙與蘇軍作戰時使用細菌戰細菌攻撃隊的隊長，戰役結束后獲得戰功獎章。

⑤、《保山縣志》中華民國，卷五。

⑥、《保山地區史志文輯》"抗日戰爭專輯之二"第313頁。保山地區行政公署史志辦公室編，德宏民族出版社，一九九零年版。

⑦、《保山市志》第575頁，保山市志編纂委員會編，雲南民族出版社，一九九三年版。

⑧、李根源，《永昌府文征.保山慘變乞賑通電》，（文稿）卷三十附録二，昆明，中華民國三十一年版。

⑨、行政院善后救濟總署滇西辦事處，中華民國三十五年《滇西災區救濟工作報告及業務計劃》"保山地區志文輯"、"抗日戰爭專輯之四"，第393頁，保山地區行政公署史志辦公室編，德宏民族出版社，一九九零年版。

⑩、魏蘭馨，保山人，已逝，文學家、歌詞由陳祖梁收集。

11、方國瑜，"抗日戰爭滇西戰事篇"，"雲南文史資料選輯"，第十九輯，第168頁，雲南人民出版社，一九八三年第一版。

12、林毓越，一九九七年五月二十四日在保山地區政協會議室對調查人員的談話。

13、保山縣人口 一九三六年、一九四二年（年底）、一九四五年三年統計數字，出自"保山市志"第84頁、第85頁，保山市志編纂委員會編，雲南民族出版社，一九九三年版。

14、熊毅廷，《保山縣志》稿大事記之五，"抗戰時期至解放前保山縣政與軍事動態"，由保山縣文化館提供，見注⑨，"抗日戰爭專輯之一"第320頁，記有："炸后，經縣府調查統計，傷者各各逃散，無法得知其數。死者有主收尸掩埋者約兩千八百多人；無主收尸由縣府發動附城鄉鎮派工掩埋者六千多人。"

15、保山縣長劉言昌，就保山縣"五四"、"五五"被炸后致雲南省民政廳廳長的報告，第284頁稱："保山縣城一九四二年五月四日、五日被日機轟炸傷亡人員數萬。"

16、同注⑥

17、《施甸縣志》第四編、第496、497頁，新華出版社，一九九七年版。

18、李家茂，《霍亂爲何蔓延滇西》載"抗日紀實"第84、85頁，雲南人民出版社，一九八八年版。

19、宋希濂，《遠征軍在滇西的整訓與反攻》，載"保山地區史辦文輯"、"抗日戰爭專輯之二"，第360頁，德宏民族出版社，一九九零年第一版。

20、同注

21、李家茂，"霍亂爲何蔓延滇西"同18

22、根據民國三十一年（一九四二年）八月，雲南省衛生實驗處處長繆安成所寫"臨時救護防疫隊工作報告"，"保山地區史志專輯"、"抗日戰爭專輯之一"，第298頁。

Witness: Dong Son. 78 Yrs. Old.
Testimony: " I saw a lot of corpses of cholera epidemic to be put into a large pit, position calling Wulitin have been set up a gas station now."
控訴人　董生　78歲

"一九四二年的日本霍亂死的人真多，我眼看到李根源動員的民衆，把没有家人收尸的尸體一齊丟到五裏亭一個大涯地裏，就是現在的加油站地址。"

"Under the heel of cholera epidemic in 1942, the day, all around the Baoshan County many many family lost relatives, crying all the days, all the countries, some children cried out for fear, some one cried with pain or with vexation, still to three months late." Testimony by Feng Desen, 81 Yrs. Old.

漢莊鎮馮德燦　81歲
"那年霍亂燎死好多好多人喲！村裏天天有人

Ai Fathen, 82 Yrs. Old, she occused: "My family has had die a tragic death, 5 persons were died and only two kept live".

控訴人　艾發珍
"我一家死得好慘啊！死于霍亂的有父艾昭、叔艾權、艾滿、祖母艾方氏、姑母成艾氏；一家七口，死了五口，我的外親黃和，夫妻一同病死，女兒回家奔喪，也傳染霍亂致死。艾山也死了，共死了13口。"

The graves covered all the hill.
滿山遍野的墳堆

The graves on graves, the heaps on heaps around the
Sand River, but the place has builded houses now.
當年拋尸捲埋的沙河已經填平

The units of construction of Japanese army in western of Yunnan province, 1942.

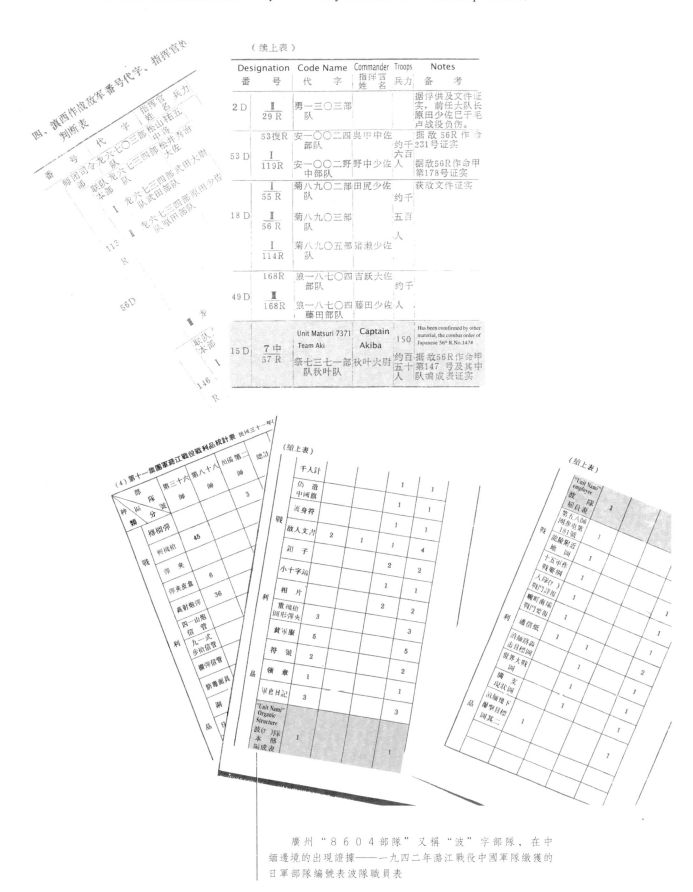

（续上表）

Designation 番 号	Code Name 代 字	Commander 指挥官姓名	Troops 兵力	Notes 备 考
2 D	$\frac{II}{29R}$ 勇一三〇三部队			据俘供及文件证实，前任大队长原田少佐已于毛卢战役负伤。
53 D	53搜R 安一〇〇二四部队	奥中中佐	约千六百人	据敌56R作命231号证实
	$\frac{I}{119R}$ 安一〇〇二野中部队	野中少佐		据敌56R作命甲第178号证实
18 D	$\frac{I}{55R}$ 菊八九〇二部队	田尻少佐	约千五百人	获敌文件证实
	$\frac{I}{56R}$ 菊八九〇三部队			
	$\frac{I}{114R}$ 菊八九〇五部队	猪濑少佐		
49 D	168R 狼一八七〇四部队	吉跃大佐	约千人	
	$\frac{II}{168R}$ 狼一八七〇四藤田部队	藤田少佐		
15 D	**7中** **57R** Unit Matsuri 7371 Team Aki 杂七三七一部队秋叶队	**Captain** **Akiba** 秋叶大尉	150 约百五十人	Has been confirmed by other material, the combat order of Japanese 56th R.No.147# 据敌56R作命甲第147号及其中队编成表证实

（续上表）

（4）第十一集团军潞江战役战利品统计表 民国三十一年

广州"8604部队"又称"波"字部队，在中缅边境的出现证据——一九四二年潞江战役中国军队缴获的日军部队编号表波队职员表

Dog's puller Yang Yiming
According to Chinese general custom, should be have a man who relative of dead person pulling the coffin from home to cemetery. But in 1942, some family whole members killed by cholera and no body pull the coffin.So, Yang yiming pulling a dog take the place of relative for coffin.

依照中國的風俗，出殯時死者親人必須牽住棺材從家裏送到墳場。但是在一九四二年許多家庭成員全部死于霍亂以致沒有人來牽棺。楊義明就拉住一條狗，代替死者後人牽棺送死者走完人生的最後一程。

He Jianyhu, 69 Yrs. Old, he accused: "The cholera epidemic covered all countries of kunming and Boashan, killed my old brother He Chunghu and He Wenji, left me followed my poor old grandmother during I have 12 Yrs. Old."

控訴人何建祖 69歲

"我一家六口，父母先亡，依居外婆家。一九四二年六月日軍施放的霍亂病傳染到外婆家裏，我哥哥何純祖，何文杰是全家的勞動力被染病死了。祇有外婆苦扯大了我們四個小孩子，那時我祇有１２歲。"

"In May 1942, my mother and my aunt has been sickened. My mother has recovered, but my aunt died, she was the 100th death person in my village." Remembered by Sha Bila.

控訴人：沙必璐（左起第二人，女灰衣）"保山市志編輯委員會"主編

"我母親馬汝珍，四二年五月也傳染上霍亂，趕快吃了藥，保住了命。但照顧我的小姑都被霍亂菌害了，小姑的死，在當時是我們村村民死于霍亂的第一百名。

To weeping oneself out during
remembered my family broken
by cholera epidemic in 1942.
幸存人拂泪哭訴

Ten sursvivors meeted together
in Sand River country, May
1999.
在沙河鄉與十位幸存人

Investigating in He village 1999
在何家村與十位牽存人

The occupation meeting in Jinji village, 1999

金鶏村控訴會

Survivor Liu Rengong talked to investigators in Jinji village, 1999: "Before May 1942, My village population was nine hundred, but after cholera epidemic dropped down to six hundred......"

左：劉仁剛　鄉老人協會副主席（在劉的小院内留影）

劉的控訴：金鶏村四二年大約有九百來人，日軍的霍亂菌致死三百多人，真是風聲鶴（霍）泪，大家口傳："今日脱了鞋子襪，不知明天八字八！"

上壽村的徐志榮家，一家六口死絶。

白雲村陳家、李家也全病死，衹剩下一個小孩子幸存。

我姑母楊琨琳，由板橋逃來我家，也被霍亂致死。

有的人家死光了，送葬由大家幫忙，沒有後代就由狗來作後代，現在還有兩個牽狗人活着，他叫楊明義，另一個叫白雲龍。

Occusator Zhu Hua,74 years old: "I lost six members in my family......"

控訴人：朱華　74歲

　　"霍亂瘟一發，我就逃到山上去，免于一死，我親戚中，死的人有：王老三、朱學寬、李成剛、陳平，在五月十二、五月十二日兩天死去的,還有兩個叔叔也死于霍亂"

Have 16 persons were died in Chang Fachong's family, included his mother, uncle.

　　我家大屋張姓親戚中，死于霍亂的：
　　１、張順全家（母張楊氏、女留鳳）
　　２、我的母親張阿兆
　　３、叔父張吉綱
　　４、全院三十多口人，死去三分之一

"How I wish for cry bitter tears ......" Survivor He Dexiang, 76 Yrs.old, his father and uncle were died in cholera epidemic 1942, "I carried my daughter left village runaway, but she died in my holding after she made a last-ditch struggle".

指控人　何德祥　76歲

　　"我家死于日本鬼子的霍亂有：父親　何家、叔祖何四爹、我的女兒也染上了，我抱着她逃出村，往山上跑，才跑過山，她就死在我懷裏。"

"Have 170 familly in my Nanau village and have two hundud more people killed by Japanese cholera assault in 1942".Witnessed by Duan wendou, 81Yrs old.
控訴人：段文門，81歲
"全村有二百人死亡，我親屬中霍亂死的人有：郭士廉、郭光、郭士林、徐健蓉。"

Accusator He changgi 70 Yrs old, his uncle He Bingheng has died in cholera epidemic 1942.
控訴人：何長啓，70歲
"我叔叔何炳恒，當年五十多歲，被日本的霍亂菌活活折磨死了"。

Survivor He Mingxuan, 83 Yrs old.
"My family has six persons killed by cholera, and has 1/3 population lost of my Liaoguan village."
控訴人：何明宣，83歲（廖官村）
"我親戚死于霍亂的有六人：何明興(堂兄)、何秉衡（叔父）、何長汝（何秉衡之子）何大興（堂弟）、何長偉（堂弟）、何明成（堂兄）。"
"一九四二年廖官村象北冬鎮，做小生意好多人，二百多人，霍亂傳染，全村死了近一百人，三分之一。

Survivor He Mingrong, 86 Yrs old, " My grand father lives at Xichang village, has more than four hundred persons there, but has 1/2 died a tragic death with my uncles and aunts......"

何明荣，86 岁

　　"我外公家在西庄，全村四五百人，死在日本霍乱病下的有二分之一还多。"

　　"我的舅舅，董友金、董兆笠和两个表妹董宝珠 A（当时十七岁），董炳珍（15 岁）都在当时病死于霍乱，接下来我的外公董明（当年八十岁），舅妈王友珍也病殁"。

　　"没有药救，什幺黄金油、黄烟水、烟锅水都当药吃，又有人刺破舌头下血流出来毒……"

Survivor Zuo Yongquan, 63 Yrs. old. "My parant with whole family were died in cholea epidemic or killed by bombing in May 1942, There is only me left. During that time, I just have six years old. So I take beg arms allday......"

控訴人：左有權　63 歲

　　"一九四二年五月四日，日機來炸，保山死了好多人，我全家不是被炸死，就是死于霍亂，我祇六歲，沒有辦法，討飯過日子。"

He Doxian, 71 Yrs old, His grandfather was died in the cholera epidemic, 1942

控訴人：何大賢，71 歲

　　"我的公公何體紹，是被日本霍亂害的，死時脚踝子抽痙"。

Witness Wang Ke, accusation: woodworker, 80 Yrs. Old. Wang's mother Wang Lishi killed by cholera 1942.

控訴人：王克，80 歲，木匠

　　"我老娘王李氏死于日軍霍亂"。

Survivor Duan Kaiguo, 68 Yrs.old, his three relatives killed by cholera and he has epidemic also, Gods help and snatched him from the jaws of death.

段開國泣訴，68歲

　　"我親戚死于日本鬼子的霍亂菌有很多人，記得的有：
伯伯段發順、二叔白雙勇、三叔白雙長，白雙長死時，
全家活下的人都怕得不得了，連哭都不敢，偷偷用板子抬了去
埋掉。白紹益家，十一口（我家）死去三口，是：白阿水、
白紹益的母親白王氏、白紹益的兄媳白趙氏。"

"My family has five persons were died in cholera (1942) included my pearant, old brothers, during I am 13 yrs. old." accusated by Zuao Wenchang.

控訴人：趙文昌　71歲

　　"我父親、母親和大哥（林鳳祥）、二哥
（林鳳翼）嫂嫂林曾氏共五人，死于日機"五四"
大炸保山之後的霍亂症。知道這件事可證明的人
有：何一庭、陳煉達、蘇炳鳳，我祇有12歲，靠
討飯長大。"

Witness He Jingxiu, 77 Yrs. old. The cholera killed He Am's family, just old mother in luck, but she is as blind as a bot no body help her for rice, she was hungry with fasting all day, thus she perished from hungry later.

控訴人：何金秀，77歲

　　"我的親人中死于日本霍亂的
人，記得有：何紹興夫婦，何阿嬢和
她的女兒（其夫何洋渙先死于日機投
擲細菌炸彈之前），一家四口人祇剩
下老媽六十多歲，是個瞎子，沒人照
顧，好可憐，不久也餓死了。

Witness: He Mingxian.79 Yrs. old. lived in Quan Tu village "When we are stayed Boashan country for building airport, the Japanese aircrafts attacking us, a lot of persons was died. I has luck escaped to back Quan Tu village, some days later, cholera epidemic covering all villages, a great deal of people were died, the corpses put around the bank of Sand River".

"我在保山修飛機場，日本人擲炸彈，炸死好多人，又掃射，我往外逃，尸體一個接一個的，我連插腳的地方都沒有，溝裏總有幾千人。我逃到官土才安了心，可不久霍亂又流行起來，死的人更多，上水河、下水河兩岸是尸體"。

Witness He Dochang, 69 yrs.old
He lived on He Goa village, has population 300-400, approximately 1/2 persons died in cholera epidemic, 19421.

控訴人 何大成 69歲
"在何家村的親戚中，死于日本霍亂的：媽媽何劉氏、表兄劉寒墨及其弟、舅舅劉誠典。在海棠村的叔叔何永晶，也病死于霍亂，那個村子三四百人死了一半，一天要抬葬四十多次"。

157

Section 2
The Zhejiang-Jiangxi Line Germ Warfare

The Japanese germ attacked on Zhijiang-Jiangxi Line around 22 counties in 1942, it's all owning to punished Chinese saved 64 American air pilots.

A Navy Task Force had transported 16 Army Air Force Bombers to within 800 miles of Japan. As huge seas rocked even the biggest ships, the midium bombers did what had never been done before. Heavy with fuel and bombs, engines to near redline, released brakes, and launched from the pitching deck of the U.S.S. HORNET.

In that trip, 15 crews came down blindly in Jiangxi Zhijiang provinces, east of China, exceped Japanese invasion force captured eight airmen, they executed three prisoners, convicting them under laws passed four months after the air raid, another P.O.W. died, but four survived three-and-a half years of neglect, abuse and torture, 64 pilots has be help sb. in danger by Chinese, and other crew opted to land in Sovied territory.

As a result, General Chief of Staff of Japanese decided the germ attack on Zhejiang-Jiangxi Line. The 13th Army included 15D. 22D. 32D. 70D. and 116D. from Hangzhou direct to west, the 11th Army included 3D.,34D. start Nanchang face to east, the other special army units included "Unit 731" and "Unit 1644". About germ warfare plan on Zhijiang-Jiangxi Line of General Chief of Staff had detail recording in "Imoto Diary".

The following summer and until to Aug. 1942, Ishii mounted a major B. W. effort against Chinese. This time the target was Zhejiang-Jiangxi Railway Line and Chinese airport around this area.

Later that May, Japanese resumed his attack. This time plague-infected fleas and other germ were dischanged over the surrounding Zhejiang-Jiangxi Line by aerial spreading.

In June, Japanese 13th A. , 11th A. attack from both sides, then the two A. in join forces in Hengfeng.

B.W. attacks by Japanese army delayed to Aug. ofter army to withdrew, they dropping cholera, typhoid, paratyphoid bacteria into water wells and reservoirs, distributing plague-infected fleas and

第二節
浙贛綫細菌作戰

日軍于一九四二年發動的浙贛綫作戰，主要是沿浙贛鐵路幹綫進行的。

浙贛幹綫是使浙江省杭州市橫穿華中地區直到江西省南昌市的一條主幹鐵路。

大面積攻擊的起因，是由于日本一九四一年發動太平洋戰爭後，美國于次年四月十八日杜立特上校率領 B-25 轟炸機 16 架自"大黃蜂號"母艦起飛成功空襲東京，而這些飛機的駕駛員大部分在返航就近飛往浙贛一帶機場時迫降，除八名飛行員被日軍捕俘外，64 名均被中國軍民搶救生還。被俘的八名飛行員，四個月後被定死刑三人，死于牢獄一人，受盡折磨最後在日本投降時重生四人。

轟炸東京後在中國東南戰區被救獲的杜立特將軍等飛行員

anthrax bacteria throughout rice field or villages.

Same times, Japanese put a lot of and unusual delicacy snacks dropping down the coner of houses, it's had been injectcd bacteria for Chinese children. Japanese provided special germ's foods for more than six thousand Chinese P. O.W.s, then released and sent home for spreading disease.

The final results were that, as a consequence of Ishii's B.W. attacks, the plague, cholera, typhoid, paratyphoid and anthrax spread throughout whole Zhejiang-Jiangxi Line twenty two surrounding counties and one million people becomes ill and over few ten thounsand were died.

Chinese searchers rescued the pilots of U.S. lost in the wilderness (Jiangxi province)
被中國人從危險中搶救出來的美國飛行員

Quyhou, Zhijiang province
浙江衢州

Chinese people used labour power building the airport for U.S. bombers.
中國人用人力爲美國轟炸機建築機場

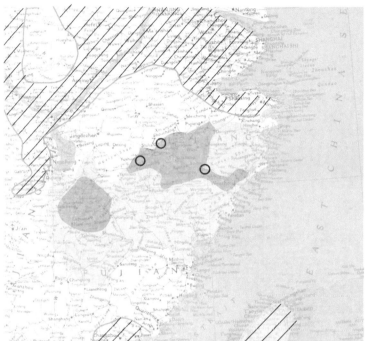

○ U.S. Force airport

The map of Zhijiang Jiangxi
Line germ attacking
浙贛綫細菌攻擊圖

諸暨 Zhuji	江蘇 Jiangsu	萬年 Wannian
義烏 Yiwu	安徽 Anhui	崇仁 Chongren
金華 Jinhua	東海 East China sea	慶元 Qingyuan
東陽 Dongyang	浦江 Pujiang	文登 Wendang
杭州 HangZhou	縣陽 Xiying	瑞安 Ruian
寧波 Ningbo	常山 Changchan	龍泉 Longquan
江山 Changshan	長汀 Changting	象山 Chiangshan'
玉山 Yushan	南平 Nanping	慈溪 Cixi
上鏡 shangrao	羅源 Laoyuan	楊子江 Changjiang
橫峰 Hengfeng	浦城 Puchang	遂昌 Suichang
鷹潭 Yingtan	永安 Yinan	廣信（上鐃）Shangrao
南昌 Nanchang	臺灣海峽 Formosa strait	鉛山 Yanshan
南京 Nanjing	永康 Yongkang	建甌 Jianou
上海 Shanghai	龍游 Longyou	書溪 Quixi
溫州 Wenzhou	合肥 Hefei	東鄉 Dongxiang
麗水 Lishui	徐州 Xuzhou	金鐃 Jinxi
衢州 Ouzhou	武漢 Wuhan	建昌 Jianchang
廣豐 Guanfeng	杭州灣 Hangshou Bay	資溪 Zixi
蘭溪 Lanxi	奉化 Fenghua	黎川 Lichuan
夏門 Xiamen	紹興 Shaxing	撫州 Fuzhou
福州 Fuzhou	蕭山 Xianshan	九江 jiujiang
臺北 Taipei	富陽 Fuyang	鄱陽湖 Puyang hu
臺灣 Taiwan	桐廬 Tonglu	樂平 Leping
福建 Fujian	建德 Jiande	進賢 Jinxian
浙江 Zhejiang	永康 Yongkang	言台橋 Jengse bridge
江西 Jiangxi	青田 Qingtian	宜黃 Yihuang
	廣昌 Guanchang	

Under the heel of cholea　蔓延區

Japanese occupied area 日軍占領區

Serious cholea area　　嚴重病區

日本大本營逐決定對浙贛綫進軍，由第 13 軍的第 15 師團、第 22 師團、第 32 師團、第 70 師團和第 116 師團從杭州西進，由第 11 軍的第 3 師團、第 34 師團從南昌東進，而細菌作戰的“731 部隊”、“1644 部隊”則指導細菌攻擊。

“井本日記”對該次細菌攻擊有詳細的記述：這次攻擊是石井指揮的細菌最大的戰役，目標是浙贛沿綫地區及其附近的空軍機場。

到五月，日機開始在這一區域進行細菌空中撒布。至六月日軍第 13 軍和第 11 軍分別從東西兩方向對中國軍隊進行夾擊，八月兩軍會師江西的橫峰。

細菌的地面攻擊則推遲到八月日軍陸軍撤退時開始，日軍把傷寒、副傷寒、霍亂、炭疽細菌和染有鼠疫的跳蚤投散于村莊的稻田及所有的水井、水源。

同時把注入細菌的餅、甜點放置于村落的屋角，讓中國孩子揀食。又向六千中國戰俘發送細菌食物，然後釋放回家，以擴散疫區。

這次進攻的結果，就讓 22 個縣的一百萬中國人患病，幾萬以上的人死亡。

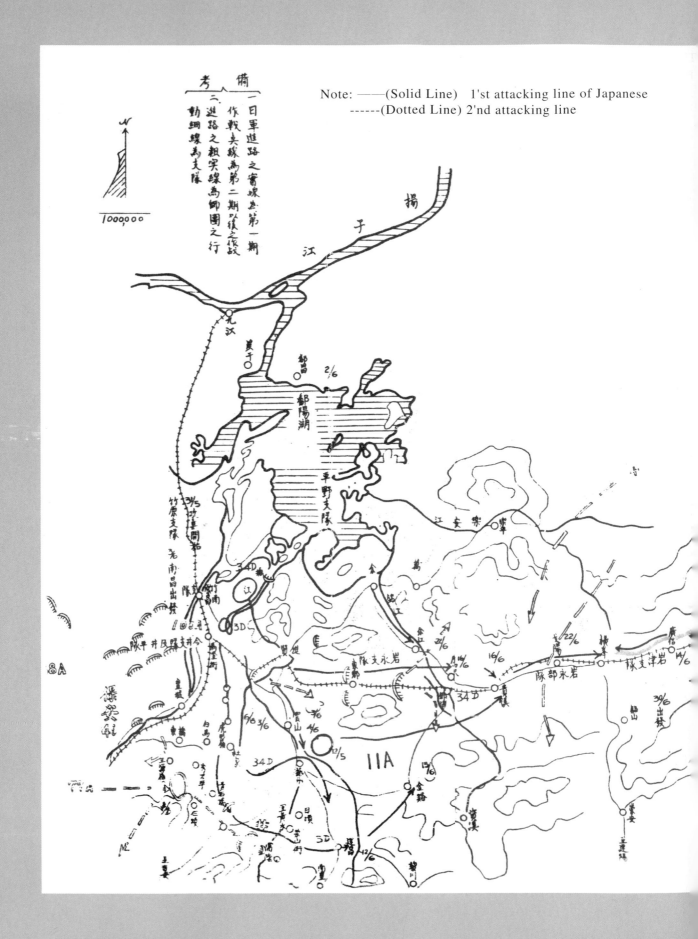

Note: ——(Solid Line)　1'st attacking line of Japanese
　　　------(Dotted Line) 2'nd attacking line

The battle map of Japanese attacking on Zhijiang-Jiangxi line, 1942
日軍浙贛綫作戰經過要圖自一九四二年五月中旬至一九四二年八月上旬

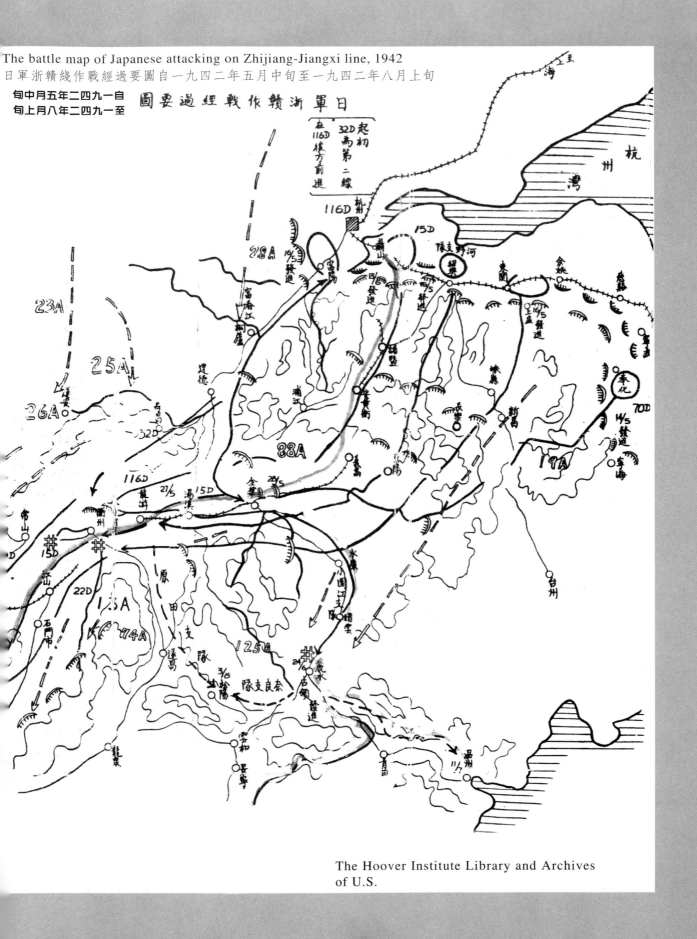

Japanese victims of a misdirected ..B.W.
細菌攻擊戰中部分日兵也感染病毒

According to the statistics of virus's infection of 13th Army has over
10,000 Japanese soldiers.
據日軍第13軍陸軍醫院同期因病毒住院統計，有一萬官兵之多。

Japanese B.W. "Unit 1644" stayed in Yiwu in June, 1942.
1942年6月日軍細菌部隊在浙江義烏

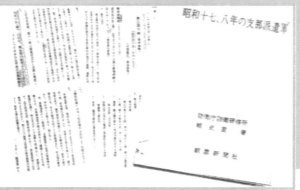

The fighting record of 13th A .in Quzhou, Zhejiang.
日軍"浙贛戰役"侵襲衢州的作戰記錄

浙贛作战期间日军第十三军人员损失表

	第 一 阶 段 (5 月 15 日～ 5 月 29 日)	第 二 阶 段 (5 月 30 日～ 6 月 15 日)	第 三 阶 段 (6 月 16 日～ 8 月 14 日)	第 四 阶 段 (8 月 15 日～ 9 月 30 日)	计
战死	281	484	442	77	1284
战伤	723	1350	609	85	2767
战病	829	983	5291	4709	11812

The recording of injuriers and deaths of Japanese 13th A. in Zhejiang-Jiangxi Line battle.
資料來源：防衛廳防衛研修所戰史室編《戰史叢書・昭和・十七・八年の支那派遣軍》，朝雲新聞社，第264頁。

Japanese Army soldiers filtering river water with the Ishii
water filter during into germ attacked area.
日軍在使用細菌攻擊後的地區用石井濾水器濾水供應日軍

The leaders of 13th A.(1942)
"浙贛戰役" 中的侵華日軍十三軍團司令澤田茂
（前排中）及各師旅團長合影（１９４２年）

"Imoto Diary" Aug.28, 1942:

"Spread fleas and rats on Shangrao,Guangfeng, it's carry plague germ allready. Put the dry plague bacteria on rices at Yushan. At Jiangshan, either put the cholera germ to the wells, or found on foods, or inject into fruits."

"井本日記" 一九四二年八月二十八日：

"在廣信、廣豐散布帶有鼠疫菌的跳蚤和老鼠。在玉山由把幹燥的鼠疫菌附于大米上。在江山，或者把霍亂菌投入井中，或附着于食物上，或注射于水果中。"

The Japanese soldiers were cooking food during the field trip of a germ warfare mission in Zhejiang.
在浙江細菌戰時，日軍的野外炊事。

167

"Have four persons died by cholera of my family (8 persons), included my mother, my brothers and my sister." Said by Zhou Yanlin, Zhaiqian village, Yushan, Jiangxi.

日軍霍亂攻擊幸存人玉山縣宅前村周延林全家八口，四口死于霍亂（母親及弟三人）

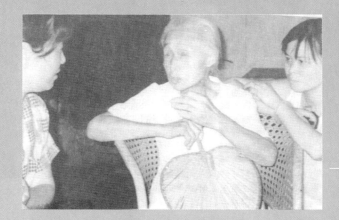

Fortunate favourite of plague of Guangfeng, Jiangxi: Zu Xiuju, but her husband has died in that moment.

日軍鼠疫戰幸存人江西廣豐縣祝秀菊，其夫死于鼠疫。

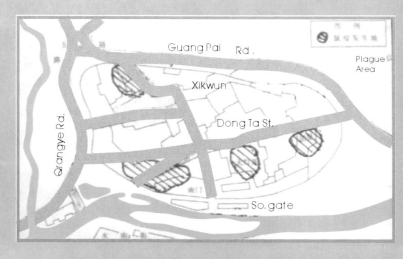

Plague on Guangfeng in 1942
1942 年廣豐鼠疫發生地區示意圖

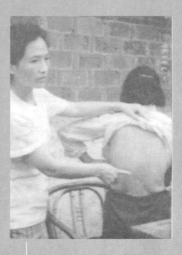

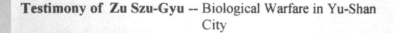

祝腮菊 Zu Szu-Gyu

Testimony of Zu Szu-Gyu -- Biological Warfare in Yu-Shan City

Before the Japanese retreated from Yu-Shan, they dumped two drums of germs into a well. The whole village got sick after drinking the water. The symptoms include vomiting, diarrhea, ... She lost ten out of thirteen of her family members.

Information adopted from "Japanese Germ Warfare Unit 731" -- A film made by the Japanese Unit 731 Exhibit National Committee

祝腮菊証言－玉山市細菌戰

日軍從玉山市撤退時在水井中倒了兩個汽油桶的細菌，全村人喝了井水後嘔吐，下痢，體中潰瘍而死。他家族 13 人中有 10 人死亡。

Scars never not die away of anthrax by Japanese B.W.

祝腮菊背上殘留的炭疽瘢痕跡。左立者爲義工王選。

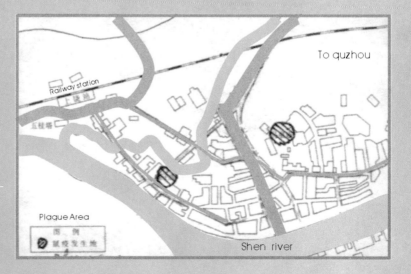

Plague on Shangrao in 1942
1942 年上饒鼠疫發生地區示意圖

Section 3
Cholera Attacked on West of Shandong

A kind of germ: Cholera

Date of started: The later 20 th of Aug. 1943

Threw by: Japanese Army Command of North China, "Unit 1855" with Jinan Deta, and 59th D. (confeessed by Shigemi in July 17, 1954)

Victimized area: 12 counties of west Shandong;

               2 counties of Henan;

               9 counties of Hebei.

     Threw cholera germ by air and by hand 1'st, then take the offensives by :

     A. Burst three embankments of Wei Rive, let heavy water ordered about infected persons runaway to other places for proliferation of cholera.(in lowland counties)

     B. 59th D., belong to 12th Army of Japanese advanced against above mentioned counties (highland) after the cholera threw for spreaded diseases also. Japanese troops separaed two parts:

     1). 53th B. has acted on the offensive Linging, Guantao, Quanxian, Qingpin and Daming three times:

     1'st attacked in middle of Sep., 1943 to ten days later.

     2'nd at the last part of Sep. to the 1'st part of Oct., 1943.

     3'rd From 10th of Oct. to next ten days.

     2). 54th B. has three times attacked also:

     1'st time occupied Qinpin, Gaolang, Shipin, Bopin, Tiaocheng, Shoughang, Langyi, Shenxian, Tanggu, Coacheng, Fanxian, from Sep. 15 to Sep. 18, 1943.

     2'nd troop exploited the victory to Puyang of Hanan province in Sep. 25 to 1'st of Oct., 1943.

     3'rd in 10th of Oct. and continued ten days.

     Result of cholera attacked, 200,000 persons were death, said by Kensan Yasaki (confessed in 1954).

The burst place of Wei River side of Quangjim Bridge (Linging) by Japanese in 1943, confessed by Shigemi Hayashi in July 17, 1954.

一九四三年臨清廣濟橋日軍決堤處，林茂美供認于一九五四年七月十七日（指證人　張偉）

第三節
魯西霍亂攻擊

攻擊使用細菌: 霍亂
攻擊發動日期: 一九四三年八月二十日後
受 害 地 區: 山東省西部十二個點
　　　　　　河南省兩個縣
　　　　　　河北省九個縣

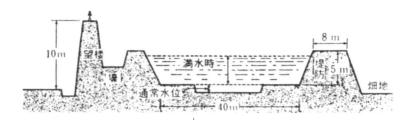

The section drawing of Wei River
衛河斷面圖

日軍在散布霍亂菌之後，采取:

A、挖決三處衛河河堤，讓大水驅趕帶民眾逃亡，
以擴大疫區；（低勢縣）

B、派遣第五十九師步兵進攻疫區（山勢縣），
武力威逼疫區病患者逃往非疫區，其進軍分為兩支:

一支由第五十三旅團，向臨清、館陶、冠縣、大名進擊，計三次: 第一次在一九四三年九月中旬至下旬，第二次在九月底至十月初，第三次在十月十日至十月二十日。

一支由第五十四旅團向南邊作三次地面進攻: 第一次于九月十五日至九月十八日占領清平、茌平、博平、臺城、堂邑、朝城、範縣。第二次在九月二十五日至十月初，占領區擴大到河南省的濮陽，第三次則從十月上旬至十月二十日，攻擊區未變。

Nanquantao's embankment has burst by Japanese in Aug. 27,
1943 (Confessed by Hirogu Naha in Dec. 27, 1954)

1943 年八月二十七日，南館陶決堤處，由難波博于一九五四
年二十月二十七日供認。

The map of cholera attacked on west of Shandong, 1943

魯西霍亂攻擊圖

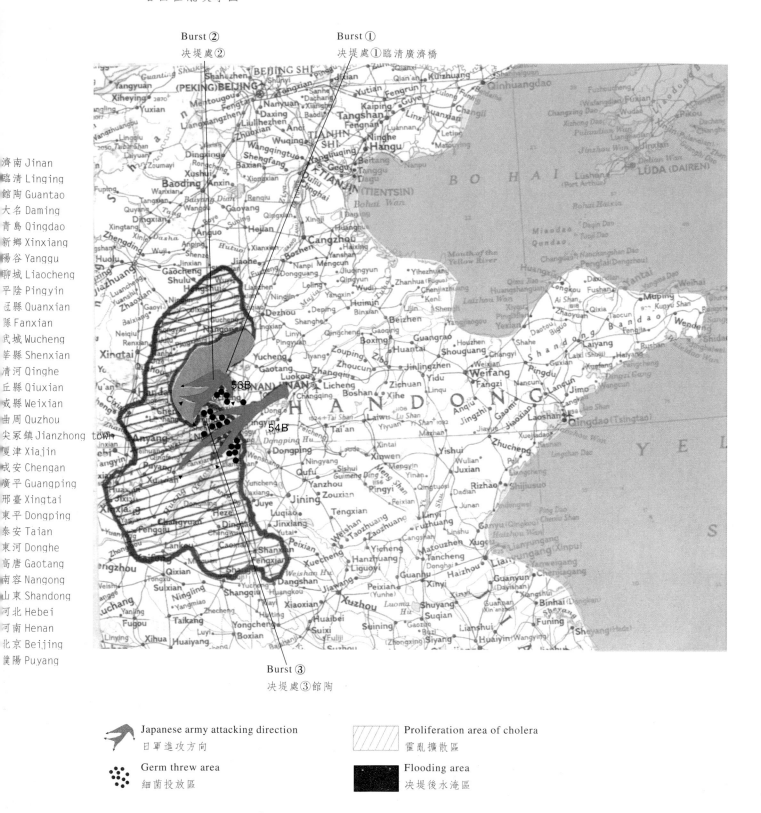

Burst ② 決堤處②

Burst ① 決堤處①臨清廣濟橋

Burst ③ 決堤處③館陶

濟南 Jinan
臨清 Linqing
館陶 Guantao
大名 Daming
青島 Qingdao
新鄉 Xinxiang
陽谷 Yanggu
聊城 Liaocheng
平陰 Pingyin
冠縣 Quanxian
範縣 Fanxian
武城 Wucheng
莘縣 Shenxian
清河 Qinghe
丘縣 Qiuxian
威縣 Weixian
曲周 Quzhou
尖冢鎮 Jianzhong town
夏津 Xiajin
成安 Chengan
廣平 Guangping
邢臺 Xingtai
東平 Dongping
泰安 Taian
東河 Donghe
高唐 Gaotang
南容 Nangong
山東 Shandong
河北 Hebei
河南 Henan
北京 Beijing
濮陽 Puyang

Japanese army attacking direction
日軍進攻方向

Germ threw area
細菌投放區

Proliferation area of cholera
霍亂擴散區

Flooding area
決堤後水淹區

Tomoyoshi Nagade (sergeant, 59th D. 54th B. 110th Detachment) confessed in Nov.1, 1954.He said:

1) Kiyoshi Hayakawa (Ishii's assistant) appointed the Chief of the Military Surgeon Department of 12th A. (garrison Shandong) in March 1943, he is a cholera profissor, has commanded cholera assault Kunming-Boashan, it was a great success.

2) "Unit 1855" made once cholera special training, has 200 non-commissioned officers to attened. Then, 59th D. hold two times same training, 1'st 20 non-commissioned officers, 2'nd 21, I directed the 2'nd one.

3) Increased the staffs of sanitation and got a raise cholera's inspection supplies.

4) Gave all the whole army an injections of preventive cholera.

5) Army attacked Wande village, Taian for cholera's sudden attacking maneuvre.

這次霍亂攻擊，造成二十萬中國人死亡。（矢疇賢三供認于一九五四年）參加這次攻擊的長田友吉（日軍第59師團第54旅團第110大隊衛生士官）于一九五四年十一月一日供出該攻擊前的準備工作：

1）一九四三年三月駐山東的日軍第12軍軍醫部長，由"七三一部隊"的早川清調任。

2）七月到北京由接受日軍華北細菌作戰部隊的霍亂培訓，共下士官200人參加。

3）第59師團在北京訓練班後，又舉辦兩次衛生下士官的霍亂訓練，第一次有20名，第二次有21名，我主持了第二次的訓練。

A lot of Chinese corpses
killed by Japanese B.W.
被細菌攻擊致死的群尸

The germ research section of Jinan Detachment of "Unit 1855"

濟南支部細菌室一角（“八一五”搗毀前）

Section 1

THE MYSTER Of CASUALTY BY JAPANESE B.W.

The Germ warfare had much longer impact comparing to the conventional weapons. for example, the anthrax becteria remains active even buried in the ground for years. The plague infected by the mice will continue for generations of the mice. We can say that the germ warfare will continue killing people for many many years.

The Japanese Army had launched the germ warfare attacks during 1940s at more than 240 counties in China and caused tremendous casualties since these villages and cities had poor sanitary condition and little epidemic prevention system.

Professor Sheldon H Harris of California State University at Northridge estimated a casualty of 200,000. However, some Japanese historians consider Harris's number too high. Keiichi Tsuneseki claims that only 106 people were died of the plague attack at Ningbo in 1940. While a Chinese "plague specialist", Mr. Chen Wengui , listed 6 casualties in his report of Changde attack in 1941.

There are two shortfalls in the Tsuneseki's theory. Although the "Unit 731" used less quantity of plague germ in the attack of Ningbo (may be less than 0.5 kilogram), they prepared and equipped 5 kilograms of the germ for the warfare in Central China area. Besides Ningbo (October, 1940), other cities consists of Yushan, Wenzhou, Taizhou, Lishui (September, 1940), Longquan, Quzhou (October), ShangYu, Cixi, Jinhua(October, 1940). The monthly production of the plague germ by the "Unit 731" was 300 kilograms in 1940. (p. 300 of Khabarovsk Trial).

Mr. Chen Wengui's investigation at Changde from 24 November 1941 to 2 December 1941 clearly indicating his 8-day report is not reliable, because the germ had not been spreaded the wider areas yet. Furthermore, Chen was not aware that the plague germ was dropped by airplane on residential area of Dongting Hu, it's put down around 100kg fleas, and again in spring1942, The survey by the governmment of Changde in 1998 reveals 10,400 casualties with names, ages, and addresses of the dead.

The Imperial Japanese Germ Warfare Crime Investigation Committee (San Francisco, USA) concluded that the total casualty in the hand of Japanese germ warfare could be as high as 748,000 after three years research effort. What a difference of this figure compare with Harris's 200,000. Please note the following conditions:

1.   professor Harris has aware only few times germ warfare attacks while there were actually more than 161 attacks launched by the Imperal Japanese Army. The reliable records tell us: 210,000 casualties at Kunming , Boashan attack (1942), 200,000 died during the west Shandong attack (1943), 50,000 dead in the Changle(Fujian province) attack, the refugee camp in Guangzhou (Canton) lost 30,000 as the result of germ spreading .There were about 45,000 casualties during the attacks along the railroad lines in the Northern China area.

2.   Professor Harris claimed that there were 3,000 people were died in the hand of "live experiment" and "live vivisection". The figure was a direct quote from Kiyoshi Kawashima's confession at Khabarovsk Trial. We should aware that Kawashinma is a liar. He has hide many crimes committed including 200,000 casualties in Shandong, Hebei, Henan's "cholera operation" in 1943 by 12 [th] and he was in charge   the chief of medical dep. of the 12th Army. Kawashima's figure of

第一節　　死亡知多少？

　　細菌武器不同于常規武器，傷害是持續性的，炭疽菌可以在土地埋葬多年而保持活性，鼠疫菌通過老鼠散播給人類，不論如何防治，老鼠身上的鼠疫菌體則始終存在并遺傳下去。因此，人們在細菌攻擊下的死亡往往是多年的、長期的。

　　日軍在中國的細菌進攻十分頻繁，有二百四十多個縣遭殃。當時中國城鄉的衛生條件極差、防疫能力幾乎為零，日軍的細菌殺傷力非常巨大。

　　對于死于日軍細菌武器的人數，美國加州大學北嶺分校哈立斯教授首先在一九九四年提出有二十

The map of Pingfan Arrangement
Drawing by　Futoo Yoshida, a member of "Unit 731"
一九四〇年日軍七三一部隊平房總部詳圖

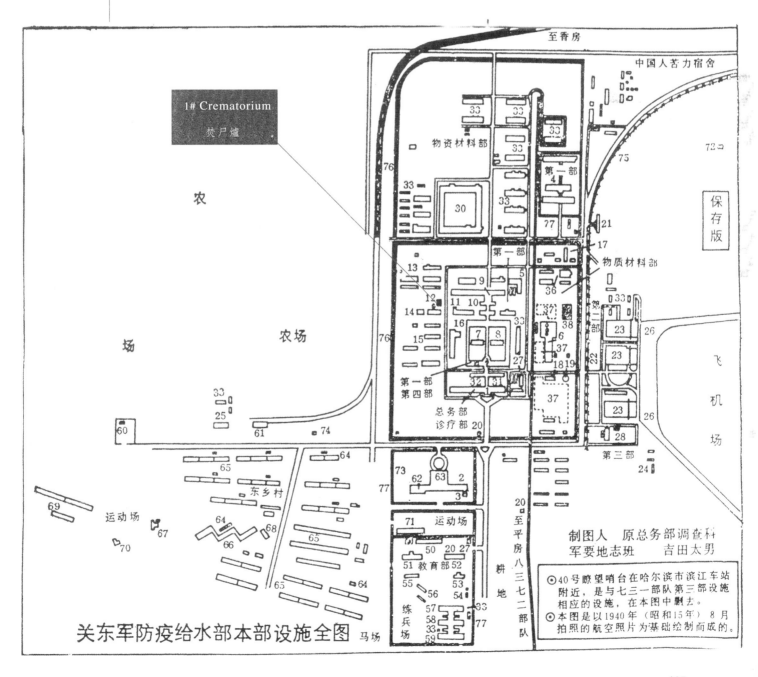

关东军防疫给水部本部设施全图

The map of Pingfan arrangement 1940

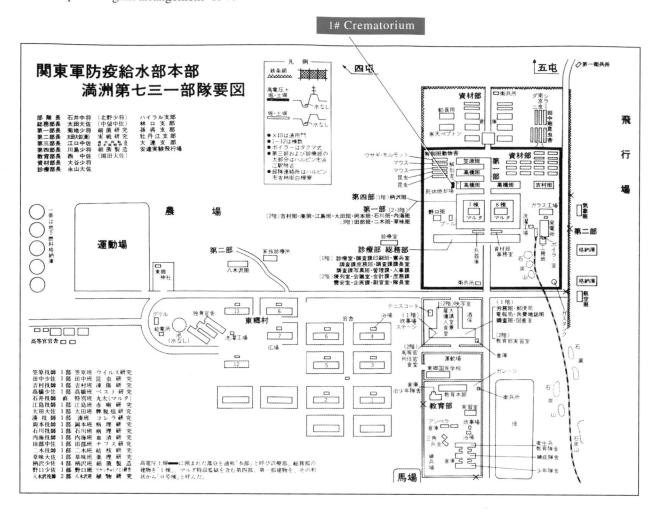

1# Crematorium

3,000 was totally wrong. It can be rebutted by the following facts:

• The number of victims before the "Unit 731" moved into the Pingfan camp was not included.

• There were 400 prisoners in the Pingfan camp while General Ishii ordering to blow-up the camp on 10 August 1945. The "Unit 731" has a cycle of 30 days in their experiment and vivisection of prisoner's life. A simple calculation tell us that there were at least 24, 000 innocent people were perished during the 5 years occupation of Pingfan camp (1940-1945).

• We can further estimate the number of victims by the fact of continuing increases of the crematoriums and experiment grounds.

★1 In 1940, there was only one crematorium (See "The map of Pingfan arrangement in 1940"). Subsequently, it was expanded to 3 crematoriums (The map of Pingfan arrangement in 1944). Obviously, there were too many dead bodies and one crematorium is not enough (The picture shows piles of dead bodies waiting to be cremated). What is the capacity of these crematoriums? At the night of August 10th, 1945, General Ishii ordered to kill all 400 Chinese prisoners and 500 laborers . These 900 victims were completely cremated in the next morning and the facilities were ready to be destroyed. Thus the average capacity for all crematoriums may be 200 bodies per day. Using Kawashima's figure of 3,000, there were only 2 bodies to be cremated each day. It would not be necessary for two extra crematoriums.

多萬人的計算。但是，一些日本史學家則表示數字誇大，史學家常石敬一認為，一九四〇年在寧波的鼠疫攻擊，祇造成一〇六人死亡，一九四一年在常德的鼠疫播散，據中國政府派赴該地調查的鼠疫專家陳文貴一九四一年十二月在報告中指出死亡人數為六人。

常石敬一的論據，有兩點缺失.

寧波的鼠疫攻擊，七三一部隊投放的鼠疫菌是較少的，根據伯力審判已公布的證詞，"七三一部隊"為一九四〇年華中之役所準備的鼠疫跳蚤為五公斤，該次華中的鼠疫攻擊點，除寧波外（十月），還有玉山（江西省、九月）、溫州、臺州、麗水（九月）和龍泉、衢州（十月）以及上虞、慈裕、湯溪、金華（均十二月），分布到寧波的鼠疫菌量不會超過半公斤，而"七三一部隊"平房的鼠疫菌當年的月產量是三百公斤（"伯力審判"第三百頁）。

陳文貴的死亡人數，應檢視陳文貴在常德停留時間。陳一九四一年十一月二十四日由貴陽到常德，同年十二月二日離開，在常德停留的八天內，鼠疫還未擴散，更不了解日機又對洞庭湖其他居民進行更多的跳蚤的投放以及在次年春再次空投鼠疫。

1# Crematorium
一號焚屍爐

The cremation of dissected bodies building up in 1940
解剖實驗後的屍體就拋入 "煉人爐"，一把火燒成灰盡

六人死亡數字，并不具代表性。一九九八年常德已完成的第一次調查，有名有姓、有住址和年齡的死亡者為 10,400 人，而且常德投放的鼠疫、跳蚤等一九四一年十一月空襲時為三十六公斤。（見"井本日記"）。

5.　　A lot of Japanese army hospital has a hand in the B.W. , Detong Army Hospital of Japanese I'st A. In winter of 1941 , with "Unit 1855", carried ten Chinese prisoners to Inner Mongolia for cold observed experiment (Takao Matsumura "The Department of Kwantung Army Epidemic Prevention and Water Supply" P.8).

In winter of 1941 , Detong Army Hospital with "unit 1855", carried ten Chinese prisoners to Inner Mongolia for cold observed experiment (Takao Matsumura "The Department of Kwantung Army Epidemic Prevention and Water Supply" P.8).

Dr. Lee Bingyan, the chief of 2'nd Field Hospital, he representated Chinese Army to Kouquan Hospital (belong to Japanese I'st A.) for take over the enemy's hospital in July 1946. He discovered a large secret room down the basement, there has had 7,000 corpses of babies, they are just four weeks to seven months old.(Chen Yin " Old Impressions ". No.1, P.268)

The remains inside of the burner of the dead bodies.[2# Crematorium]

二號焚尸爐類內部殘迹

＜實驗場＞，一九三八年設立海拉爾實驗場，一九三九年增設佳木斯實驗場，一九四０年再增設陶賴紹實驗場和東寧實驗場，一九四一年更增設城子溝實驗場和安達實驗場。每個實驗場均須附有飛機場和防、檢疫及安全保密機制，投資很大，也顯然是原有實驗場不能適應實驗需要。實驗場的活人人靶靶量據韓曉《日軍七三一部隊罪惡史》記載的調查材料，陶賴紹實驗場在一九四一年九月連續進行兩天三次的活靶炭疽實驗，有三十名中國人被置于靶心致死。日軍戰俘"七三一部隊"成員的軍醫上田彌太郎于一九五三年十一月十日供稱："我所知道兩次警備實驗，就殺害了二百人"。如果一個實驗場每五日作一次實驗，每次十人被實驗，六個實驗場被害人數為 16,830 人。每次被害二十人，則實驗被害總數為 33,660 人。如果"七三一部隊"死亡總數三千人，又何須擴建這麼多實驗場？

其四，"七三一部隊"被害人，大多數通過"特別輸送"管道由憲兵運交給平房。現已在日滿檔案中已查出十二個案計 1,203 人的"輸送"資料，而大量檔案已被日軍焚毀，可見川島三千人之說是不可信的。

其五，"平房"之外，"七三一部隊"還在細菌攻擊地進行活體解剖。如石橋直方指控：一九四０年寧波之役後，親眼目睹在杭州由日本憲兵和便衣密探從寧波抓來兩名男性中國人，當場由"七三一部隊"給解剖了。又如一九四二年九月，日機在浙江省義烏縣崇山村投播鼠疫菌引發鼠疫後，于十月派兵進駐該村，立即在村內的"林山寺"進行三天的活體解剖，數十村民致死。

至于"七三一部隊"系統外，其他細菌戰部隊和日軍陸軍軍醫所作的活試和活剖，哈立斯也未計入，這些有：

★1　日軍"一００部隊"據成員中村中佐指認："日軍憲兵隊每星期都往一００部隊送活人作試驗。該部隊成立于一九三八年，至日本投降的七年間，則可能有成千以上的人死于該部隊。

而另一個成員三友一男在"伯力"時則供認："在本部的後面也有這樣的小屋，每屋至少監押三十至四十人……監押着準備作細菌試驗的中國人"。

★2　日軍"一八五五"部隊（北京）、"一六四四部隊"（南京）、"八六０四部隊"（廣州）、"九四二０部隊"（新加坡），這些細菌部隊所作活試、活剖的次數也是驚人的。一九八九年七月二十一日韓國《中央日報》刊登當年服務于濟南支部（屬"一八五五部隊"）的翻譯員崔享振的證詞指出：一九四一年至一九四二年他在任職期内，有一千多名中國俘虜和韓國流浪漢被當成人體實驗對象，悲慘地死于濟南支部。

在遠至印度洋北岸的泰國曼谷，日軍"九四二０部隊"也在那裏進行殘酷的活體試驗，英國雷諾德.蕭特爾（Leonard Short）記述："在曼谷海關的地下室房間的黑色牆壁上，我能够得到的姓名顯示了在凶惡的醫藥實驗，活的戰俘受到了直接的殺害"。（見丁道爾少將 《東南亞盟軍司令部醫務管理處戰時日記》，一九四五年九月一日至三十日）。

★3　日軍各陸軍軍醫進行的活試和活剖廣泛存在，如：上述的崔享振也證實，駐濟南的日軍軍醫在一九四一年及一九四二年"對離部隊八公裏遠的一個村子五十多戶、三百多村民進行霍亂人體試驗……經過十五天左右，因霍亂死了二十人。

而太原、撫順"日軍戰俘管理"的檔案上，則記載下有四十九名日本軍醫在一九四五年至一九五五年所供認的對一百八十個中國人從事活體解剖的審詢原文。

★4　日軍對各地的"中國戰俘營"進行的細菌屠殺，已查到的記錄中，包括一九四二年在日軍第十三軍所轄的南京戰俘營和玉山戰俘營曾分別對六千戰俘采取散發細菌食物。同年八月，對衢州戰俘營二千戰俘也用同樣方式殺害。

The ruins of 3# crematorium
of Pingfan

第三號焚尸爐（殘迹）

駐華的醫科大學、研究所進行的活試、活剖:《黑龍江文史資料》第二十二輯記述了日軍在該省設立的"三島理化研究","一九四五年八月二十一日地方維持會組織一些人到三島所掩埋死難尸體……在這所陰森院落的西北角,有一個長十米、寬八米、深二米的大坑,……共發現五十四具尸體,其中十四具無頭。"

南滿醫科大學所進行的活體解剖數字也是駭人聽聞的,曾在該校任活剖助理的張丕卿證明,一九四二年至一九四三年一年間,他在該院就參與對二十五名中國人的活剖。

哈立斯對細菌攻擊下,蔓延于一九四五年戰後的情況,雖有提及,但記述不多。近期的不完全統計,戰後死于日軍細菌遺害的人數為 109,239 人。

實際上,日軍細菌戰造成的死亡數字,將超過二百萬或是更多,因為:

一、此七十四萬八千人死亡的數字,是不完全統計,日軍細菌攻擊點中有許多沒有進行死亡報告的調查(如對重慶的攻擊等)。

二、已做的調查仍限于較少的攻擊點,如緬甸全境是日軍一九四二年至一九四五年撒布細菌的重點區,盟軍當時已發現日軍在緬境廣泛散布玻璃型細菌彈(稱為"聖誕球炸彈),而當時中國的情報已指出一九四三年的頭幾個月內已有三萬枚玻璃細菌彈運進南方。日軍新加坡電臺一九四五年五月二十四日甚至公開播發出:"目前印度和緬甸都有英、美軍隊,他們知道將成熱帶疾病的犧牲品"。

又如廣東沿海十 數縣在歷史上并未發生過霍亂"瘟疾",然而在一九四三年後有一百萬以上的民眾,死于霍亂,這一點已有蛛絲馬跡可以查到出于日軍"八六O四部隊"所為,其目的為完全堵死中國的出海口,祇是至今還沒有進行調查。

三、細菌戰的遺害調查也才起步,很多攻擊點的情況,如魯西的臨清縣,是一九四三年日軍"霍亂作戰"的重點之一,至一九九九年仍年年復發霍亂,死亡多少?

四、細菌攻擊下,疾病蔓延是嚴重的。一九四二、四三年日軍對黃河河套的鼠疫攻擊,當時致死人數據綏西等十個縣報告為1,525 人,另有二百萬鼠疫患者,這些人是否存活?并沒有下文。又如一九四二年對華北的細菌進攻,也造成二千萬農民患疾,事後死亡多少?

五、大量的日軍醫院配合細菌專業部隊進行許多活體試驗和活體解剖,死亡人數均難以計算,以山西大同日軍陸軍醫院為例:

1941 年冬"1855 部隊"張家口支部,在內蒙與大同陸軍醫院合作,用 10 個中國戰俘作凍傷實驗和子彈貫穿實驗。(松村高夫"關東軍防疫給水部"P.8.)

1946 年 7 月當晉綏軍區第二野戰醫院院長李炳炎奉命到大同陸軍醫院所轄之口泉煤礦醫院接管時,發現該地下密室中藏有中國四周至七個月大的嬰尸七千具。(成鷹"老印象",第一輯.P.268)

细菌战死亡人数（不完全统计）

The number of dieth by B.W.,(incomplete stalistics)

序号	Name 地名	Virosis 菌種	Number of dieth死亡人数						Attacking date 攻擊日期	Notes 注释
	（浙江省）Zhejiang province		1940	1941	1942	1943	1944	1945		
1	Shangyu 上虞	Plague/鼠疫	120						Dec. 1940 一九四0年十二月	
2	Quzhou衢州	Plague/鼠疫	2000	3000	7600	1254	10000		Oct.4.1940 ①一九四0年10月4日	Qiu Mingxuan" Evidence of a Crimese", Shan Xia publisher,1999 邱明軒"罪證",三峡出版社,一九九九年
		Cholera/霍亂							march.1941 ② 一九四一年三月	
		Typhoid/傷寒							Aug.1942 ③一九四一年十二月	Unit Canoyashi.15th D. 奈良部隊,15師團
		Anthrax/炭疽							Aug.8,1942 ④一九四二年八月	Same as "Quzhou",15th D. 同衢州,15師團
3	Changshan 常山	Plague/cholera 鼠疫／霍亂／			2500	1506	958	10000	Aug.19,1942 一九四二年八月十九日	Same as "Quzhou",15th D. 同衢州,15師團
4	Jiangshan 江山	Plague/cholera 鼠疫／霍亂／			2000		11		Aug. 1942 一九四二年八月	Same as "Quzhou",15th D. 同衢州,15師團
5	Longyou 龍游	Plague/cholera 鼠疫／霍亂／				2948				Same as "Quzhou",15th D. 同衢州,15師團
6	Kaihua 開化	Plague/cholera 鼠疫／霍亂／								Same as "Quzhou",15th D. 同衢州,15師團
7	Jinhua 金華	Plague/鼠疫	1617		2000				Nov.27,1940 ①一九四0年十一月二十七日	Osamu Shibo confession ,Jan. 1945 榛葉修供詞,一九四五年一月八日
									Nov.28,1940 ②一九四0年十一月二十八日	
		Anthrax/炭疽			1000				June–Aug,1942 ③一九四二年六月至八月	15th D. 15師團
8	Ningbo宁波	Plague/鼠疫	106						Oct.22/27,1940. 一九四0年十月22日,27日	
9	Dongyang東陽	Plague/鼠疫		118						Injected from Yiwu 義烏鼠疫傳染
10	Yiwu 義烏	Plague/鼠疫		257	1057				① Oct.2,1941 一九四一年十月二日	The result of Yiwu investingation 義烏調查結果
									② Sep.1942 一九四二年九月	"Watch and Think" July, 1999, the thinks, 1,081 persons were death.
									③ Oct.1942 一九四二年十月	一,"觀察與思考"一九九九年七月號認爲死亡爲 1,081人
11	Yunhe 雲和	Plague/鼠疫 Dysentery/痢疾			3,357				Aug.26.1942 ①一九四二年八月二十六日	
12	Maoyuan 茂元	Plague/鼠疫			No figure 未統計				1942-1945 ②一九四二至四五年	
13	Lishui 麗水		No figure 未統計						1940 ①一九四0年	
		Typhoid/傷寒 Cholera/霍亂					5,000		June 1942 ②一九四四年六至八月	"Unit Canoyashi"arrived June 24, 1942, depature at Aug. 3
		Plague/鼠疫							June17.1944 ③一九四四年六月十七日空投	"奈良部隊"一九四二年六月二十四日到麗水,八月三日赴松陽。"
		Plague/鼠疫							Aug.1944 by air ④一九四四年八月,空投	
		Plague/鼠疫							Sep.1944 by air ⑤一九四四年九月,空投	
14	Yinkang 永康								June.1942 一九四二年六月	Unit Canoyashi 奈良部隊
15	Taizhou 臺州								Sep.1940 一九四0年九月	

序号	Name 地名	Virosis 菌種	Numbe of dieth 死亡人數						Attacking date 攻擊日期	Notes 注釋
			1940	1941	1942	1943	1944	1945		
	（浙江省）Zhejiang province									
16	Lanxi蘭溪	Plague/鼠疫 Cholera/霍亂		12		3,000			①By air .1941 一九四一年 1941空投 ②Aug.1942 一九四二年八月	Reported by the staff of sanitation dep. of Zhe,jiang 浙江衛生廳職員報告。 15th D. 15師團
17	Zhuji諸暨	Plague/鼠疫 400 Cholera/霍亂 Typhoid/傷寒		1,000					①Dec.19.1941 by air 一九四一年十二月十九日 ②Aug.1942 一九四二年八月	15th D. 15師團
18	Wenzhou溫州	Plague/鼠疫 Cholera/霍亂		1,000 3,000					①Apr.21.1941 一九四一年四月二十一日 ②July.1942 一九四二年七月	空投
19	Xingden新登	Plague/鼠疫		300					Apr.21.1941. 一九四一年四月二十一日	空投
20	Qingyuan慶元	Plague/鼠疫 200			50				①Dec.1940 一九四０年十二月， ②1943 by air 一九四三年，	空投 空撤
21	Wengyang翁墻	Plague/鼠疫					3,000		Sep.1944 一九四四年九月	Army occupied 地面部隊入侵
22	Jinyun縉雲	Plague/鼠疫			3,000				Jane.1942 一九四二年六月	
23	Jinnin景寧	Plague/鼠疫			3,000				1942．一九四二年	
	Ying,jiao永嘉	Plague/鼠疫			1,000					
24	Qingtian青田	Plague/鼠疫		1,000					July .1942 一九四二年七月	
25	Suichang松陽	Typhoid/傷寒 Dysentery/痢疾 Cholera/霍亂			4,500				Aug.1942 一九四二年八月	"Unit Canoyashi"arrived at Aug.3. "奈良部隊" 八月三日到達
26	Cixi慈溪		210						Dec.1940, by air 一九四０年十二月，	空投
27	Tangxi湯溪	Typhoid傷寒		No figure 未統計	1,000				①By air .1941 一九四一年 ②Sep.1942 一九四二年九月	空投
28	Longquan龍泉	Plague/鼠疫		165					Dec.1940 一九四０年十二月	
	Jiangxi province(江西省)									
29	Yushan玉山	Plague/鼠疫	300			3,500			①Aug.1940 一九四０年八月 ②Aug.1942 一九四二年八月	
30	Ganzhou贛州	Plague/鼠疫			NO figure 未統計				By air 1942 一九四二年，	空投
31	Guanfeng廣豐	Plague/鼠疫		4,000					Aug.19.1942 一九四二年八月十九日	15th D. 15師團
32	Shangrao 上饒（廣信）	Plague/鼠疫		5,000					Aug.19.1942 一九四二年八月九日	15th D .15師團
	Hubei Province （湖北省）									

199

序号	Name 地名	Virosis 菌種	Numbe of dieth 死亡人數						Attacking date 攻擊日期	Notes 注釋
	Hubei Province		1940	1941	1942	1943	1944	1945		
33	Hankou 漢口	Plague/ 鼠疫							1940 一九四〇年	
34	Yidu 宜都	Plague/ 鼠疫							1943 一九四三年	
	Fujian Provinec （福建省）									
35	Jianou 建殴	Plague/ 鼠疫			180				By air ,1942 一九四二年,	空投
36	Xiapu 霞浦	Plague/ 鼠疫							1942 一九四二年,	空投
37	Nanqing 南清	Plague/ 鼠疫							1941 by air 一九四一年	空投
38	Chengzhou 漳州	Plague/ 鼠疫							1941 by air 一九四一年	
39	Longxi 龍溪	Plague/ 鼠疫		100					① 1941，一九四一年	
						200			②1943,一九四三年	
40	Changle 長樂	Cholera/ 霍亂					50,000		1944，一九四四年	蔣開惠證言
41	Fuqing 福清	Plague/ 鼠疫							1944，一九四四年	
	Nnortheast of China （東北）									
42	Nongan 農安	Plague/ 鼠疫				298			① 1940，一九四〇年七月	Ibid as Zhanhuang 同贊皇
		Plague/ 鼠疫				4，500			②1942,一九四二年	The epidemic prevention station of county 農安縣防疫站
43	Changchun 長春	Plague/ 鼠疫							① 1938 一九三八年	
		Plague/ 鼠疫							② 1940 一九四〇年	
44	Harbin 哈爾濱	Plague/ 鼠疫				300			① Sep.10,1935 一九三五年九月十日	
		Typhoid/ 傷寒 Plague/ 鼠疫							② Aug.1941 一九四一年八月 ③ 1945-1949	
45	Dedu 德都	Cholera/ 霍亂							1941 一九四一年	
46	Nace 拉古	Cholera/ 霍亂	106						1940 一九四〇年	The Culture of History Materials of Mudanjiang "牡丹江文史資料"
47	Shanhu 三河區								1942 一九四二年	
48	Del'nes river 得爾布爾河	Anthrax/ 炭疽							1942 一九四二年	
49	Hailar 海拉爾	Typhoid/ 傷寒 Cholera/ 霍亂 Plague/ 鼠疫							1944 一九四四年	
	Henan Province （河南省）									
50	Nanyang 南陽	Plague/ 鼠疫							1942，一九四二年	

序号	Name 地名	Virosis 菌種	Number of dieth 死亡人數						Attacking date 攻擊日期	Notes 注释
	Henan Province (河南省)		1940	1941	1942	1943	1944	1945		
51	Xinxiang 新鄉	Typhoid/傷寒			100				1942 一九四二年	
52	Huaxian 滑縣	Typhoid/傷寒							1942 一九四二年	
53	Junxian 浚縣	Typhoid/傷寒							1942 一九四二年	
54	Neixiang 內鄉	Typhoid/傷寒			80				Apr.14,1940 一九四〇年四月十四日	
55	Boai 博愛	Cholera/霍亂			1,000				Oct.1938 一九三八年十月	
56	Buying 濮陽	Typhoid/傷寒							Aug.16,1939 一九三九年八月十六日	
57	Linxian 林縣	Cholera/霍亂							Nov.1944 一九四四年十一月	Rehappended cholera in 1984. 一九八四年再度發生霍亂
58	Fengqiun 封丘	Cholera/霍亂							July,1944 一九四四年七月	
59	Southeast of Henan 豫東南	Typhoid/傷寒							1944 一九四四年	
	Hebei Province (河北省)									
60	Dinxian 定縣	Plague/鼠疫	70						① Feb-Apr.1941 一九四一年二月至四月	
		Plague/鼠疫			NO figure 未統計				② Feb.1942 一九四二年二月	
61	Jishi 冀氏	Typhoid/傷寒							Feb.7,1944 一九四四年二月七日	
62	Wanxian 完縣	Typhoid/傷寒		150					1941 一九四一年	
63	Zhanhuang 贊皇	Cholera/霍亂		60					Apr.6,1941 一九四一年四月六日	
64	Neiwuang 內黃	Cholera/霍亂		NO figure 未統計					Oct.1938 一九三八年十月	
65	Jizhong 冀中	Cholera/霍亂		70					1941 一九四一年	
		Plague/鼠疫		NO figure 未統計					1942 一九四二年	
66	North of Hebei 冀北	Typhoid/傷寒		NO figure 未統計					Aug.1938 一九三八年八月	
67	Shunde 順德	Dysentery/痢疾		NO figure 未統計					1937 一九三七年	
68	Cangzhou 滄州								1937 一九三七年	
69	Sincheng 新城	Cholera/霍亂							1940 一九四零年	
70	North China Railway regions 華北鐵道兩則	Typhoid/傷寒		45,000(1938)					Aug.1938 一九三八年八月	
71	Deltoid Area of Beijing\Tianjin\Baoding 北京、天津、保定三角地區	Cholera/霍亂							Feb.-Apr.1941 一九四一年二月至四月	
72	Yingxian 應縣	Dysentery/痢疾							Nov.1942 一九四二年十一月	
73	Yanbei 雁北	Plague/鼠疫							Apr.1942 一九四二年四月	

序号	Name 地名	Virosis 菌種	Number of dieth 死亡人數						Attacking date 攻擊日期	Notes 注釋
	Inner Mongolia (內蒙)		1940	1941	1942	1943	1944	1945		
	Suiyuan 綏远	Plague/鼠疫			313					Telegraph of dep. of sanitation 衛生署代電
115	Wulin 五臨	Plague/鼠疫			205					
	Anhui Province (安徽省)									
116	Wuwei 無爲								July 24,1940 一九四〇年七月二十四日	
117	Guangde 廣德	Plague/鼠疫			160				1943 一九四三年	
	Guangdong Province (廣東省)									
118	Yangjiang 陽江	Cholera/霍亂	1000						1939 一九三九年	Apr.8,1951 "So. Daily" "南方日報" 一九五一年四月八日
119	Pinghu 平湖	Tuberculosis 結核							Nov.17,1937 一九三七年十一月十七日	
120	Shigu 石鼓	Tuberculosis 結核							Nov.17,1939 一九三七年十一月十七日	
121	Shaoguan 韶關	Cholera/霍亂							1939 一九三九年	
122	Loching 樂昌	Cholera/霍亂							May-June,1941 一九四一年五、六月	
	Guangzhou 廣州 (難民營)	paratyphoid 副傷寒			30,000				1942-1943 一九四二年至一九四三年	
123	Wengyuan 翁源	Plague/鼠疫							1942-1943 一九四二年至一九四三年	
124	Fanyu 番禺									"The Resist Ten Days Pres." June 5,1940
										"抗戰旬報"，一九四〇年六月五日"
	Guangxi Province (廣西省)									
125	Quilin 桂林	Plague/鼠疫 Cholera/霍亂							1939 一九三九年	
									1942, 一九四二年	
126	Nanning 南寧	Plague/鼠疫		70					1942, 一九四二年	
	Sichuan Province (四川省)									
127	Chongqing 重慶	Cholera/霍亂							1939	
									1940	
	Yunnan Province (雲南省)									
128	Kunming 昆明	Cholera/霍亂			210,000				May-July,1942 一九四二年五月至七月	
129	Baoshan 保山									

130　"Unit 731" before move into Pingfan, 8yrs. Killed 300 persons each yr, total killed 2,400
　　　平房之前，**1932-1939**（**8 年**），每年 **300 人**致死，計 **2,400 人**
131　"Unit 731" moved in Pingfan , 5 yrs. killed 20,000，1940-1945（平房五年，二萬人致死）
132　Sunwu Deta. Sent 60 persons there for experiment were died (孫吳支隊，一次送去六十名活試致死)
　　　Chinese labourers be killed in :(修築用民工被殺)
133　①Sunwu Deta. (孫吳支隊) has 1,000 be killed, investigated by the Dep . of Police of Hailongjian
　　　1940 年起建（**1940-1945**），死 **1,000 人**（黑龍江公安廳正調查,**1945 年**）
134　② "Unit 2645" 300 people were died （**2645 部隊**）殺死 **300 人**
135　Around the villages of "Unit 731"(七三一部隊在附近村莊)
　　　①Takeo Kazune witnessed: "In 1944, Hailar Deta. sent secret agents to Monglia to spreaded bacteria in water
　　　　sources".
　　　"**1944 年**在海拉爾，他們多次派人秘密潛入蒙古部落，在居民毫無查覺下，將霍亂菌、傷寒菌投
　　　　入水井和飲用水源。"
　　　② Kozo Okanoto pointed out : "Our Data . got once experiment of plague bacteria spreading and preventing in
　　　　the mountain village beside unit for B.W. research." 山本習明（秘書）：**1944 年** " 支隊在附近山村組
　　　　織一次鼠疫傳染防疫戰實習。"
136　"Unit 1855" "一八五五部隊"
　　　"Some prisoners sent to Unit 1855 transported by truck from P.O.W .camp in Fengtai, I known three times, I'st
　　　six prisoners, 2'nd five ,and 3' nd six also . " Confessed by kiichi Hirakawa in Dec. 1944.
　　　日本 " 戰争責任研究"，一九九三年第二期 **P.49**
　　　平川喜一證詞：（一九四四年十二月）
　　　" 當时豐臺有俘虜收容所，從那里用汽車將俘虜送到北京。連續運來了三次（6 人，5 人，6 人）".
137　"Unit 731" killed 500 labourers during "815"
　　　731 撤出平房基地时，殺掉參加勞務的中國勞工（彼得.威廉斯，大衛.瓦雷斯 " 七三一部隊 "）
138　Dr. Kozo Okamoto made vivisection in Hailar, killed 99 people.
　　　岡本耕造在海拉爾活體解剖鼠疫 " 患者 " 九十九名
139　Jinan Deta . of "Unit 1855"濟南支部
　　　①Hengzhen Cui stating his witnese of over 1,000 victims died of live experiment and live dissection in
　　　1941-1942, and made the cholera experiment on 300 villagers outside of Jinan in 1941-1942, after 15 days , 20
　　　victims were died ("The Korea Central Daily" July 21,1989)
　　　韓 " 中央日報 "**7/21/1989**，崔享振揭發：有一千多名中國俘虜被活體試致死（一九四一年至一九四
　　　二年）.軍醫們還對離部隊 **8** 公里遠的一個村子五十多户三百多村民進行霍亂人體實驗，經過十五天左
　　　右因霍亂死了 **20 人**。
　　　② Killed by experiments of Jinan Deta . from 1939-1940 and 1943-1945 , 2,500 were died.
　　　濟南支隊在一九三九年至一九四 **0** 年、一九四三年至一九四五年的活試，活剖死亡二千五百人。
140　"Unit 1644"(" 一六四四部隊 ") According to Xin Jinlong's file charges in Capital Court of Nanjing Dec.1
　　　1945: "In 1942, has 100 Prisoners killed ", by unit 1644 for experiment in three months .Thus figure, has 2,000
　　　people were died..
　　　謝金龍于一九四五年十二月一日向 " 南京首都地方法院 " 控告，一九四二有中國戰俘 **100 人**，三個
　　　月内被殺，一年 **400 人**，**1940-1945**，五年致死二千人。
141　Sandao physics and Chemistry Research Inst. Killed 200 persons
　　　三島理化所，殺 **200 人**。
142　"Unit 100" has 1,062 people died there .
　　　" **100 部隊** " 死亡一千零六十二中國人.
143　Killed by live experiments and vivisections by surgeons of Japan's Army hospitals, Kanisawa Herikuda said :
　　　"May be few ten thousads killed", may be 20,000 died of whole army's hospitols."
　　　各地軍醫活體解剖，已查明 **180 人**，湯淺謙説：" 也許有幾萬人 "，故估計死二萬人。
144　Chinese P.O.W. camp, according to : ① the Khabarovsk Trial ;② Investigation of Quzhou;③ The Mateerials
　　　of Culturc & History of Jilin" No.14 . Has 8,000 prisoners he killed in three POWs camp of 13 th A.
　　　日軍第三者事家 **13** 軍中國俘虜營，根據：①伯力審判；②衢州調查③吉林文史資料 **14** 輯.有八千戰俘
　　　致死
145　Jinan, Xinhuayuang, the P O W camp of Japan 12th A . in Shandong , has 1,000 prisoners were deid there.
　　　濟南新華院（**1941-1943**），山東第十二軍俘虜營，死亡戰俘一千。
146　Mukden , American P O W , died 150 by live experiments.
　　　沈陽，沈陽美俘虜營死亡一百五十名。
147　After "8.15"(戰后死亡)
　　　After "8.15" were died(戰后死亡) 109,239
　　　Total 總計：748,027

Section 2
The Map of Germ Attacks

The Japanese Army's germ attacking, in the case of working in large area, the main measure they use was air spreading by plane. The recording of " Imoto's Diary " said that the plan of G. Chief of Staff, was the same method. Each germ unit or germ team all had incorporated air team. As we know there at least were seven germ air teams (or air squad) worked with each germ unit, like the "Unit 731" air team. There were 11 air planes equipped. They had had:

"Nomiryu" style knocking plane

97-1 style heavy knocking plane

97-2 style heavy knocking plane

97' style transport plane

99' style double light

99' style single light

Eagle style

Patriotic style

Emergency recovery vehicle

Every germ attacking air team had owned its exclusive airport. For example, in the "Unit 731", the airport was put at out of the fence . The one of unit 1644's (Nanjing) was put on "Imperial place Airport" cross the street of "Unit 1644" , Japanese Navy and Japanese Army has equipped B .W. air teams also.

Chapter co The Death.

Besides of the air team of the Germ warfare , in Japanese Navy and Japanese Army, there also exclusive germ warfare pilot team established. For example, the county magistrate of Yongjang county sent a telegraphic report to The Government Chairman of Zhejiang Province in Feb.26 1941: "In Feb.19, 1941, Japanese set up the unit of Yangtze River Navy's Special Agent with eighteen aircrafts, command by Lieutenant Colonel Jinrei Funeda will be take germ spreading attacks to around the Jiangxi, Anhu, Zhejiang. Jiangsu, Shandong provinces". Since the germ warfare was special, the pilot team was some of kind belonging to each germ warfare Army. Here we have a collateral evidence, it pick up from Peter Williams and David wallace's book "The Unit 731". In the 8th chapter of the book, the author tell us that the Allied forces once happened got a Japanese air pilot's training note in islands of Pacific. In the note there were some information about "Bacillus bomb" and "Number 7 special bomb". The attacking object was water dams, animals and people.

In attending at the germ warfare, the Japanese germ air teams were most activity in 1942, As we know in January, Febraury of the year, the air teams were gathered at Shuiyuan, Hetao area and spreaded plague. In March, April, they worked for the China-Burma war-area water resource infecting. In May, they were busied on cholera attacking Baoshan, Kunming. From June, they had begin to spread germ on Zhejiang Jiangxi Line, the offensive was went on to fall of the year. After that they back to China-Burma area again to spread germ in water, the renge was much bigger than ever.

Enter 1943, the Japanese germ air teams were seriously challenged, because the U.S Air force had got the control of the air of the China-Burma area in the beginning of 1944, and the renge was developed reached the whole Burma and China war zone. The Japan's lower speed air planes were shot down by the U.S. air force one after another. The Japanese Army's offensive was restricted seriously from the U.S air force.

To suitable the China-Burma frontier decisive battle of 1943 fall to 1944, Tokyo, the government of Japan ordered teams to finish the air-dropping "Cristmas Ball" to the all district of Burma. It turned the south Asia war zone into a fear area of "Death Line".

Even though, the Japanese germ air team's plane was loss horribly. For the reason, the U.S. air force bombed Japan, the production of air plane went down, and battle with the U.S .Air Frce in Pacific area needs a large quantity of planes, so the government had no any more power to supply the germ air teams.

So the Japanese germ warfare scale went down. From the beginning of 1943 they lost the control of the air, their germ attacking was slow down..

第二節　細菌攻擊

日軍的細菌攻擊,大面積主要依靠于飛機撒布,"井本日記"所記載的日軍參謀本部的細菌作戰手段,也指明以飛機為主。

各細菌部隊均編入航空隊,已知至少有七支細菌航空隊(或航空班),配備有數十架飛機,如"七三一部隊"航空隊(稱"8273部隊")有飛機十一架,型號為:

吞龍式爆擊機

九七式重爆一型

九七式重爆二型

九七式運輸機

九九式雙輕

九九式單輕

隼式

愛國式

緊急式救援機

細菌戰航空隊有自己專用的機場,如"七三一部隊"航空隊機場,設于"七三一部隊"本部的牆外,"一六四四部隊"(南京)航空隊機場設于本部大樓馬路對面的"故宮機場"。

除細菌戰部隊航空隊外,日軍陸軍和海軍另有專門的細菌航空兵,如一九四一年二月二十六日,浙江省永嘉縣縣長向浙江省政府主席的電文報告稱:"皓(19)日,敵機十八架在蕪湖編成楊子江海軍特務隊,由船田仁禮中佐負責指揮。聞將對我贛皖浙蘇魯戰區後方施放細菌"(浙江省檔案館世藏,35-58-10),由于細菌戰的特殊技術性,這些航空兵必然是在細菌部隊掌控下作業的.彼得·威廉斯,大衛·瓦雷斯所著"七三一部隊"書中第八章,論及盟軍在太平洋島嶼截獲一個日軍航空兵飛行員訓練生的筆記,筆記中指出:"杆菌炸彈和特別炸彈第七號的資料,以及攻擊目標蓄水池、動物和人。"印證了陸軍和海軍還設有專門為細菌作戰的航空隊。

細菌航空隊的出擊,以一九四二年為最多。這一年一、二月航空隊集中于綏遠、河套地區的鼠疫散播,三、四月主攻目標是緬甸戰區的水源"毒化",五月霍亂攻擊保山、昆明,六月開始是浙贛綫的細菌投放,攻勢繼續到年秋,而後又再次對緬甸進行大面積的空中播放。

進入一九四三年後,細菌航空隊受到空中的嚴重挑戰。美國空軍在年初獲得了中緬邊境制空權後,進一步擴大制空權至緬甸全境和中國戰區,日軍細菌航空隊的低速飛機,紛紛被美機擊落。大大制約了日軍細菌戰的功勢。

東京為配合一九四三年秋至一九四四年的中緬邊境決戰,命令日軍細菌航空隊冒險完成全緬的"聖誕球"空投,使南亞戰場形成一個恐怖的"死亡帶"。

然而,日軍細菌航空隊的飛機損失慘重,日本本土遭美機轟炸後飛機產量下降,又迫于供應太平洋美日激戰所需之戰機,無力再保證細菌航空隊的飛機補充了。

于是,日軍細菌戰的規模,自失去制空權的初期起(一九四三年)即走向下坡。

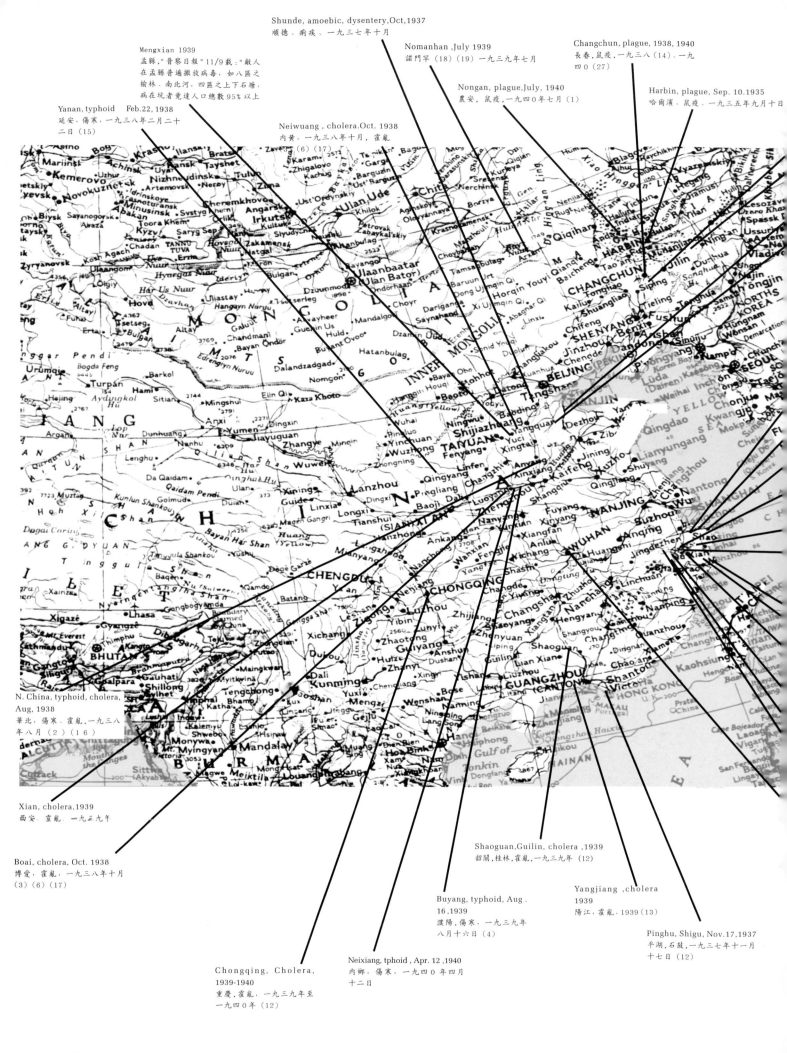

Shunde, amoebic, dysentery,Oct,1937
順德、痢疾、一九三七年十月

Mengxian 1939
孟縣,"晉察日報" 11/9 載:"敵人
在孟縣普遍撒放病毒,如八區之
榆林、南北河,四區之上下石塘,
病在坑者竟達人口總數95%以上

Nomanhan ,July 1939
諾門罕 (18)(19)一九三九年七月

Changchun, plague, 1938, 1940
長春、鼠疫,一九三八 (14)、一九
四 0 (27)

Yanan, typhoid Feb.22, 1938
延安、傷寒,一九三八年二月二十
二日 (15)

Nongan, plague,July, 1940
農安, 鼠疫,一九四0年七月 (1)

Harbin, plague, Sep. 10.1935
哈爾濱、鼠疫、一九三五年九月十日

Neiwuang , cholera.Oct. 1938
內黃、一九三八年十月、霍亂

N. China, typhoid, cholera,
Aug, 1938
華北、傷寒、霍亂,一九三八
年八月 (2)(16)

Xian, cholera,1939
西安, 霍亂,一九三九年

Boai, cholera, Oct. 1938
博愛、霍亂,一九三八年十月
(3)(6)(17)

Shaoguan,Guilin, cholera ,1939
韶關,桂林,霍亂,一九三九年 (12)

Yangjiang ,cholera
1939
陽江, 霍亂, 1939(13)

Buyang, typhoid, Aug .
16,1939
濮陽,傷寒,一九三九年
八月十六日 (4)

Pinghu, Shigu, Nov.17,1937
平湖,石鼓,一九三七年十一月
十七日 (12)

Neixiang, tphoid , Apr. 12 ,1940
內鄉,傷寒,一九四0年四月
十二日

Chongqing, Cholera,
1939-1940
重慶, 霍亂,一九三九年至
一九四0年 (12)

208

ncheng, cholera ,1940
城．霍亂，一九四〇年（5）

Nace. plague
拉古，鼠疫一九四〇年

Changzhou, 1937
滄州，一九三七年

Wuwei, aircraft sprayed germ, Luly 24,1940
無爲，飛機瀰播細菌，一九四〇年七月二十四
日（21）

Shangyu ,plague, Dec .1940
上虞，鼠疫，一九四〇年十二月（24）
Zhuji, cholera, typhoid, Oct,5, 1940
諸暨，傷寒，霍亂，一九四〇年十月五日（29）

Cixi, plague ,Dec .1940
慈谿，一九四〇年十二月鼠疫（25）

Ningbo, plague. Oct.
寧波，鼠疫，一九四〇年（11）（22）

Jinhua, plague, typhoid, Nov. 27-28 1940, Dec. 1940
金華，鼠疫，一九四〇年十一月二十七日，二十八日
（8）（11）一九四〇年十二月（23）

Taizhou, plague, typhoid ,Sep. 1940
臺州，鼠疫，傷寒，一九四〇年九月（10）
（11）

Tangxi,typhoid, Dec. 1940 (24)
湯溪，傷寒，一九四〇年十二月

Venzhou, plague, cholera, Sep .1940
州，鼠疫，霍亂，一九四〇年九月（10）
11）

Lishui, plague, Sep. 1940
麗水，鼠疫，一九四〇年九月（10）（11）

Quzhou, plague, typhoid, Oct. 4 ,1940
衢縣，鼠疫，傷寒，一九四〇年十月四日（7）（8）（9）

ongquan,plague, Dec.1940
龍泉，鼠疫，一九四〇年十二月（25）

ingyuan, plague,Dec.1940
元，鼠疫，一九四〇年十二月（25）

ushan, plague ,Sep. 1940
山，鼠疫，一九四〇年九月（10）
11）

Hankou, plague,1940 (26)
漢口附近,鼠疫

Germ attacks record before 1940
一九四〇年前日軍細菌攻擊記録

209

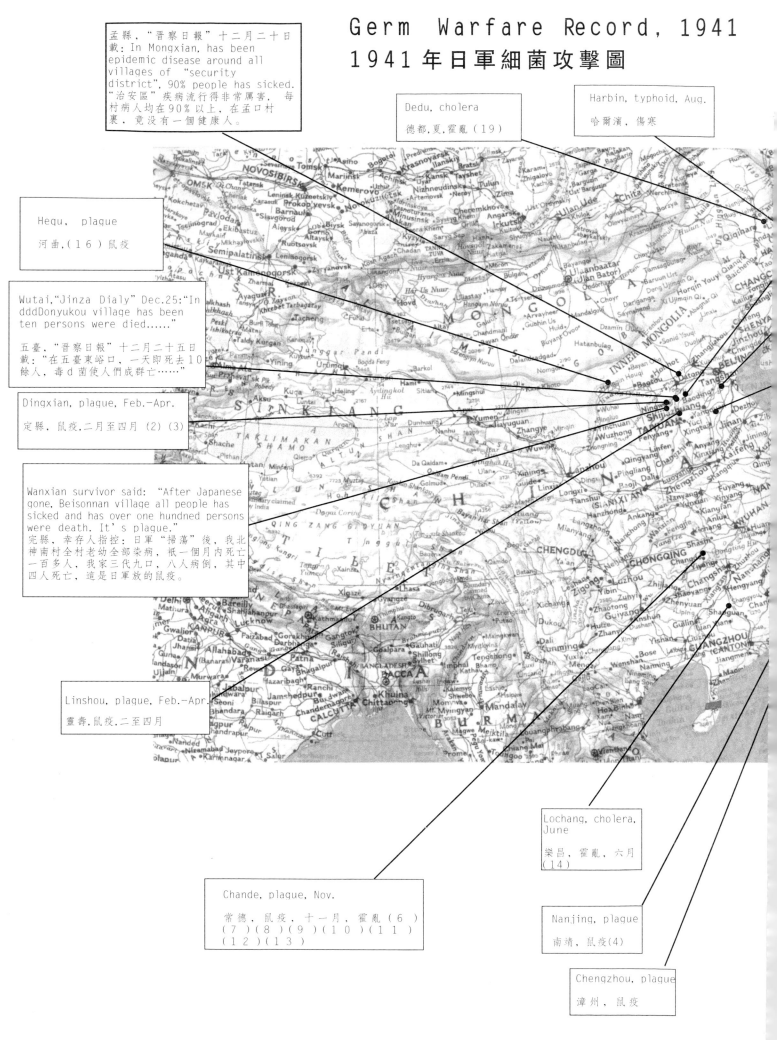

Germ Warfare Record, 1941
1941年日軍細菌攻擊圖

孟縣，"晉察日報"十二月二十日
載：In Mongxian, has been
epidemic disease around all
villages of "security
district", 90% people has sicked.
"治安區"疾病流行得非常厲害，每
村病人均在90％以上，在孟口村
裏，竟沒有一個健康人。

Dedu, cholera

德都,夏.霍亂（19）

Harbin, typhoid, Aug.

哈爾濱，傷寒

Hequ, plaque

河曲,（16）鼠疫

Wutai,"Jinza Dialy" Dec.25:"In
dddDonyukou village has been
ten persons were died......"

五臺，"晉察日報"十二月二十五日
載："在五臺東峪口，一天即死去10
餘人，毒d菌使人們成群亡......"

Dingxian, plaque, Feb.-Apr.

定縣，鼠疫,二月至四月（2）（3）

Wanxian survivor said: "After Japanese
gone, Beisonnan village all people has
sicked and has over one hundred persons
were death. It's plaque."
完縣，幸存人指控：日軍"掃蕩"後，我北
神南村全村老幼全部染病，祇一個月內死亡
一百多人，我家三代九口，八人病倒，其中
四人死亡，這是日軍放的鼠疫。

Linshou, plaque, Feb.-Apr.

靈壽,鼠疫,二至四月

Lochang, cholera,
June

樂昌，霍亂，六月
（14）

Chande, plaque, Nov.

常德，鼠疫，十一月，霍亂（6）
（7）（8）（9）（10）（11）
（12）（13）

Nanjing, plaque

南靖,鼠疫(4)

Chengzhou, plaque

漳州，鼠疫

Notes

Zhanhuang, cholera ,Apr.6
贊皇，霍亂（1） 四月六日

The deltoid area of Beijing, Tianjing and Baoding
北京、天津、保定三角地帶 （17）

Jizhong
冀中

Guangde, plaque, Feb.
廣德，鼠疫，二 月（15）

Zhujin, Dec.19 （18）
諸暨，十二月十九日

Yiwu, plaque, Oct.
義烏、鼠疫、十月

Quzhou, plaque, March 1941
衢州,鼠疫,三月

Qingyuan ,Longquan, plague
慶元、龍泉 ,鼠疫流行（5）

Xiapu, plague
霞浦，鼠疫

Longxi ,plague
龍溪，鼠疫（4）

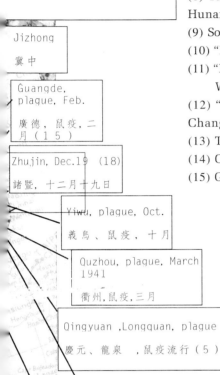

(1) Guo Chengchou. Liao Yingchang "Factual Account of Japanese Army's Biological Warfare Against China", P. 246, Yanshan Press ,1997.

(2) Ibidem (1)

(3) The circulate a notice of the command of Dingxian, China (Dec. 14, 1941)

(4) Ibidem (1) p.338-339

(5) Lu Dihuan (Hebei province medical school professor) "have some informations about Japanese airplane threw down plague germ on Zhejiang province." Ibidem as (1) P.351-353

(6) Ibidem (1) P.351-353

(7) "The plague Report of Changde, Hunan"(Dec. 12, 1941)

(8) Yung Giyung "The report of under going about prevention and cure plague in western Hunan".

(9) Some archives of plague on Changde, ibidem (1) P363-376

(10) "Probe the history of Syowa," No.1 Bunei Fuynsyu

(11) "Imoto Diary", Yoshiaki Yoshimi "The Centrol of Army With Germ Warfare a Vocational Work a Diary of Japanese Officer" (1995)

(12) "Imoto Diary" "at Nov. 20 1941, the plague diseases has been run sampant around Changde, it's looks as if hit the target, I belive firmly that can be come on diseases".

(13) The Kharbarovsk Trial

(14) Cai Mantian testimony, ibidem (1) P.421

(15) Gen. Gu Zhutong's report by telegraph.

注釋

(1) 郭成周，廖應昌"侵華軍細菌戰紀實"，P.246，燕山出 版社，1997

(2) 同（1）

(3) 中國河北省完縣軍區司令部通報（一九四一年十二月十四日）

(4) 同(1)，P.338-P.339

(5) 河北省醫學院陸滌寰教授"關于日機在浙江，福建兩省投 擲鼠疫菌情況"。同(1) P.338-340

(6) (1) p.351-353

(7) "湖南常德鼠疫報告"（一九四一年十二月十二日）

(8) 容啟榮"防治湘西鼠疫經過報告書"

(9) 常德有關鼠疫的歷史檔案資料，同(1) P.363-376

(10) "探索昭和史之謎"（上），文藝春秋社

(11) "井本日記"：吉見義明"陸軍中央與細菌戰，日軍軍官 業務日記（1995）。"

(12) "井本日記"："十一月二十日，常德流行鼠疫，其勢甚 猛，看來只要命中，確實可以發病。"

(13) 伯力審判庭

(14) 蔡滿天證詞同(1) P.421

(15) 顧祝同將軍電報：

(16) 同(1) P.91

(17) 同(1) P.92

(18) "人民日報"，一九五０年二月九日

(19) "日軍731罪惡史"P.268，"黑龍江文史資料"第三十 一輯

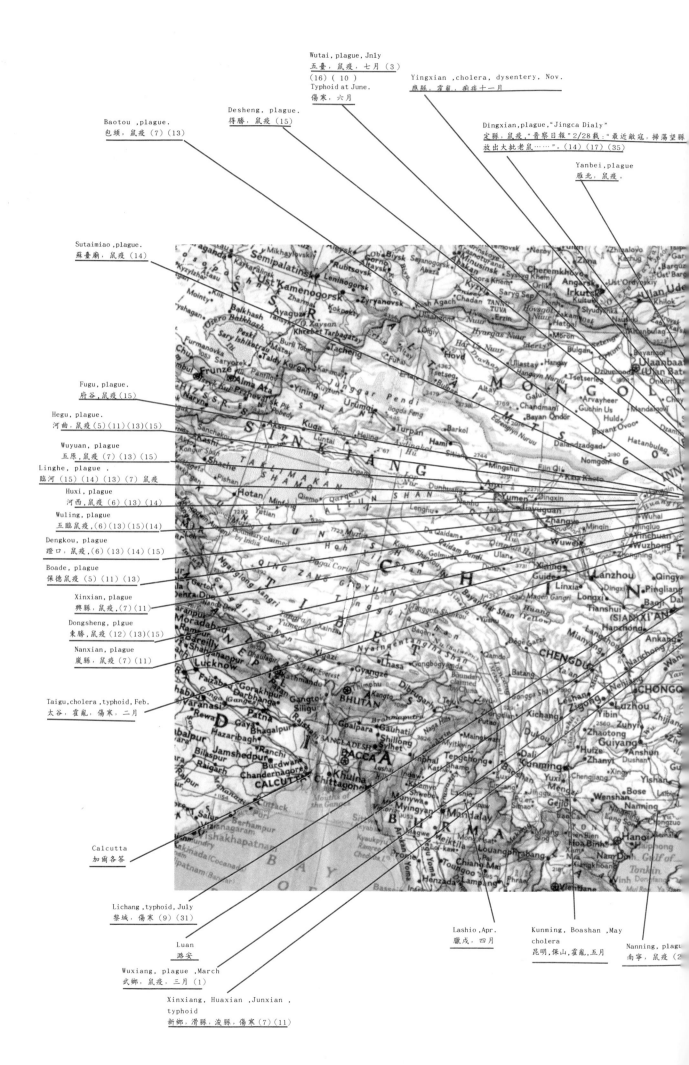

Wutai, plague, Jnly
五臺，鼠疫，七月（3）
(16)（10）
Typhoid at June.
傷寒，六月

Yingxian ,cholera, dysentery, Nov.
應縣，霍亂，痢疾十一月

Baotou ,plague.
包頭，鼠疫（7）(13)

Desheng, plague.
得勝，鼠疫(15)

Dingxian,plague,"Jingca Dialy"
定縣,鼠疫,"晉察日報" 2/28載："最近敵寇,掃蕩望縣
放出大批老鼠……"。(14)(17)(35)

Yanbei,plague
雁北，鼠疫。

Sutaimiao ,plague.
蘇臺廟，鼠疫(14)

Fugu, plague.
府谷,鼠疫(15)

Hegu, plague.
河曲，鼠疫(5)(11)(13)(15)

Wuyuan, plague
五原,鼠疫（7）(13)(15)

Linghe, plague .
臨河(15)(14)(13)(7) 鼠疫

Huxi, plague
河西,鼠疫（6）(13)(14)

Wuling, plague
五臨鼠疫,（6)(13)(15)(14)

Dengkou, plague
蹬口,鼠疫,（6）(13)(14)(15)

Boade, plague
保德鼠疫(5)(11)(13)

Xinxian, plague
興縣,鼠疫,（7）(11)

Dongsheng, plgue
東勝,鼠疫(12)(13)(15)

Nanxian, plague
巽縣,鼠疫（7）(11)

Taigu,cholera ,typhoid, Feb.
太谷，霍亂，傷寒，二月

Calcutta
加爾各答

Lichang ,typhoid, July
黎城，傷寒（9）(31)

Luan
潞安

Wuxiang, plague ,March
武鄉，鼠疫，三月（1）

Xinxiang, Huaxian ,Junxian ,
typhoid
新鄉,滑縣,浚縣,傷寒（7）(11)

Lashio ,Apr.
臘戌，四月

Kunming, Boashan ,May
cholera
昆明,保山,霍亂,五月

Nanning, plague
南寧，鼠疫（2

214

Germ Assaults Record, 1942
一九四二年細菌攻擊圖

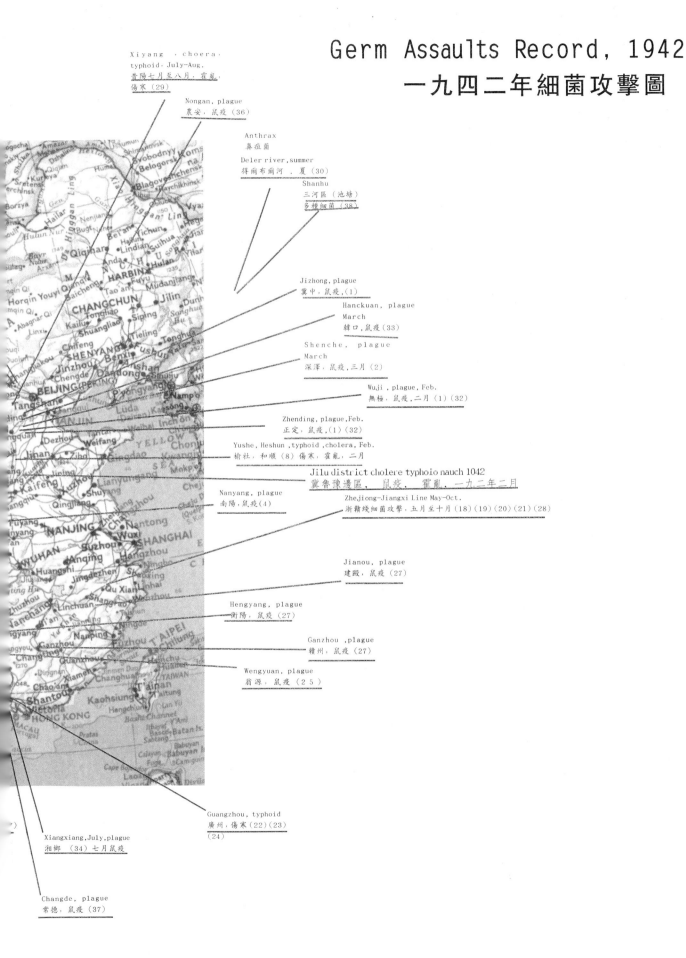

Xiyang , choera,
typhoid, July-Aug.
昔陽七月至八月，霍亂，
傷寒（29）

Nongan, plague
農安，鼠疫（36）

Anthrax
鼻疽菌

Deler river, summer
得爾布爾河 . 夏（30）

Shanhu
三河區（池塘）
多種細菌（38）

Jizhong, plague
冀中，鼠疫，(1)

Hanckuan, plague
March
韓口,鼠疫(33)

Shenche , plague
March
深澤，鼠疫，三月（2）

Wuji , plague, Feb.
無極，鼠疫，二月（1）（32）

Zhending, plague, Feb.
正定，鼠疫,(1)(32)

Yushe, Heshun , typhoid , cholera, Feb.
榆社，和順（8）傷寒，霍亂，二月

Jilu district cholere typhoio nauch 1042
冀魯豫邊區， 鼠疫， 霍亂，一九二年二月

Zhejiong-Jiangxi Line May-Oct.
浙贛綫細菌攻擊，五月至十月（18）（19）（20）（21）（28）

Nanyang, plague
南陽，鼠疫(4)

Jianou, plague
建甌，鼠疫（27）

Hengyang, plague
衡陽，鼠疫（27）

Ganzhou ,plague
贛州，鼠疫（27）

Wengyuan, plague
翁源，鼠疫（2 5）

Guangzhou, typhoid
廣州，傷寒（22）（23）
（24）

Xiangxiang,July,plague
湘鄉 （34）七月鼠疫

Changde, plague
常德，鼠疫（37）

215

Notes (1942)

(1)   Guo Chengchou, Liao yingchang, "Factual Account of Japanese Army's Biological warfare Against China" P.246, Yanshan press ,1997

(2)   Ibid (1) p.247

(3)   Ibid (2)

(4)   Ibid (2)

(5)   Ibid (2)

(6)   Ibid (2)

(7)   Ibid (2)

(8)   Ibid (2)

(9)   Ibid (2)

(10)   Ibid (2)

(11)   Ibid(2) P.250

(12)   Ibid(2) P.254

(13)   Chinese Sanitation Office express mail "Fang 031" # 9845,Yinjian

(14)   The Wartime Antiepidemic Unit Office "Tendays Report of Epidemic Diseases", No .2, middle of March ,1942.

(15)   Ibid (14) No.3

(16)   Shanxi Medical Sechool "The medical appraisal report of Japanese discharged plague rats on Wutai, Shanxi" May 13 ,1956

(17)   Ibidem   (2) . p .261-162

(18)   The Khabarovsk Trial.

(19)   The member of "Unit 1644" Jinjiang Detachment Osamu Shiba's confession, Jan. 8, 1945

(20)   "Imoto Diary" May 27 ,1942 and May 30, 1942

(21)   Ibid (2) p.389- P.396

(22)   Maruyama's speech, Nov.1995, ibid (2) P.406-P.408

(23)   "The witness of Mutsuo Inoue", "Too Daily" # 37296, Aug .13 , 1995.

(24)   Prof. Sha Dongxun's spcech on "The Forum for Fight Against Aggression War and Safeguard Peace," Harbin ,1995

(25)   Cheng Anliang's witness, ibid(2) p.421

(26)   Tani kasukawa "The Japan's germ warfare on Guandong."

(27)   "Imoto Diary" July 26 1942

(28)   Ding Xiaogiang "The Biological Warfare on Zhejiang", carried on" Watch and Think" No. 4. No. 5 ,1999

(29)   Confessioned by Noriichi Sumioka

(30)   Confessioned by Hirazakura and by Sanshi

(31)   Witness of Kanisawa Herikuda

(32)   "Jeifang Daily" March 28, 1942

(33)   Ibid (20), March 15,1942

(34)   "Xinhua Daily" July. 1942

(35)   "The Report of 7th Chapter Sanitation Section of Jizhou."

(36)   Ibid (1) P.94

(37)   Liu Yaling "The whole story of germ warfare on Changde " P.26

(38)   The khabarovsk Teial.

注釋 ＜一九四二年的細菌攻擊＞

(1) 郭成周，廖應昌 "侵華日軍細菌戰紀實"，P.246 ,燕山出版社，1995
(2) 同（1）P.247
(3) 同（2）
(4) 同（2）
(5) 同（2）
(6) 同（2）
(7) 同（2）
(8) 同（2）
(9) 同（2）
(10) 同（2）
(11) 同（2）P.250
(12) 同（2）P.254
(13) 中國衛生署快郵代電，一九四二年六月十三日 "O三一防字" 第9845號，寅儉代電。
(14) 中國戰時防疫聯合辦事處 "疫情旬報"，一九四二年三月中旬第2號。
(15) 同（14）第3號
(16) 山西醫學院 "關于在山西五臺縣施放鼠疫老鼠的醫學鑒定書"，一九五六年五月十三日。
(17) 同（1）P.261-P.262
(18) 伯力審判供證：
　　　　a、 第十三軍司令部偵察科長三品隆行（"伯力審判" P.420）
　　　　b、 伯力法庭 "起訴書"（"伯力審判" P.26）
　　　　c、 國家公訴人演詞（"伯力審判" P.478-P.479）
　　　　d、 川島清供詞（"伯力審判" P.61 P.270-271）
　　　　e、 柄澤十三夫供詞（"伯力審判" P.68）
　　　　f、 古都良雄供詞（"伯力審判" P.378-P382）
(19) "一六四四部隊" 九江支部榛葉修供詞（一九四五年一·月八日）
(20) "井本日記" 一九四二年五月二十七日、五月三十日
(21) 同注（1），P.389-396
(22) 丸山茂（"八六O四部隊" 成員）談話（一九九五年十一月）注（1）P.406-408
(23) "八六O四部隊" 成員井上睦雄證言："東奧日報" #37296，1995年8月13日
(24) 中山醫科大學,沙東迅教授在一九九五年哈爾濱 "反對侵略維護和平座談會" 上 的論文。
(25) 陳安良證詞，同（1）P.421
(26) 糟川良谷 "日軍在廣東的細菌戰"
(27) "井本日記",七月二十六日
(28) 丁曉強在 "細菌戰在浙江"（浙江 "觀察與思考"，一九九九年第四、第五期）一文中指出：日機于一九四二年八月在麗水碧湖鎮上閣圩、沙崗圩投下死鼠和跳蚤，目擊人有碧湖鎮的湯益友、江壽雲等。不久該地發生鼠疫，蔓延36個村莊。據 "東南日報" 報導，碧湖平原死于鼠疫人數至少在千人以上。我們在碧湖鎮上的調查，死亡平民有名有姓的有六百二十三人，此統計未計入當時在鎮上駐守的軍政機關之死亡人數。
(29) 住岡儀一供詞
(30) 平櫻、三友供詞
(31) 湯淺謙證詞
(32) "解放日報" 一九四二年三月二十八日
(33) 同上，一九四二年三月十五日
(34) "新華日報" 一九四二年七月
(35) 冀中第七分區衛生處報告
(36) 同（1）P.94
(37) 劉雅玲 "常德細菌戰始末" P.26
(38) "伯力審判" "加強對蘇細菌戰"

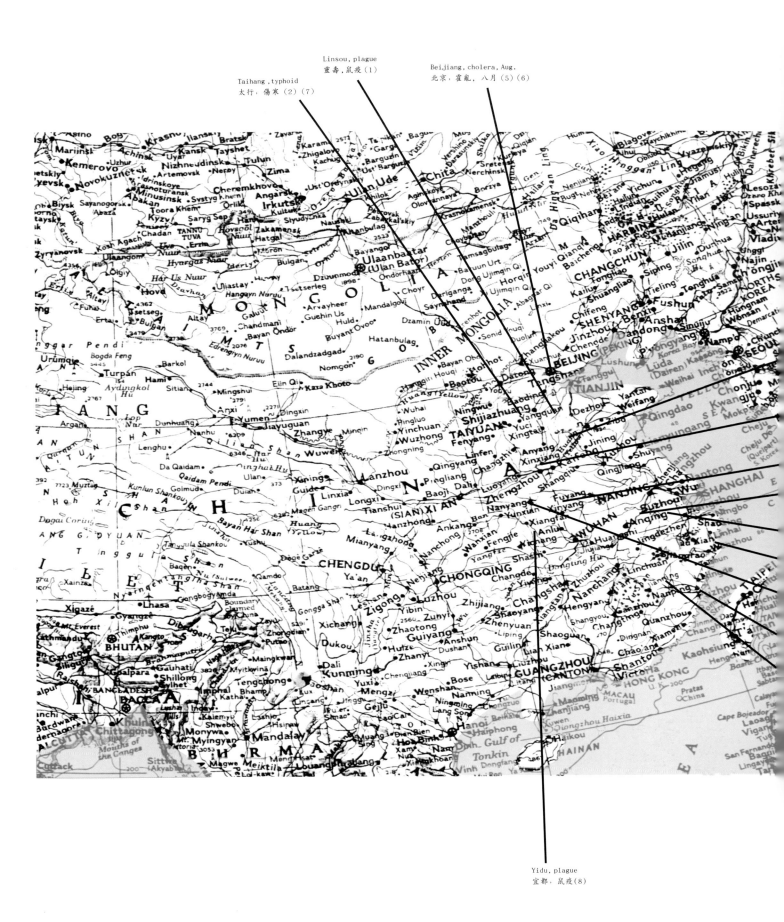

Linsou, plague
靈壽，鼠疫（1）

Taihang ,typhoid
太行，傷寒（2）（7）

Beijiang, cholera, Aug.
北京，霍亂，八月（5）（6）

Yidu, plague
宜都，鼠疫（8）

218

Germ assaults,1943
一九四三年細菌攻擊圖

West of Shandong, cholera, typheid
魯西,霍亂(3),傷寒(9)

Xinxiang,typhoid
新鄉,傷寒(4)

So. of Hen an, typhoid, three times by aircrafts
豫南,傷寒,三次空投

Langxi, plague
郎溪,鼠疫

Guangde, plague
廣德,鼠疫

Wengyoung, plague
翁墻,鼠疫

Nanyang, plague
南陽,鼠疫

Changle, clorea
長樂,霍亂(9)

Longxi, plague
龍溪,鼠疫

Notes

(1)Quo Chengchou, Lio Yingchang "Factual Account of Japanese Army's Biological Warfare Against China" P.247, Yanshan press, 1997.

(2) Ibid (1)

(3) Detail to ck . Section 3 , 3'rd Chapter

(4) Ibid (1) p.248

(5) Ibid (4)

(6) Tomygashi Nagada confession.

(7) Cofessioned by Kenisawa Herikuda

(8) Ibid (1) P.95

(9) Witness by Jiang Kihui, Changle ,Fujian

注釋 1943
（ 1 ） 郭成周，廖應昌 "侵華日軍細菌戰紀實"，P.247 ,燕山出版社，1997
（ 2 ） 同（ 1 ）
（ 3 ） 見本書 "魯西霍亂攻擊"
（ 4 ） 同（ 1 ）P。248
（ 5 ） 同（ 4 ）
（ 6 ） 長田友吉供詞（日軍第五十九師團第五十四旅團第一一O大隊，衛生軍曹，于一九五四年十一月一日）
（ 7 ） 湯淺謙供詞
（ 8 ） 同（ 1 ）P.95
（ 9 ） 福建省長樂縣嶼頭蔣家村蔣開惠證詞。

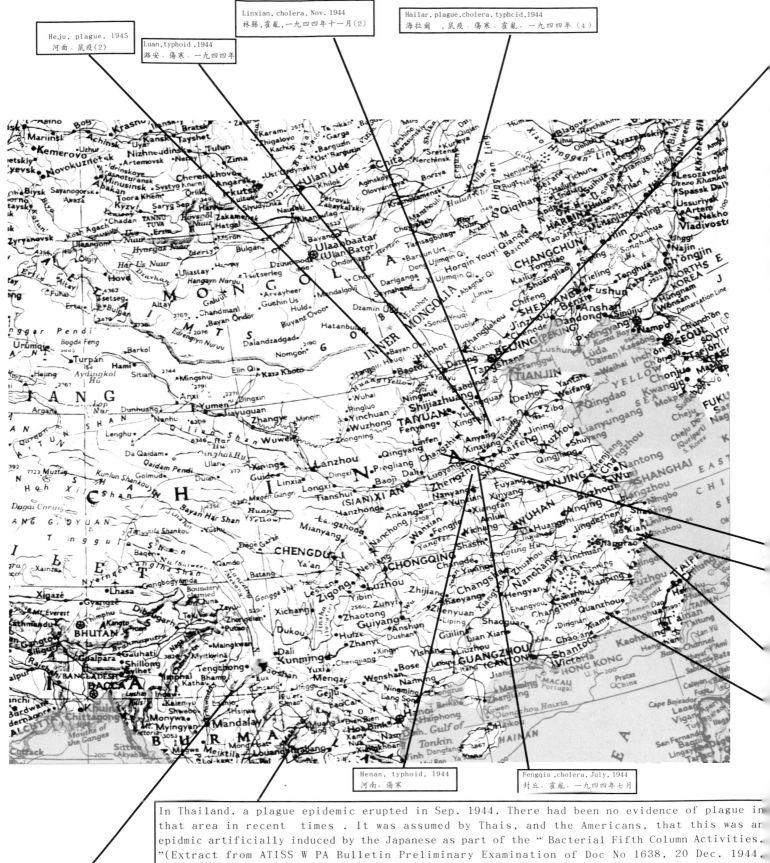

Heju, plague, 1945
河曲、鼠疫(2)

Luan,typhoid ,1944
潞安、傷寒、一九四四年

Linxian, cholera, Nov. 1944
林縣,霍亂,一九四四年十一月(2)

Hailar, plague,cholera. typhcid,1944
海拉爾　,鼠疫、傷寒、霍亂, 一九四四年（4）

Henan, typhoid, 1944
河南, 傷寒

Fengqiu ,cholera, July, 1944
封丘, 霍亂, 一九四四年七月

In Thailand. a plague epidemic erupted in Sep. 1944. There had been no evidence of plague in
that area in recent times . It was assumed by Thais, and the Americans, that this was an
epidmic artificially induced by the Japanese as part of the " Bacterial Fifth Column Activities.
"(Extract from ATISS W PA Bulletin Preliminary Examination of Doc No 1638, 20 Dec. 1944,
Riodriguez Jr. Collection.)
1944年9月在泰國爆發了一場鼠疫，那個地區近代從未發生過鼠疫，泰國人和美國人都認爲：這場鼠疫的流行
是由于日本"細菌第5項行動"人爲引起的。

THE news of Japanese B. W. activity in Burma, filtered into Intelligence Headguarters of American
in Dec. 1944. Three months earlies, Burmese fighters discovered some "20 cubic cm ampoules (yellow
and half clear)" that, upon analysis, was disclosed to contain cholera bacilli.　"The Burmese
claimed that the ampoules were dropped from Japanese airplanes. (Harris "Factories of Death")
1944年12月，美軍情報部獲得情況指出：三個月之前，緬甸抵抗戰士發現了一些"有黃色半透明的20立方厘米的針
劑瓶"，經分析後發現含有霍亂菌。發現針劑的緬甸人説，這些針劑是日本飛機投下的。（哈立斯"死亡工廠"）

Jishi, typhoi ,Feb. 7. 1944
冀氏、傷寒，一九四四年二月七日

Germm Warfare Re rd 1944-1945
1944-1945 細菌攻擊圖

Notes 1944-1945

（1）　Peter Williams, David Wallace "Unit 731: Japan's secret biological warfare in World War Ⅱ ", p.140,Taipei.

（2）　Quo Chengchou, Lio Yingchang "Factual Account of Japanese Army's Biological Warfare Against China", P.248 ,Yanshan press ,1997

（3）　Ding Xiaogiang "The Biological Warfare on Zhejiang", carried on "Watch and Think". No. 6. 1999.

(4)　Akiji Yamamoto Remembering, Han Xiao, Jin Chengmin "The witness of crimes of unit 731" No.2. P.91. P.53.

(5)　Li Beingxim, Xu Junyuan, Shi Yuxin "A Complete Record of Atrocities Committed by Inviding Japanese Troops in China", P.812-813, Hebu press, 1955

(6)　Peter Williams, David Wallace "Unit 731", P.93 has pointed out:

"In Aug. 1944 when Ishii's friend Kajitsuka visited Pingfan, Kitano reported that large quantities of plague had been dropped from high altitude over densely populated Chinese territory South of Shanghai".

注釋　1944-1945

（1　）彼得·威廉斯，大衛·瓦雷斯 "七三一部隊"，P.140 臺北，中文版，1992

（2　）郭成周、廖應昌 "侵華日軍細菌戰紀實"，P。248　燕山出版社，1995

（3　）丁曉強 "細菌戰在浙江 "（ "觀察與思考" 一九九九年第六期）證實：

1、　日本在一九四四年六月十七日于麗水縣城區慶橋到太平場投撒細菌，月擊人有莊祖光、李岳、李常春、李金花、李岳齊、李壽樟、李友清等相繼患鼠疫死亡。

2、　同年八月 "王贊光看到日機在麗水城內大水門與小水門一帶投下兩枚炸彈，後來家居的 "協勝米廠" 老板許瑞啓和王的妻熊淑英等染鼠疫而死。計有 37 個村莊的 857 人罹難。

（4　）山本明司回憶，韓曉、金成民 "日本七三一部隊罪行見證" 第二部 P．91、P．53

（5　）李榮新、徐後元、石玉新 "侵華日軍暴行總錄"，P812-P813，河北出版社 1995

（6　）彼得·威廉斯、大衛·瓦雷斯 "七三一部隊" P.93 指出：

"一九四四年八月當石井的朋友尾訪問平房時，北野宣稱在上海南邊人口稠密的中國占領區曾從高空投下大量的鼠疫跳蚤 "。

Yuo ,dysentery, July 1945
曲沃、痢疾，一九四五年七月

Lishui
麗水（3）（6）

1) 一九四四年六月十七日，鼠疫，城區，空投 June 17, 1944, plague
2) 一九四四年八月，城區，空投, Aug .1944, plague
3) 一九四四年九月下旬，城區，空投跳蚤 The 3' rd ten aqys of Sep. 1944, plague.
4) 一九四四年九月十六日，日軍撤退時 Sep. 16. 1944

Yunhe, plague
雲和，鼠疫，一九四五年

福清（1）（6）Fuqing

Section 3

The position of strategy

Japanese has had adopted germ assaults for operational use in battle strategies.

On may 23 1940, the "Asahe News" (Tokyo) printed the commendation of The Army Minestry for "Unit 731"'s outstanding statement that "the unit overcoming all hardships, contributed to the securing of an advantageous tactical operation position of a large brigade force."

It's declared Japanese B.W. has been mounted the important strategy position.

If one links the sites of biological attacks launched by the Japanese army during WWII (1942 and 1944) to construct a map showing their distribution, one can see that the Japanese army had adopted biological assaults for operational use in important battle strategies.

The map 1. Yellow River Region (Hetao), west of Shanxi: Numerous plaque B.W. assaults. The scope reached 13 counties, creating death from germ infection along the river, and impeded the eastward movement of Mao's communist army.

日軍細菌攻擊記錄
1941年　河曲（鼠疫）
1942年　河曲、荒縣、岢嵐、得勝、包頭、武台屆、府谷、五原、河西、保德、五隅、砣○、東勝

Japanese germs attacked on
1941　Hegu (plague)
1942　Hequ. Wuzam. Narzian. Xinxian

Japanese grms attacked on:
1941 Hegu (plague)
1942 Hequ,Lanxian, Xinxian, Desheng, Baotou,
    Sutimiao,Fugu,Hexi, Bode, Wuling, Dengko
    Dongshen,etc. countys.

日軍攻擊記錄
1941年 河曲（鼠疫）
1942年 河曲、嵐縣、興縣、得勝、包頭、蘇臺廟
府谷、五原、河西、保德、五臨、磧口、東勝等13個縣

Japanese occupied
area 日占區

第三節 戰略地位

如果把日軍細菌攻擊占連接來，則可以明顯地看出日軍進行的細菌戰已在日軍各大戰役中具有重要的戰略地位。

日軍細菌戰在日本發動的戰役中占有重要的戰略地位，早在一九三九年日蘇諾門罕戰役後，日本軍方即已加以肯定。一九四０年五月二十三日"朝日新聞"公布了陸軍省給"七三一部隊"的嘉獎令，令詞指出："這支部隊克服重重困難，為大部隊取得有利的戰略地位做出了貢獻。"（"朝日新聞"，一九四０年五月二十三日）

《一號圖》 日軍對黃河河套以及對晉西各縣沿黃河東岸地區的細菌擊，有明顯的防堵者中共軍隊東進的戰略意圖。

黃河自晉南的風陵渡以上，谷深水急，少有渡口，日軍派有精銳的第一軍駐守，陝北共軍東渡較難。而自晉西的興縣、嵐縣以上，沿河套西至磧口，長達一千公里的河流平展，是延安共軍東進的最佳選擇地。

日軍對華北的細菌攻擊示意圖（二號圖）

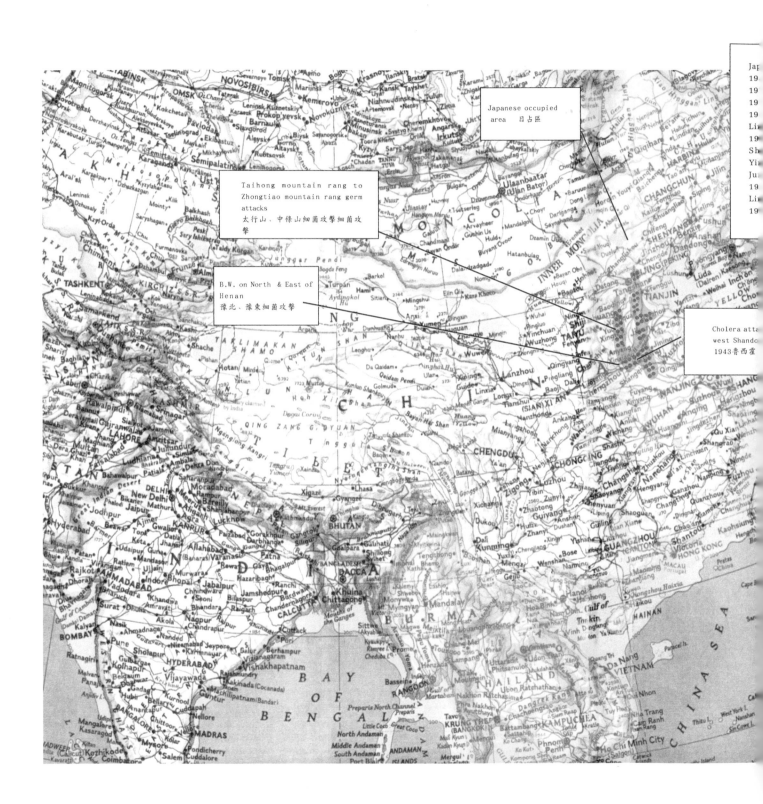

Japanese occupied
area 日占區

Taihong mountain rang to
Zhongtiao mountain rang germ
attacks
太行山、中條山細菌攻擊細菌攻擊

B.W. on North & East of
Henan
豫北、豫東細菌攻擊

Cholera atta
west Shando
1943魯西霍

oai.

nxian, Wutai,
Mongxian, Jizhong, Zhesnhuang.

bei, Wutai, Dingxian, Hanchuan,
ng, Jiluyu, Lichang, Luan, Taigu,
Yushe, Xinxiang, Wuxiang, Huaxian,

andong, Xinxiang ,Yunan Taihong,

gqiu,Jishi, Linxian Luan

日軍細菌攻擊記錄
1938年　內黃、博愛.
1939年　孟縣
1940年　新城
1941年　定縣、完縣、五臺、靈壽、保定、孟縣、冀中、贊皇.
1942年　冀魯豫、黎城、潞安、太谷、應縣、和順、榆社、新鄉、武鄉、滑縣、浚縣.
1943年　魯西、新鄉、豫南、太行、靈壽.
1944年　封丘、豫東、冀氏、林縣、潞安.

Map No. 2
To have enough to do on force, Japanese can not occupied all the countries of North China, they are no choice.
Let to Mao's army controlled these regions , so Japanese made the B.W. attacked there for strategical intentions.

二號圖
　日軍限于兵力，不能占領華北的全部鄉村，祇得讓中共軍隊控制。因此，日軍對廣大華北游擊區進行反復地細菌攻擊。

No.3 The map of Japan's B.W assaults on zhejiang
日軍對浙江的細菌攻擊示意圖（三號圖）

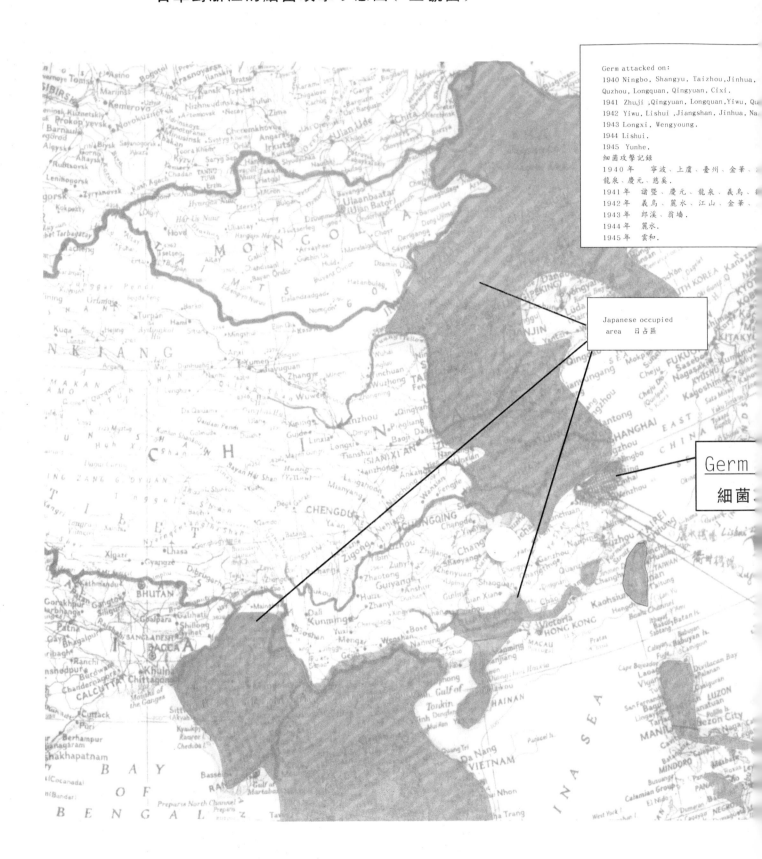

Germ attacked on:

1940 Ningbo, Shangyu, Taizhou,Jinhua,
Quzhou, Longquan, Qingyuan, Cixi.

1941 Zhuji ,Qingyuan, Longquan,Yiwu, Qu

1942 Yiwu, Lishui ,Jiangshan, Jinhua, Na

1943 Longxi, Wengyoung.

1944 Lishui.

1945 Yunhe.

細菌攻擊記錄

1940 年 寧波、上虞、臺州、金華、

龍泉、慶元、慈奚.

1941年 諸暨、慶元、龍泉、義烏、

1942年 義烏、麗水、江山、金華、

1943年 邱溪、翁墻.

1944年 麗水.

1945年 雲和.

Japanese occupied
area 日占區

Germ

細菌

Map No. 3
The Chinese army of zhejiang has had two seriously inperilling to Shanghai-Nanjing and the U. S. bombers will be use the airports around there to bombing Japan.
So that, the Japanese G. Cheif Staff made dicided to assaults to Zhejiang by B.W. in 1940-1944

三號圖

駐浙江的中國軍隊嚴重威脅上海－南京的日軍，而浙江的機場群又能為美國轟炸機轟擊日本提供前進基地，故日軍參謀本部遂決定發動對浙江的細菌攻擊，時間長達四年之久。

U.S. Air force bombers with in easy reach to Japan from Lishui air base, Zhejiang China ("Asahi News" Apr. 3 1942)

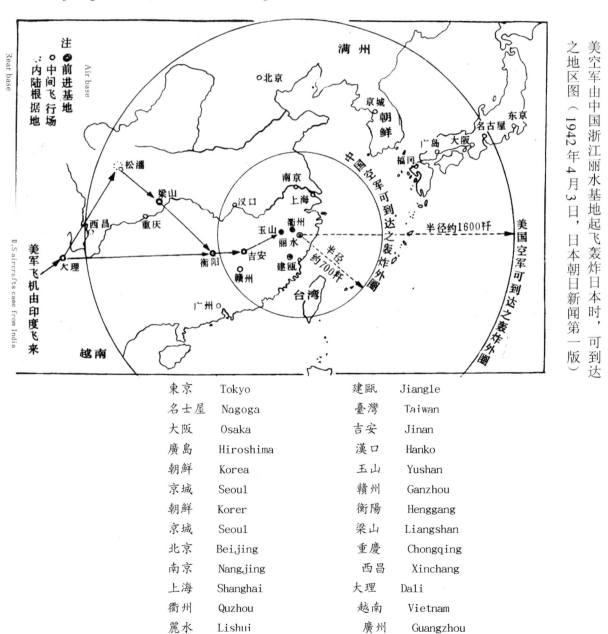

東京	Tokyo	建甌	Jiangle
名士屋	Nagoga	臺灣	Taiwan
大阪	Osaka	吉安	Jinan
廣島	Hiroshima	漢口	Hanko
朝鮮	Korea	玉山	Yushan
京城	Seoul	贛州	Ganzhou
朝鮮	Korer	衡陽	Henggang
京城	Seoul	梁山	Liangshan
北京	Beijing	重慶	Chongqing
南京	Nangjing	西昌	Xinchang
上海	Shanghai	大理	Dali
衢州	Quzhou	越南	Vietnam
麗水	Lishui	廣州	Guangzhou

The Japanese objective point of B.W. attacked to west of Heunan province (Nanyang),
West of Hubei province and North of Hunan province (Changde , Xiangxiang) for raised a
death obstacle in Front of Wuhan.

日軍爲保衛武漢所作細菌攻擊示意圖（四號圖）

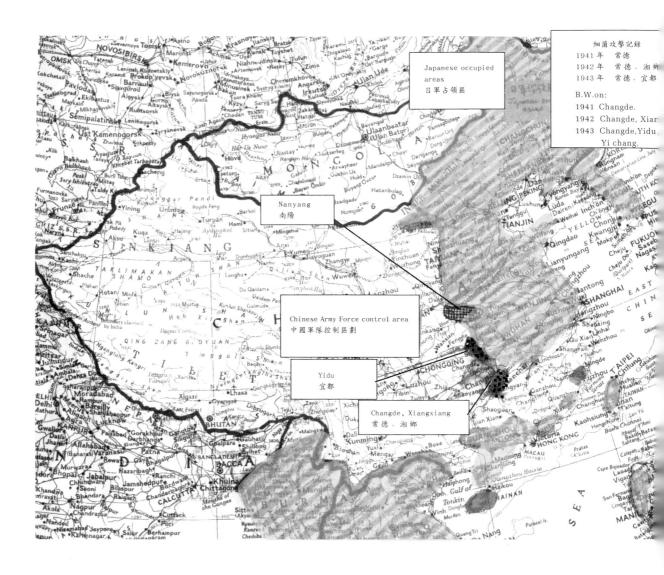

四號圖

　　　日軍對豫西、南陽，鄂西和湘北（常德、湘鄉）的細菌攻擊，旨在武漢前綫製造出
一條死亡障礙，阻止中國軍隊的反攻。

Map **No. 5**
Chinese 3'rd Army force have 400,000 soldiers control three provinces of Southeast of China but just
have one road from Ganzhou (Jiangxi province) through many moutains range connect to the Chinese
command centra.
Japanese used B.W. attacked this highway in order to cut short this umbilical cord.

日軍爲切斷中國東南戰役軍隊的細菌攻擊示意圖

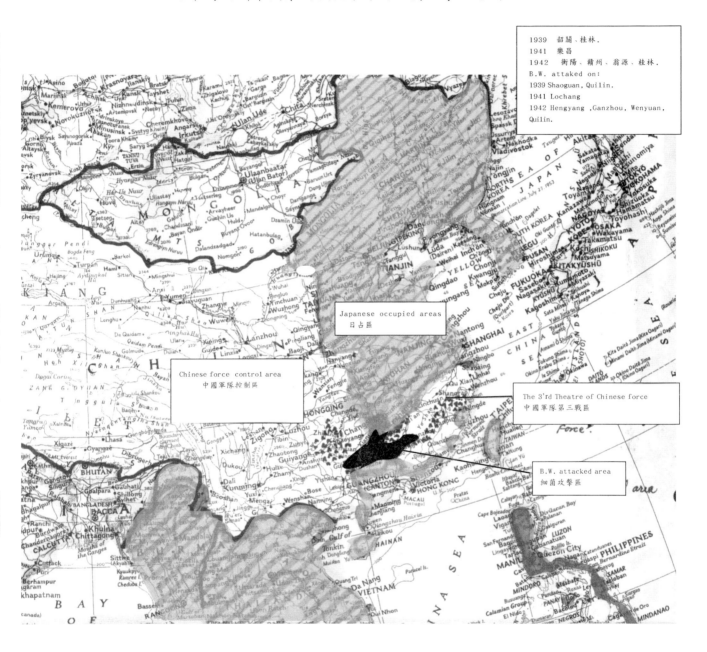

五號圖
　　中國第三戰區的 **40** 萬軍隊控制東南三省，但祇有一條公路從江西贛州翻越萬重大山與大
後方連接，日軍對這條線的多次細菌攻擊顯然在于切斷這條生命的臍帶。

Chinese military materials supply should be through few small harbors late in 1939, because the important sea ports has been occupied by Japanese .Thus, Japanese commanded the unit of B.W. attacked to all these rest of harbors.

日軍以細菌戰封鎖中國軍隊出海示意圖

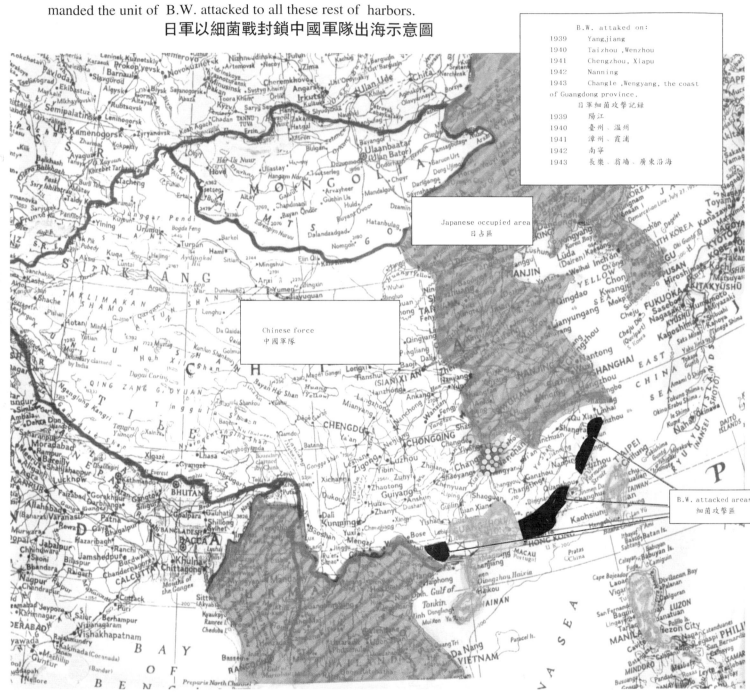

B.W. attacked on:
1939	Yangjiang
1940	Taizhou ,Wenzhou
1941	Chengzhou, Xiapu
1942	Nanning
1943	Changle ,Wengyang, the coast

of Guangdong province.

日軍細菌攻擊記錄
1939	陽江
1940	臺州、溫州
1941	漳州、霞浦
1942	南寧
1943	長樂、翁墻、廣東沿海

Japanese occupied area
日占區

Chinese force
中國軍隊

B.W. attacked areas
細菌攻擊區

六號圖

中日戰爭進入到1939，中國失去了所有大的海港，祇能依靠小的港灣進行軍事物資的補給。

因此，日軍從戰略角度發動了對剩餘口岸的細菌攻擊。

No. 7

In spring 1942, Japanese commanded an army to march North of Burma, and spreading bacteria on China-burma border in an instant. up to May carried a large germ threw in Kunming-Boashan near the Burma as a resalt of this assaults two hundred thousand people were died late to 1943, Japanese situation in China-Burma has been take a sudden turn and then develop rapidly until after 1944, Japanese army stepped back to Thailand from Burma and made broad cast sowing bacteria on all Burma with a parst of Thailand for obstructed Allied army's counter attack.

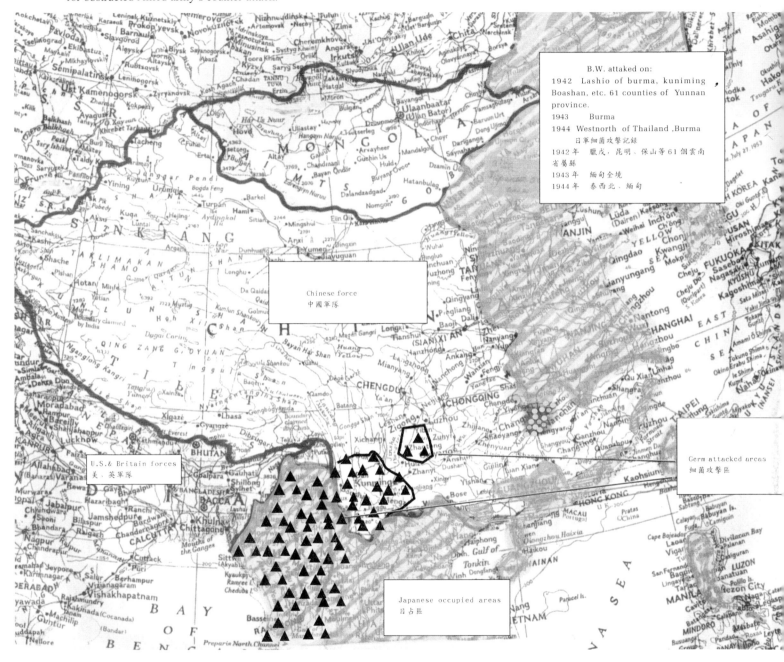

B.W. attacked on:
1942 Lashio of burma, kuniming, Boashan, etc. 61 counties of Yunnan province.
1943 Burma
1944 Westnorth of Thailand ,Burma
日軍細菌攻擊記録
1942年 臘戌、昆明、保山等61個雲南省屬縣
1943年 緬甸全境
1944年 泰西北、緬甸

Chinese force
中國軍隊

U.S.& Britain forces
美、英軍隊

Germ attacked areas
細菌攻擊區

Japanese occupied areas
日占區

七號圖：

　　一九四二年春，日軍揮師緬北，在中緬邊境散布細菌。至同年五月在昆明，保山進行大規模的霍亂攻擊，造成二十多萬人死亡。

　　一九四三年後日軍在中緬地區的情勢急轉直下，至一九四四年日軍從緬甸向泰國後撤，隨即在緬甸全境和泰國部分地區投放大量細菌,阻止了盟軍的反攻。

Section 4
第四節　活體解剖

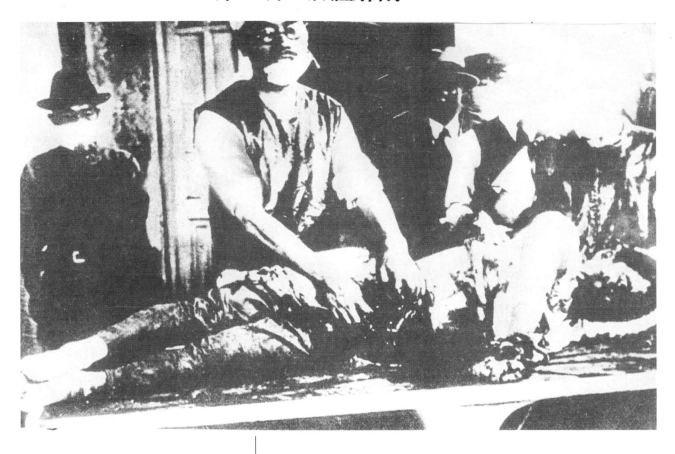

A live body to be dissecting
一個活人正在被解剖

This is Kurumi Zawa, once the anatomy technician of "Unit 731"
曾在七三一部隊擔任解剖技手的胡桃澤

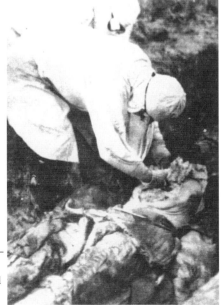

Take viviseetion on field
在野外的活體解剖

Mother & her new-born baby
sired by kobayashi, a technician,
were infected with syphilis, then
killed by unit 731 doctors.
姑娘被强奸後懷孕，後被感染梅
毒，爲實驗梅毒在妊娠中，生産
後的種種生理變化，進行解剖母
子二體。

Dissecting the child
as the gunea pig
小孩被當成實驗動物
被進行解剖

A survivor Chao Yuchan

赵玉春

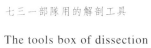

七三一部队用的解剖工具

The tools box of dissection

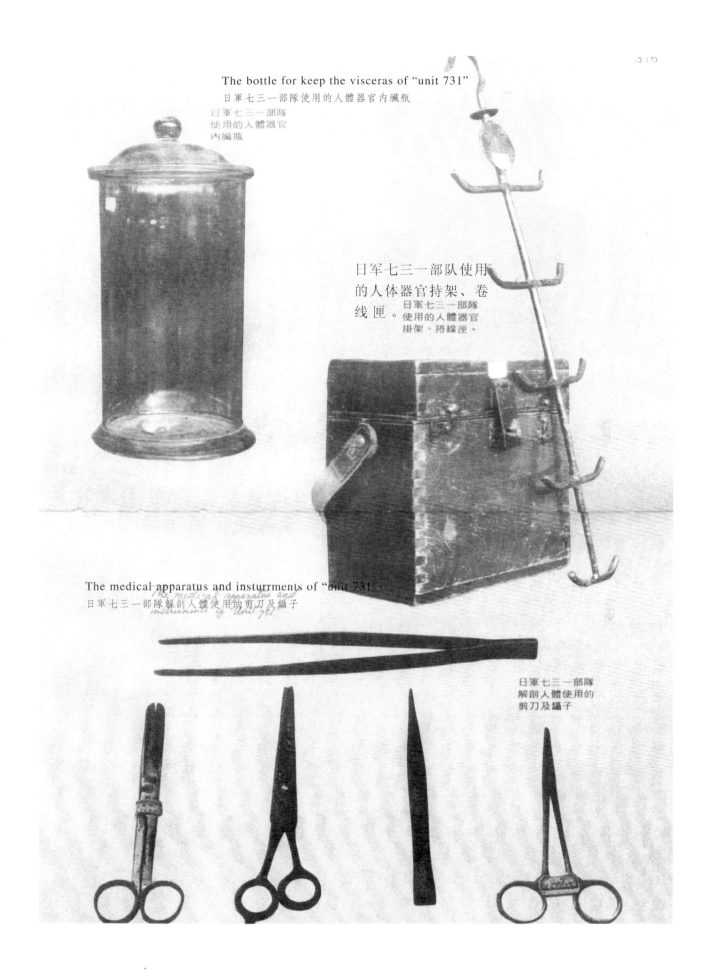

The bottle for keep the visceras of "unit 731"
日軍七三一部隊使用的人體器官內臟瓶

日軍七三一部隊
使用的人體器官
內臟瓶

日军七三一部队使用
的人体器官持架、卷
线匣。日軍七三一部隊
使用的人體器官
掛架、捲線匣。

The medical apparatus and insturrments of "unit 731"
日軍七三一部隊解剖人體使用的剪刀及鑷子

日軍七三一部隊
解剖人體使用的
剪刀及鑷子

Wang Chuliang
王菊蓮(受害人)

The remains of the laboratories used for live human dissections
日軍 "七三一" 部隊人體解剖室遺迹

The tablet of spectre in the
basement of former
Nanman Medical Uni.

在前"南滿醫科大學"地下室的
"群靈碑"

How many vivisections they did?

Here we can use two Japanese medical workers who did working on the vivisection's confession to answer the question:

(1) The specialist of Pathologist, ex-member of " Unit 731 ": Ishikawa Katanaomaru said: " About the number of the objects of vivisection what I had did, may be I made the recording of the world." ("Magazine of Japan Pathology Institute", the 34 term) 1940 Autumn, Ishikawa Katanaomaru was working at Nongan of Jiling Province, he had took 57 people from the pestis contagioner, the contagioner who were contaced the germ spreaded by the "Unit 731 ". He himself made vivisection on and killed the 57 people he chosen. (Morimura's book "Den of human eating monster")

(2) Ex-military surgeon Kanizawa Herikuda who was working at the Shanxi Luan army hospital said at "The 7. 7 Incident 50th Anniversary Commemoration Meeting" in 1987, "Army hospital was the plactice place of operation for the military surgeon of Japanese Army". "Every hrmy hospital had did the vivisection". Kanizawa Herikuda had said earlier at the "Administrative Unit of Prisoner of War" in 1955, "While I was working at Luan in that three years, I did so. I have killed 18 people, including prisoner and inhabitant by doing vivisection."

活體解剖知多少?

用兩位從事活體解剖的日本醫生的自白來回答:

1) 病理學家,"七三一部隊"成員石川大刀丸述説:

"就解剖的人數來説,我創造了世界記錄"("日本病理學會雜志"第34期)石川的記錄是多少?

森村誠一在"食人魔窟"第一部中指出:"一九四O年石川在吉林省農安從七三一部隊散布的鼠疫感染中,選出五十九人,由其活體解剖 "。

2) 山西潞安陸軍醫院,軍醫湯淺謙説:"陸軍醫院是侵華日軍陸軍醫生練習手術的場地,每一個日軍醫生都進行過活體解剖⋯⋯。"

(一九八七年在紀念"七七"事變五十周年會上演説)

湯淺謙早在一九五五年于戰俘管理所已筆供承認:"我在潞安的三年裏,就是這樣,通過活體解剖,慘殺了十八名俘虜及和平居民。"

Instruments of torture used by Unit 731 to discipline live persons.
731 部隊中用來解剖活人的器具

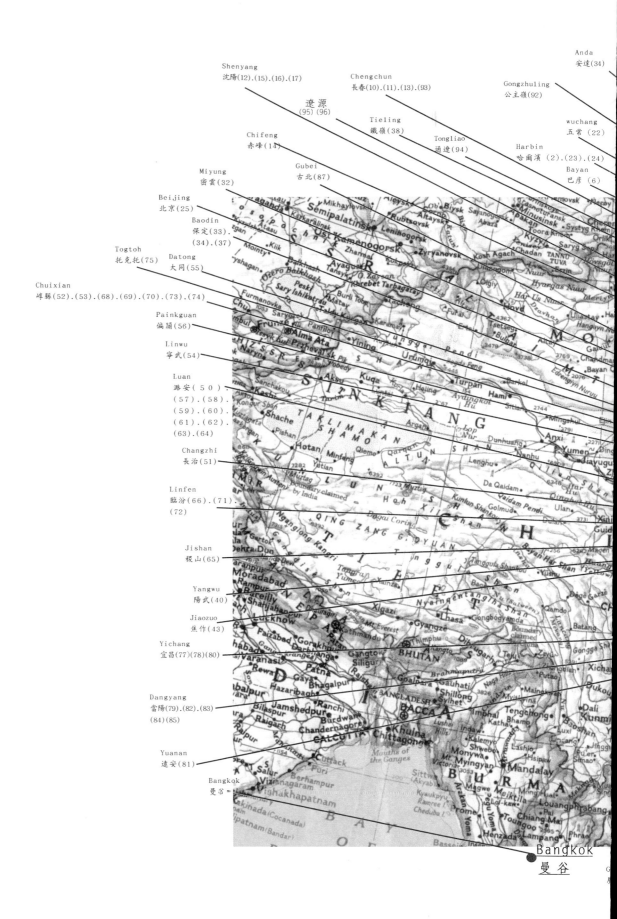

Anda
安達(34)

Shenyang
沈陽(12).(15).(16).(17)

Chengchun
長春(10).(11).(13).(93)

Gongzhuling
公主嶺(92)

遼源
(95)(96)

wuchang
五常（22）

Chifeng
赤峰(14)

Tieling
鐵嶺(38)

Tongliao
通遼(94)

Harbin
哈爾濱(2).(23).(24)

Miyung
密雲(32)

Gubei
古北(87)

Bayan
巴彦(6)

Beijing
北京(25)

Baodin
保定(33).
(34).(37)

Togtoh
托克托(75)

Datong
大同(55)

Chuixian
崞縣(52).(53).(68).(69).(70).(73).(74)

Painkguan
偏關(56)

Linwu
寧武(54)

Luan
潞安（50）.
(57).(58).
(59).(60).
(61).(62).
(63).(64)

Changzhi
長治(51)

Linfen
臨汾(66).(71).
(72)

Jishan
稷山(65)

Yangwu
陽武(40)

Jiaozuo
焦作(43)

Yichang
宜昌(77)(78)(80)

Dangyang
當陽(79).(82).(83)
(84)(85)

Yuanan
遠安(81)

Bangkok
曼谷

Bangkok
曼谷

242

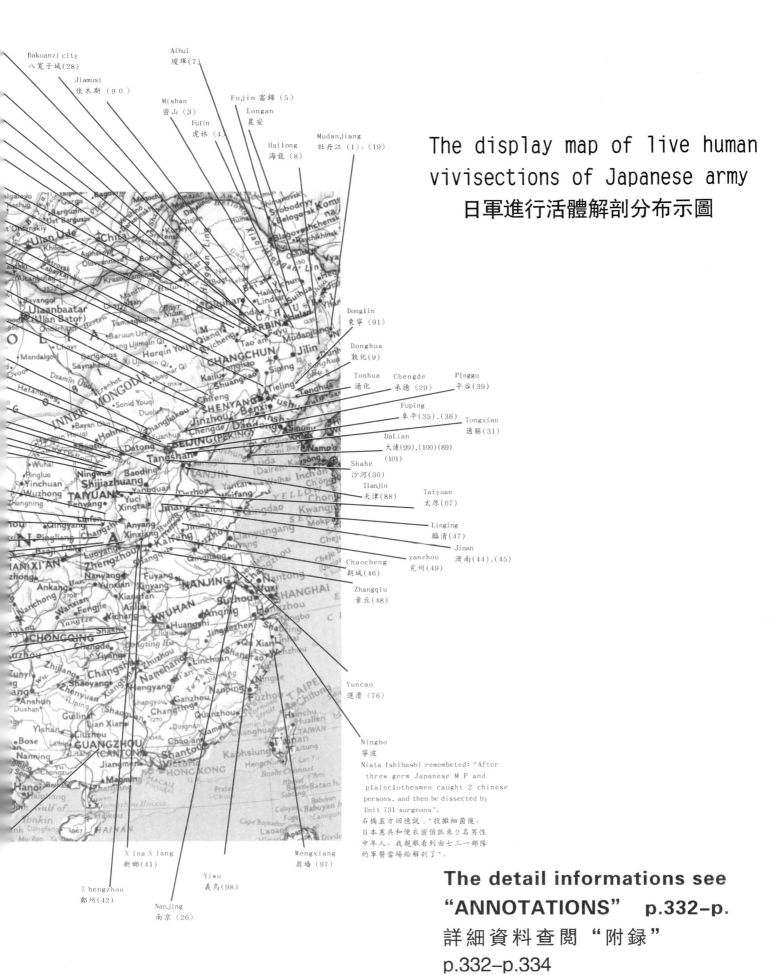

Bakuanzi city
八寬子城(28)

Jiamusi
佳木斯（９０）

Mishan
密山（3）

Fulin
虎林（4）

Aihui
璦琿(7)

Fujin 富錦（5）

Longan
農安

Hailong
海龍（8）

Mudanjiang
牡丹江（1）。(19)

The display map of live human
vivisections of Japanese army
日軍進行活體解剖分布示圖

Donglin
東寧（91）

Donghua
敦化(9)

Tonhua
通化

Chengde
承德（29）

Pinggu
平谷（39）

Fuping
阜平（35）.(36)

Tongxian
通縣(31)

DaLian
大連(99).(100)(89)
(101)

Shahe
沙河(30)

Tianjin
天津(88)

Taiyuan
太原(67)

Linging
臨清(47)

Jinan
濟南(44).(45)

yanzhou
兗州(49)

Chaocheng
朝城(46)

Zhangqiu
章丘(48)

Yuncao
運漕 (76)

Ningbo
寧波

Niata Ishibashi remembeted: "After
threw germ Japanese M P and
plainclothesmen caught 2 chinese
persons. and then be dissected by
Unit 731 surgeons".
石橋直方回憶說：" 投擲細菌後，
日本憲兵和便衣密偵抓來２名男性
中年人，我親眼看到由七三一部隊
的軍醫當場給解剖了 "。

**The detail informations see
"ANNOTATIONS"   p.332-p.**
詳細資料查閱 " 附錄 "
p.332-p.334

X ina X iang
新鄉(41)

Wengxiang
翁墙 (97)

Z hengzhou
鄭州(42)

Yiwu
義烏(98)

Nanjing
南京(26)

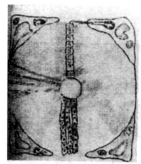

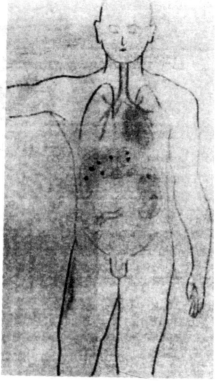

This chartings of pathology of human experiment in "unit 731" draw by Japanese B.W crimend and reported to U.S.

日軍細菌戰戰犯向美國提供的實驗人體報告中的病理繪圖

Tamura Yoshio's confession (10/10/1954)

In the ending of December 1943, I was a technician and working in the Nanman Medicine University pathology experiment room. While that time I have had killed an worse 18 years old boy for my vivisection study.

田村良雄口供

（1954年10月10日）

四三年十二月下旬，我在僞滿醫笠大學精神神經科病理實驗室任技術員時，有一名十八歲的男孩患早發性痴呆癥住院治療，因看護不好，兩脚再度凍傷。我爲了學技術，晚間，秘密地讓我們給活活解剖。

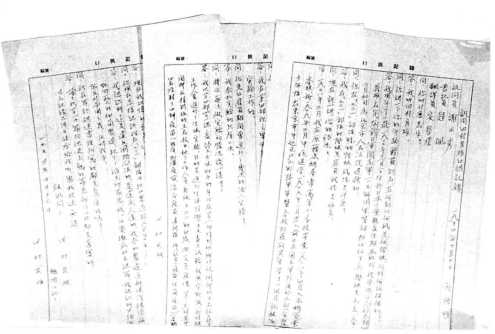

CHAPTER IV

THE POWS OF AMERICA

第 四 章

美國戰俘

The charge that Ishii and his confederates used American POWs as human experiment or vivisection was discovered four cases:

The I'st case happened in the camp of Mukden POWs.

According to a register of F.B.I. in 1956, has recorded: Mr James J kelleher, Jr. office of Special Operations, DOD (Department of Defense) has volunteered further comments to the effect that American Military Forces after occupying Japan, determined that the Japanese actually did experiment with "B.W." agents in Machuria during 1943-1944 using American prisoners as test victims.

The 2'nd case occurred in Shinagawa POWs camp.

The "New York Times" reporter Robert Tuembull wrote: "Enemy Tortured Dying Americans with Sadist Medical Experiment" on 2 Sep. 1945, reported that two American doctors charged Japanese doctors using seciouslly ill American captives as "guinea pigs" for B.W.experiments. The story indicated that Japanese doctors comfirmed the American physician's allegations. Tokuda Hisikichi, a certain captain allegedly injected various pathogens into his American patients as part of B.W. experiments.

The 3'rd one arisen in POWs camp of Shanghai in 1942, Japanese compelled five hundred American POWs endured human experiments, management by Tatao Minato, his is a member of "Unit 731", Ishii's helper.

The fourth case happened in kyushu's camp of POWs. Has nine American pilots were died by vivisection.

In October 1942, about 1,000 US troops had been singled out and marched to Manila, the capital of the Philippines. They went aboard the Japanese vessel "The Totori Maru."

一九四二年十月，大約有一千名美國戰俘被挑揀出來，行軍到馬尼拉，菲律賓的首都，他們登上了日本船"鳥取丸"。

關于石井及其同伙以美國戰俘爲實驗品和活體解剖的罪行已發現四起:

第一件是沈陽美軍戰俘營,這裏共押禁美、英戰俘一千四百八十五名,由菲律賓用船于一九四二年十一月十一日送進沈陽。

一九五六年三月美國聯邦局調局一分内部備忘録記載:

DOD(陸軍部)特別行動辦公室的詹姆斯·凱勒爾先生主動進一步説明了美軍在占領日本後已經確認于一九四三年至一九四四年間,滿洲的日本人已把美國戰俘作爲實驗犧牲品用細菌戰病原體作實驗.

第二件是由"紐約時報"一九四五年九月二日的報告所揭發,報以"敵人用殘虐的醫藥實驗折磨致死美俘"爲題,報導指出:"兩名美國醫生指控東京品川戰俘營的日本醫生,確認了美國醫生的指控。一名叫TOKUDA HISIKICHI 的大尉,作爲人體實驗的一部分,給他的美國病人注射了各種各樣的病原菌。"

第三件發生于一九四二年,據《日軍731部隊罪惡史》P.83、P.266指出,日軍在上海美俘營,對五百美俘進行活體試驗,具體工作由"七三一部隊"的凑技師負責。

第四件發生于日本本土,美國戰俘飛行員在九洲大學被活剖.

A long march to Mukden of Allied POWs
盟國戰俘在赴沈陽的長途行軍

The route taken by the 1000, American prisoners to Mukden began with what became known as the Bataan Death March. "We were subjected to beatings, killings, forced marches during the that of the day. We were deprived of food, water, and any medical attention whatsoever." As remembered by Pappy Whelchel.

巴丹死行軍—美國的一千戰俘去沈陽之路。爸爸威陸其爾留下的記憶:在炎熱的天氣裏,遭受痛打、殺害和強迫行軍。我們被剝奪了食物,水和任何的醫藥。

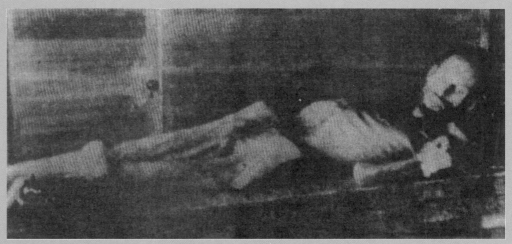

The final stage of
starvation, Mukden POW.
因饑餓實驗而待斃的盟軍戰俘

Medical orderly Ishibashi witnessed:
"I saw the malnutrition experiments.
They were conducted by the project team
under the technician Yoshimura. He was
a civilian project team under the technician
Yoshimura, a civilian member of Unit 731.
The purpose of the experiments, I believe, was to find
out how long a human being could survive just with water
and biscuits. Two marudas were used for this experiment. They continuously circled a prescribed course within the grounds of the Unit carrying, approximately, a 20-kilogramme sandbag on their backs. One succumbed before the other, but they both ultimately died. The duration of the experiment was about two months. They only received Army biscuits to eat, and water to drink, so they would not have been able to survive for very long. They weren't allowed a lot of sleep either."

醫務助理石橋的證言:
我看到了營養不良的實驗,由技術員吉村手下的工作隊執行。他是"七三一部隊"的文職人員。我相信實驗的目的在于發現一個人祇用水與餅乾能活多久。兩個"原木"作這個實驗。他們背着大約二十公斤的沙袋,在總部院內,沿着一定的路綫不停地循環,一個人首先倒下,但是最後兩個人都死了,這個實驗期限大約兩個月。他們祇給餅乾吃和喝水,所以他們不可能活很久,他們也不准有充分的睡眠。

Among the list of those men who had worked in the dysentery group of "Unit 731" was Tsuneji Shimada. He confirmed that he had, for seven years, "been attached to the Minato group, the dysentery group"(a group run by researcher minato). He had been with them from early 1939 until the end of the war.

"Researcher Minato visited there frequently. He frequently went with one of my professors with bacterial strains... I went there once to see what it was like".

"Blood samples were taken from the Americans and British prisoners."

"Normally we gave American infected materials to drink and carried out autopsies to ascertain the symptoms. We had to observe the progress [of the disease] and we had to ascertain the potency of the various viruses."

"Because we also carried out the same experiments at the headquarters of "Unit 731" [at Pingfan]."

And he believed there was a balloon bomb factory at Mukden." Unit 731" put cholera and typoid germ into balloon bombs.

曾經在七三一部隊的赤痢組工作的名單中有島田恒二。

他肯定有七年的時間，「他是屬於湊班，即赤痢班」（該班由研究員湊領導），他同他們在一起自一九三九年初，一直到戰爭結束。

「湊研究員常去瀋陽。他常同我的一個有細菌學修養的教授一同去．．．．我去過一次，看看那裡是什麼樣．．．．他們從美國和英國的戰俘抽了血的樣本．．．．我們給美國人感染的東西去喝並作解剖以確定病症。觀察（疾病的）進展，並且確定各種細菌的力量．．．我們在七三一部隊總部（平房）作相同的實驗。

Allied POWs in Mukden.
在沈陽的美國和西方人戰俘

Naoji Uezono spoke at length for the TVS documentary. He was a member of Unit 731 for four years. He was the Unit's printer and, as such, he had the opportunity to read all the most secret documents as he printed them.

"As regards the white prisoners at Hoten [Mukden], many of our scientific teams went there and I don't know for what purpose but they certainly did go there... Whenever important experiments or assessments were carried out in the Unit, at least fifteen or sixteen copies of a report had to be prepared for circulation to senior officers. There were so many in the four years I was there that I don't remember precisely what was in the reports about the prisoners at Mukden. But, to the best of my recollection, those prepared were almost wholly related to malnutrition and I also seem to remember the phrase: "It is considered unwise to bring these prisoners to Pingfan."

"Unit 731 was also working in the military hospital at Mukden. So the fact that it was necessary for our scientists to visit the prisoner-of-war camp as well indicates that some type of work was going on there."

植園直寺為「南方電視」記錄片敬述很詳盡。他是七三一部隊成員達四年之久。他是該部的印刷員，在所個職務上，他有機會閱讀他所印的最機密的文件。

「關於在奉天（瀋陽）的白種人戰俘，很多我們的科學隊去過：我不知道他們究竟去了……無論何時，在我們所隊作重要的實驗或鑑定，貢低限度一個報告要繕十五份或十

Allied POWs
盟軍俘虜

Testimony of Max McClain – US POW, a survivor of Mukden.

He testified that he and his fellow POW George Hayes were getting injections regularly. "I know he was (killed by those injections)…He knew it too. He said' I don't know what they mess me …'…He died that night".

馬克‧麥克南證言一美軍在沈陽戰俘，細菌實驗幸存者．
Max 和他的好友哈頁斯常被定期注射．"我知道他是被那些注射殺死，哈頁斯自己也知道，在他死前曾對我：爲會麼要坑害我．"

Testimony of Art Campbell – US POW, a survivor of Mukden. He described being frozen for twenty four hours and then taken to a hot room to be thawed out just like the Unit 731's Frost Bite Laboratory: "They froze until I was unconscious,……"." I can not describe how much it hurts. It hurts so much that I beg the Japs. to kill me".

他描述過去的經驗：被冷凍24小時，然後加溫解凍，和731部隊的凍傷實驗方法一樣．"他們（日本人）把我冷凍直到昏迷"，"那種疼痛簡直無法形容，痛到我要求日本人把我殺了．"

Testimony of Robert Peaty – A Former British Senior
Offcer and POW, Survivor of Mukden
"The Japanese tried to keep me out of the hospital,
away from the sick people, as far as they could. They
made it pretty obviously. I would be very unwelcome to
pry into any sort of sickness of them health." He kept a
daily diary of life in Mukden. Culled from one pages of a
daily diary recorded on scraps of paper torn exercise
books or saved from the daily ration of a single toilet paper.

（Robert Peaty）皮悌

證言－英國高級官員
沈陽戰俘在沈陽時他每天用從練習簿上撕下來的碎紙或當
天節省下僅有的一頁廁所紙，記載日記：
　　"日本人盡量阻止我去醫院，不讓我同病人接觸，他們十分
清楚地表示，不歡迎我查詢任何有關戰俘的疾病或健康
問題……．許多事情雖然在當時我們不清楚，但是現在回
憶起來那些在醫院所發生的事情，一定是由七三一部隊的
科學家所作的．"

Robert Peaty in POWs camp at Mukden
皮悌在沈陽戰俘營

252

For Greg Rodriquez, one of the oddest incidents took place when he was too sick to leave the barracks.

"A Japanese came in and looked me over and then placed mirror in front of my nostrils. At the time, I thought: 'Well, he just checking to see if I'm still breathing.' But, after a little while he came back again with a feather. He ran that feather up and down under my nostrils-and, later on, I discovered this was one of the methods used to get prisoners to ingest bacteria. It is also a was of collecting bacteria."

Greg Rodriquez has a theory. "The people who died were mostly Americans. I wonder if the British and Australians were the control group for the experiments, and we Americans were always given the doses, the real shots…"

"What ever that was they had on those feathers, infected my who body because I inhaled something…There was some kind on bacteria germ…" Greg Rodriquez said he has been suffering from unknown fever ever since.

Greg Rodriquez
葛來格·羅垂科斯

當葛·來格·羅垂科斯臥病不能離開營房時，一件最奇异事情一一發生了。

"一個日本人走進來，仔細看我，然後在我鼻孔前放一個鏡子，當時我想，他不過是在檢查，看我是否還呼吸。但是，一會兒他來，用一個羽毛在我鼻孔上下動。以後我發現這是一種使戰俘攝取細菌方法之一，那也是一個收集細菌的辦法，"

"那羽毛上所沾的不知道是什麼東西，因爲由鼻腔吸入之後我全身發燒，肯定是細菌類的東西。"

Charley Wilson 查理維樂生

傑克羅伯茲(Jack Robert)證言－英國皇家陸軍醫藥團員‧瀋陽戰俘

第一個冬天，四百三十人死了。因為地凍得像岩石一樣的堅硬；如果把他們埋葬起來將有極大的困難。皮悌少校同美國高級官員磋商，但最後由日本人決定。所有的屍體都運到一個簡陋的棚裡堆起來，有些用臨時木頭釘成的棺材，有些用布或口袋纏裹。據羅伯茲的回憶，很多「像木頭棍子」般堆積起來。這時候羅伯茲已經十分習慣於這一群有組織的訪問者，這些人顯然不是軍人，也不是文職人員，他們穿半軍裝的制服，神秘的從某地而來，命令日本的醫藥助理發給不同的藥。有一次來訪，我記得他們每天早晨拿出一個大的燒瓶，告訴我們是葡萄糖溶液，給病人注射以幫助他們從饑餓症狀康復。．．．但有

Testimony of Jim Byrd, survivor of Mukden: "They measured our skull, our height that is when they took our blood test also".

金柏（Jim Byrd）證言－美軍在沈陽戰俘營幸存者"他們量我們的頭圍及身長，又抽血檢驗".

Relief supplies arriving at
Mukden POWs camp
美機向沈陽美俘營空投食物
（"八．一五"後）

"....They were experimenting on
us...no questions on my mind. The
ones that I saw got shots (injections)
came out feet first...They (were)
dead."
Sam Castrione（譯音）證言－美軍在
沈陽戰俘
"毫無疑問他們（日本人）是用我
們來做實驗，那些我見到曾接受注射
的人全都斃命了."

Testimony of Frank James(Survivor of Mukden,
American POWs)
Frank James was assigned to burial detail. "I was
pretty sick myself but wouldn't go to the hospital
because nobody that went in ever came out. I went
round to the hut and there must have been, I reckon,
340 bodies stacked there. Each body had a tag attached to his toe. There were two or three men
who I took to be Japanese doctors there. They
were all masked, 100 percent. All the time they
were there, their faces were covered. Another
fellow and I were told to lift the bodies up and put
them on autopsy tables. Then, they began to cut
them open. They went deep into the stomach, the
bile, the small intestine and they also took what
looked like pancreas and lungs. They also operated
on the heads and took part of the brain... The
specimens were trucked away from Mukden."

弗蘭克·杰木斯（Fank James）證言－美軍沈陽戰俘
"我病得很重，但不願去醫院，因爲進去的人從沒有能够
活着出來的.我走到停尸棚的周圍轉一圈，算一下，那裏堆
者340個尸體，每個尸體的脚趾上有一個牌子，有兩、三
個人站在那裏，我想他們是日本醫生；他們都戴面具，把臉
完全掩蓋起來.我和另外一個人被命令把尸體抬起來放在解
剖的桌子上．然後他們把尸體割開，切開胃、膽、小腸，好象
是把胰臟和肺帶走.他們也剖開了頭部，拿走腦的一部
份…….樣本由卡車裝走.

Drawn by Mukden P.O.W.

Life of the POWs in Mukden, drawn by a POW

沈陽戰俘所繪的戰俘生活圖

Some veterans today-veterans captured and imprisoned in World War II's Pacific theatre-have a story to tell and an agonizing chapter of their lives to resolve. These veterans...have not received justice... These men are victims of a terrible secret, born 44 years ago deep in Manchuria in Japanese POW camps. Theirs perhaps has been the longest and best kept secret of World War II, long denied by Japan and long concealed by the US Government.

Bit by bit, and year by year, despite our government's public statements of ignorance, the truth has been leaking out. We know now that Mukden was more than just another Japanese POW camp for Allied soldiers.

Operated by Japanese scientists from "Unit 731", Mukden was the site for deadly chemical and biological experiments, for injections, body dissections, blood and feces tests, freezing of body parts, infection of wounds with anthrax, the applications of plague bacillus, cholera, dysentery, and typhoid.

That...was what was waiting for many of the American figthing men who survived the Bataan Death March. Along with our soldiers at these terrible camps were also men from China, Great Britain, Australia, and the Soviet Union. We don't know how many survived, but we do know that the US government knew of the experiments at the war's end.

(Statement of Congressman Pat Williams, Dem. Montana, before the Subcommittee on Compensation, Pension, and Insurance of the Committee on Veterans' Affairs, House of Representatives, Ninety-Ninth Congess, Second Session, 17 September 1986, Serial No.99-61, P.3)

　　今天一些退伍軍人在第二次世界大戰太平洋戰場上被俘虜、監押的老兵有一段故事要傾訴，他們的生活中有一段極為痛苦的經歷．這些老兵尚未得到正義，這些人是一個可怖的秘密的受害者，它發生在44年前滿洲深處的日本戰俘營裏.他們的遭遇也許是二次世界大戰中保守最長、最嚴密的秘密，長期以來這個秘密一直被日本政府否認、被美國政府隱瞞。

　　絲絲縷縷，月月年年，盡管我們的政府公開聲稱毫無所知，事實真相還是慢慢地泄露出來．現在我們知道，當年的奉天并不僅僅是一個關押盟軍士兵的日本戰俘營。

　　來自731部隊的日本"科學家"把奉天當作了致使的化學和生物實驗的實驗場，用來進行注射、肢解、血液和糞便化驗、肢體冷凍、給傷口感染炭疽，應用鼠疫菌、霍亂、痢疾、傷寒。

這些……就是很多在巴丹半島死亡行軍幸存下來的美國戰士面臨的命運。在這些恐怖的戰俘營裏，同我們的士兵在一起的還有中國人、英國人、澳大利亞人和蘇聯人．我們不知道一共有多少人逃過了劫難，但我們確實知道，美國政府在戰爭結束時就知道了這些實驗。

（美國眾議院退伍軍人事務委員會退伍軍人補償、撫恤和保障委員會第99屆大會第2次會議，蒙大拿州眾議員帕特.威廉斯，1986年9月17日）

P.O.W.s camp of Mukden
沈陽戰俘營

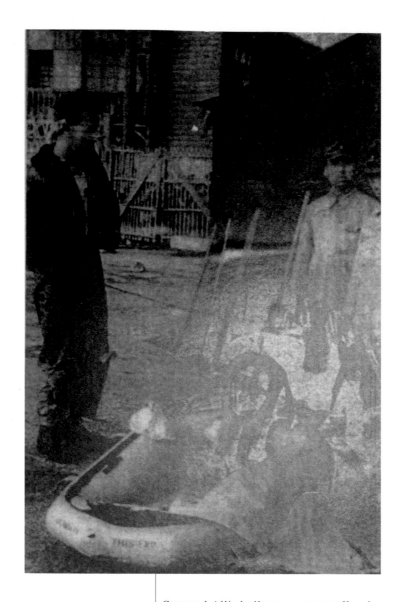

Captured Allied pilot were sent to Kyushu University for live human dissection experiment.

　1945年轟炸日本的盟軍飛機被擊中，飛行員跳傘被俘，這些俘虜被送到九州大學，做活體解剖．

CHAPTER V
THE EVIL LEGACIES OF JAPANESE
B.W. IN CHINA
第 五 章
細菌戰在中國的遺害

The map of evil legacies of Japanese germ warfare in 1945
一九四五年日軍細菌戰遺害圖

Plague 鼠疫
Persons were died: 死亡人數
Guamgye 光澤 24 人
Nanchang 南城 230 人
Nanfeng 南豐 23 人
Lichuan 黎川 97 人
(Leeli "The B.W. of Zhejiang - Jiangxi
Line"), 李力 "浙贛綫細菌戰".

Notes:

①"Japanese army's biological warfare monagrah", p.6, has been show clearly: Number tens of thousands rats released by "Unit 731" under these fled in 1945, result in over 20,000 peaple died around 22 counties of North Manchuria. (Dr.Tein-Wei Wu, Socity for Studies for Japanese Aggression Against China, N.Y.)

② 300 persons to perished from plague on Hohhot and 400 persons died on Hequ at 1945--1946, it's according to Guo Chengchou, Liao Yingchang "Factual account of Japanese army's biological warfare against China", Yan-Shan Press, 1997.

③Tha plague around Quzhou and Yiwu epidemic killed Chinese persons still to 1957 (Xuan Wang, a represantative of the Lawsuit Research Conference of the Victims of Japanese Army's Biological Warfare).

④ It has been established by The Japanese Germ Warfare Crime Investigation Committee 1999: The people of Baoshan under the heel of cholera still to filled up the Sand river at 1951.

⑤Some Linqing's victims let the menber of J.G .W.C. I .C. to knew: "The cholera has been continued to now, come on every summer time around Linqing, but slow down the pace."

⑥A lot of victims by Japanese anthracolemus attacked still under heel of disease in Jinhua.

⑦Qinyuan plague disease has 70 persons to died.(Leeli "The B.W. of Zhejiang-Jiangxi Line")

注釋

①、 "日軍細菌戰專輯"（吳天威、日本侵華研究社，紐約）記載："七三一部隊"在一九四五年逃亡時，釋放出數萬支老鼠，造成北滿二十二個縣發生鼠疫，有二萬餘人死亡.

②、 郭成周、廖應昌 "侵華日軍細菌戰紀實"（北京燕山出版社，一九九七）指出：一九四五年至一九四六年呼和浩特鼠疫再次復出，三百人致死，在河曲則有四百人死亡.

③、 在浙江省義烏、衢州，鼠疫仍然存在至一九四七年 "侵華日軍細菌戰受害訴訟研究會"（代表王選）浙江的調查：衢州的鼠疫至一九四八年才消失.

④、 一九九九年美國 "日軍細菌戰罪行調查小組委員會" 在去雲南保山調查時得知：日軍于一九四二年投放細菌所造成的霍亂疾始終未滅，年年復發，延至一九五一年填平沙河之後才未再發生（一九四二年間大量霍亂死尸丟于沙河沙灘）.

⑤、 美國 "日軍細菌戰罪行調查小組委員會" 一九九九年在山東臨清縣調查時，民眾均稱："一九四二年日軍霍亂攻擊所造成的霍亂症，一直持續到現在，每年夏天都會復發，雖經幾十年防治仍未根絕，但情勢已弱".

⑥、 到目前爲止，金華縣仍有大批受日軍于一九四二年施放炭疽病的受害人還在挣扎.

⑦、 慶元，鼠疫死亡７０人（李力 "浙贛細菌戰"）.

The map of plague epidemic area of Harbin after "8.15"
"七三一" 部隊撤退後哈爾濱鼠疫發生地點圖

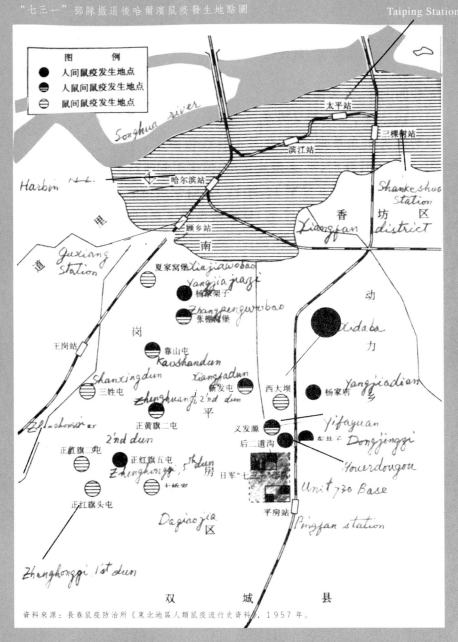

Taiping Station

Persons died by plague recording:
死亡記錄：
1946 135 人
1947 56 人
1948 1 人
1950　18 人
1951　2 人
(Guo Hongmao "The 3'rd plague epidemic in North East of China") (郭洪茂 "東北第三次鼠疫大流行")

資料來源：長春鼠疫防治所《東北地區人類鼠疫流行史資料》，1957 年。

"Unit 731" put down three pcs. plague spreaders on three villages near the Pingfan in Aug 1945, and the "Unit 731" beat a hasty in Aug. 10 1954, a lot of plague fleas run away into residential area of villages.

Few days later, the plague epidemic covered around these area, 1'st Yifayuan village has 39 persons were death.

The city of Harbin near to Yifayuan 20 kms, plague fast infected to there, bring about one hundred citizens were died in 1946 to 1954.

一九四五年 "八‧一五" 前，"七三一部隊" 曾將三枚 "鼠疫菌投擲器" 分別投到平房附近的正黄旗三屯、正黄旗四屯和義發源三個村莊，這種由玻璃管制成的蓄有鼠疫的裝置，長10CM，直徑5CM。

加上 "七三一部隊" 在逃亡時臨時用火燒毀老鼠飼養區，又讓老鼠和跳蚤四散逃命，分散于平房四周的村落，從而造成靠近平房的農村于是年發生鼠疫，並流傳到哈爾濱市區。

一九四五年九月當平房農民第一次在告別長達十五年的日軍占領後，準備第一個 "金收" 時，鼠疫首先在靠平房最近的二道溝村張彦廷發生。村民靖如先去張家幫忙辦喪事，回家後也患病死亡，接著靖如先家十九口，有十二口相繼死去。

之後，鼠疫又在東井子、義發源兩個村流行。其中義發源死39人。

哈爾濱市離東井子村二十公裏，鼠疫得以迅速傳入市區，1946年至1954年間共發生六次，感染二百多人，有一百人死亡。

While they were burning up the animal houses before retreating in defeat, they sent out all the animals infected a artificially. Thus, it caused the plague in Yifayuan, Houerdaogou, Dongjingzi near Pingfan District. 103 people died of it. This is the dead body of a patient of the plague.

　　七三一部隊敗退前，在燒毀動物捨的同時，將染疫動物全部放出，致使平房附近的義發源、後二道溝、東進子發生了鼠疫，死亡１０３人。圖爲鼠疫患者屍體。（一九四五年秋）

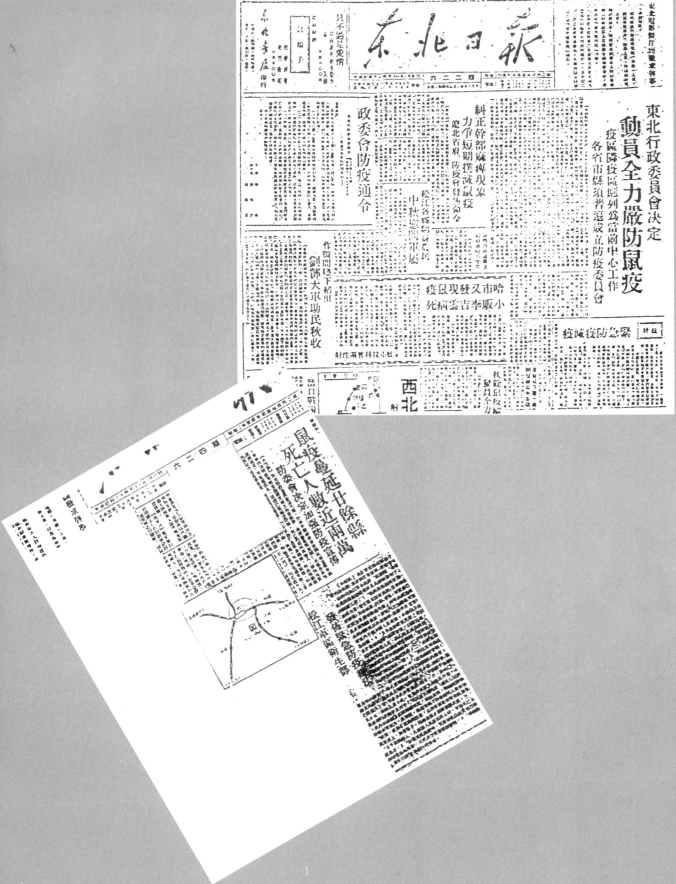

Plague victim near Pingfan, (1946)
平房附近農民死于鼠疫（一九四六年）

The map of evil legacies of Japanese germ warfare in 1946
一九四六年日軍細菌戰遺害圖

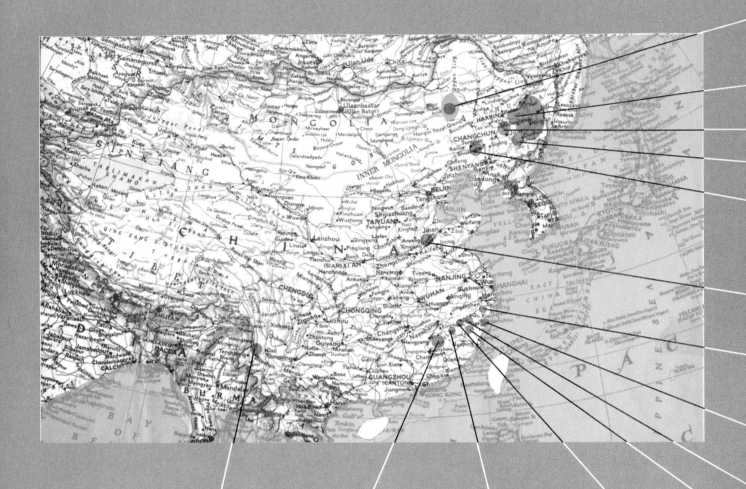

Persons were died killed by plague in Jiangxi

鼠疫死亡人數

地區	Number of death 死亡人數
南城 nanchang	171人
南豐 nanfeng	62人
臨川 linchuan	43人
黎川 lichuan	47人
撫州 fuzhou	55人
金溪 jiangxi	24人
廣昌 Quangchang	1人

(Leeli "The B.W.of Zhejiang-Jiangxi Line"

李力 "浙贛綫細菌戰")

Shangrao, plague ,17 persons were died

上饒，鼠疫流行，１７人死

Attacked with the epidemic of cholera in Baoshan

保山地區繼續流行霍亂

The plague happened around Zhaoan, Zhaonan, Kaitong has had 1,400 persons were died.
洮安、洮南、開通發生鼠疫1，400人死亡③

Harbin plague
哈爾濱，鼠疫③

Cholera, Yushu and Yingji counties
榆樹、永吉二縣發生霍亂

Yanbian, plague
延邊，鼠疫，死3，000人．

Kaiyuan, plague, 3,000 died
開源，鼠疫，死3，000人②

Epidemic disease of cholera continued around Linqing
臨清縣附近霍亂繼續流行

Happened the positive reactions of antibodies of plague in rats on Yiwu
義烏持續有鼠疫菌抗體陽性反映存在

Wenzhou, plague, 123 persons were died
溫州，鼠疫，123人死

Yueqing, plague, 4 persons were died
樂清，鼠疫，4人死

Ruian, plague ,12 Persons were died
瑞安，鼠疫，12人死

A lot of disabled persons of anthracolemus diseases in Jinhua
大批炭疽病患者在金華

Plague, Wenchang, 6 persons died, Qinyuan 70 persons died
鼠疫，文城死6人，慶元死70人

Plague, Quzhou area 16,200 people were died
衢州地區，仍有鼠疫霍亂、傷寒、痢疾、死亡16，200人 ④、⑤

Notes: The evil legacies of Japanese germ warfare at 1946

1) Yanbian, plague, Lin Bingxin, Xu Junyuan, Shi Yuxin, "A complete Record of Atrocities committed by Invading Janpanese Troops in China", P.58, Yanshan Press, 1997.

2) Li Siwen, Du yuanyou, Zhu Zhaoli, Shang Guohua " The germ warfare crimes of Japan's Kwangtung Army in Kaiyuan Old City".

3) About Harbin's plague, recording to "the crimes history of unit 731" P.300.

4) Qiu Mingxuan "Evidence of a crimes" P.14: In 1946 epidemic of plague, cholera, anthrax, typhoid, dysentery has 135,000 persons diseased and 16,200 people were died.

5) "Da Ming Press"(Quzhou) report:

"Epidemics diseases rampant in Changshan, same as a horse without a bridle cannot control roll up around this county's 21 towns & villages has been many many death there and nobody get gather in paddys. Some whole family no one kept alive, the coffin supplie's have fallen short. Too horrible to look!"

日軍細菌戰在一九四六年的遺害（注釋）

1）、延邊發生鼠疫，見李秉新、徐俊元、石玉新"侵華日軍暴行總錄"第五十八頁，燕山出版社，一九九七年。

2）、李師文、杜源佐、朱肇禮、尚國華"日本關東軍細菌戰在開源老城的罪行"。

3）、哈爾濱鼠疫，見"日軍731罪惡史"，黑龍江文史資料第三十一輯，P.300，1991

4）、邱明軒"罪證"，14頁：1946年衢州、龍游、江山、常山、開化受害致病135000人，致死16200人。

5）、衢州"大明報"、"常山縣疫病猖獗，勢如無羈之馬，如今二十一個鄉鎮已無一片净土，死亡累累，禾倒于田無人收割，全家滅口也有新聞。棺材供不應求……"

Some victims of anthracolemus attacked on Jinhua (Zhejiang province) struggle for existence on the brink of death until now
炎疽攻擊下的幸存人仍在痛苦挣扎

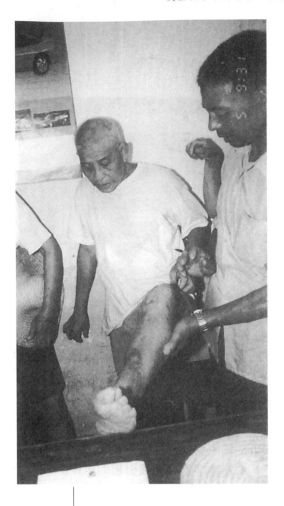

Condemn the evils of germ warfare(Jinhua)
金華人的控訴

Victim of anthrax by Japanese (Jinhua)
金華炭疽病受害人

Victim by anthrax, Wang Chunlian, Tangxia village, Jinhua
金華塘下村炭疽菌致殘人　王春蓮

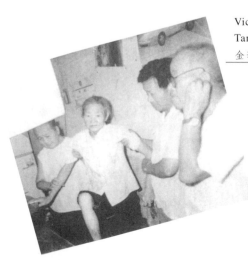

Yangjingrong's leg have cut off for keeping his life, Jinhua
金華日軍炭疽菌受害幸存人楊金榮劃掉一脚後存活下來。

The emergency meeting record of epimedic prevention in Quzhou from Nov. 11, 1946 to Dec.14, 1946
為衢州發生鼠疫而召開緊急防疫會議的記錄（一九四六年十一月）

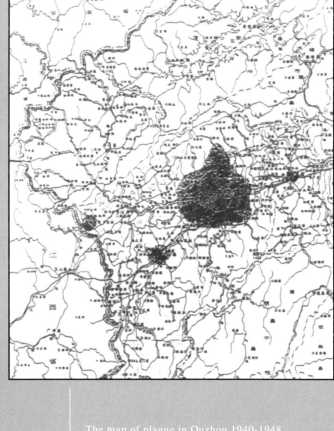

The map of plague in Quzhou 1940-1948
一九四○年至一九四八年衢州鼠疫流行分布
繪制人（日本）常石敬一（一九九○年作成）

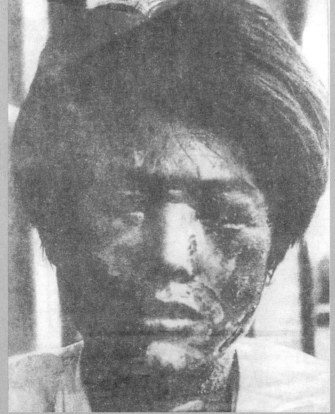

Survivor injured by B.W. in Mudenjiang.
被遺棄的細菌炸彈所傷害的東北牡丹江市的受害者

The map of evil legacies of Japanese germ warfare in 1947
日軍細菌戰在一九四七年的遺害

Tonglian, inner Mongolia, plague were 25,089 death.
通遼、內蒙、鼠疫，25，089人死亡③

The epidemic of cholera continued to 1951 around Baoshan.
保山地區的霍亂一直持續到一九五一年

鼠疫死亡人數 Killed by plague in Jiangxi④

南城 Nanchang	7人		
南豐 Nanfeng	12人	金溪 Jinxi	6人
臨川 Linchuan	19人	崇仁 Chongren	79人
黎川 Lichuan	14人	南昌 Nanchang	17人
撫州 Fuzhou	16人		

Yu Hanmou (Governor of Quzhou)telegraph at Nov. 25, 1947, "Discovered plague in Shangrao, 69 persons killed..."
衢州公署余漢謀一九四七年十一月二十五日電："上饒……發現鼠疫"，69人死亡

鼠疫死亡人數

Has attacked with the epidemic of plague included: Qiqihar, Zhaojing, Zhaodong£¬Zhaoan, Zhaonan, Dalai, Jinglai, Zhanyu, Antong, Harbin, 7,500 persons were died.
大面積地區發生鼠疫，流行區包括：齊齊哈爾、肇京、肇源、洮安、洮南、大賚、鎮賚、哈爾濱、瞻榆、安廣、開通、7,500人死亡①

Songjiang,Nenjiang, plague
松江、嫩江鼠疫②

Epidemic disease of cholera continued on Linqing
霍亂繼續在臨清流行

The positive reactions of antibodies of rats has continued stayed around Yiwu county.
義烏老鼠身上的鼠疫菌抗體陽性反映繼續存在

A lot of disabled victims of anthracolemus still to struggle for existence on the brink of death around Jinhua.
在金華、許多炭疽病受害人挣扎在死亡綫上

Quzhou, The telegraph by the Sanitation Dep. Office of Zhejiang. No. W.S#2816 in March 5, 1948
"The Magistrate of Quzhou county: Plague has occurred on there in last year, epidemic situation was very grave......"
衢州：浙江衛生處代電（衛三字第2816號）一九四八年三月五日
"衢縣縣長鑒：查該縣上年發生鼠疫，疫情頗屬嚴重……。"

Plague,persons to died④
鼠疫死亡人數
溫州 Wenzhou   42人
瑞安 Ruian   27人
樂清 Yueging   3人

Nanxi county happened plague,15 persons died.
a,蘭溪縣發生鼠疫，死亡15人
"The prevention and cure of Chinese epidemic disease", magazine 7th 1992: "Plague epidernic was continued still to may 1948".
b,據《中國地方病防治》雜志一九九二年第十卷載……
"衢州鼠疫至一九四八年五月止才未流行。"

The Notes

The evil legacies of Japanese germ warfare in 1947

① Cheng Ying "Old Impression",No.1, p.253, Society Publishing House, 1998.

② Li Bingxian, Xu Junyuan, Shi Yusin "A complete Record of Atrocities Committed by Japanese Troops in China", P. 540, Hebie Renmin Publishing House, 1995.

③ Ibid. ②

④ Leeli "The B.W. of Zhejiang-Jiangxi Line".

日軍細菌戰在一九四七年的遺害（注釋）

①成鷹 "老印象" 第一輯，第二百五十三頁，社會出版社，一九九八年

②李秉新、徐俊元、石玉新 "侵華日軍暴行總錄"，第五百四十頁，河北人民出版社，一九九五年

③同注②

④李力 "浙贛綫細菌戰"

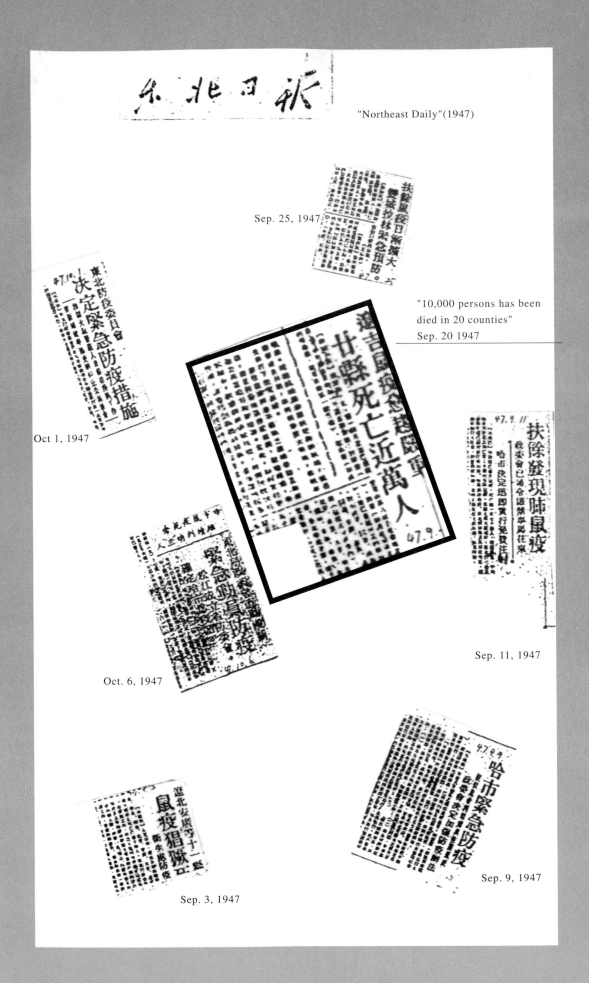

東 北 日 報

"Northeast Daily"(1947)

Sep. 25, 1947

"10,000 persons has been died in 20 counties"
Sep. 20 1947

Oct 1, 1947

Sep. 11, 1947

Oct. 6, 1947

Sep. 3, 1947

Sep. 9, 1947

"Da Ming Press" Quzhou, March 9, 1947
"Palgue diseases picked up on Jianjun Village and Beijiatong village a great many deaths have taken place here lately...."
衢州《大明報》(1947,3,9)一版

Most whole family members all died by the Japan's cholera in 1942, no descendants to bury them dead bodies, then the Government organized few groups put the bodies to the sand beach of Sand River and used sands covered. After 1942, the cholera back againt during every flashing seasons years and years. Nine years later, Government orders filled up the Sand River for eliminated the scourge of cholera.

一九四二年日軍在雲南保山沙河沿岸投放霍亂菌,造成許多家死絶,被害人尸體無人收葬而弃投于沙河河灘或以沙掩之,形成沙河附近村莊年年春汛後發生霍亂,此照片即填河後留存的沙河一角.

Plague disease infected line of N.E. of China in 1945-1947
1945-1947年東北鼠疫大流行時鼠疫發生地區與傳播路線圖

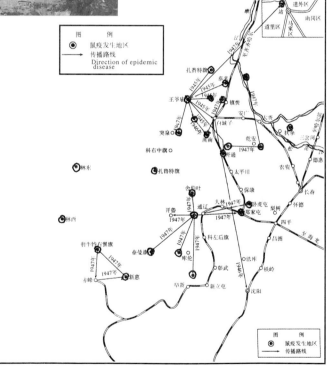

科左後旗 Kezuohouqi
鎮賚 Zhenlai
突泉 Tuquan
白城子 Baichangzi
安廣 Anguang
洮南 Raonan
大賚 Dalai
乾安 Quianan
開通 Kaitong

哈爾濱 Harbin
鬆花江 Songhua river
道裏區 Daoli district
馬家區 Majia district
南崗區 Nangang district
齊齊哈爾 Qigihat
札賚特旗 Zhalaitegi
王爺廟 Wangfumiao
泰來 Tailai

四平 Siping
海龍 Hailong
鄭家屯 Zhongjiadun
卧虎屯 Efudun
通套 Tongliao
捨伯吐 Shebeitu
開魯 Kailu
奈曼旗 Naimanyi
庫倫 Kulun

太平川 Taipingcheean
扶餘 Fuyu
三岔河 Shanchahe
德惠 Dahui
長春 Changchun

The map of evil legacies of Japanese germ warfare after 1948
一九四八年至今日軍細菌戰遺害圖

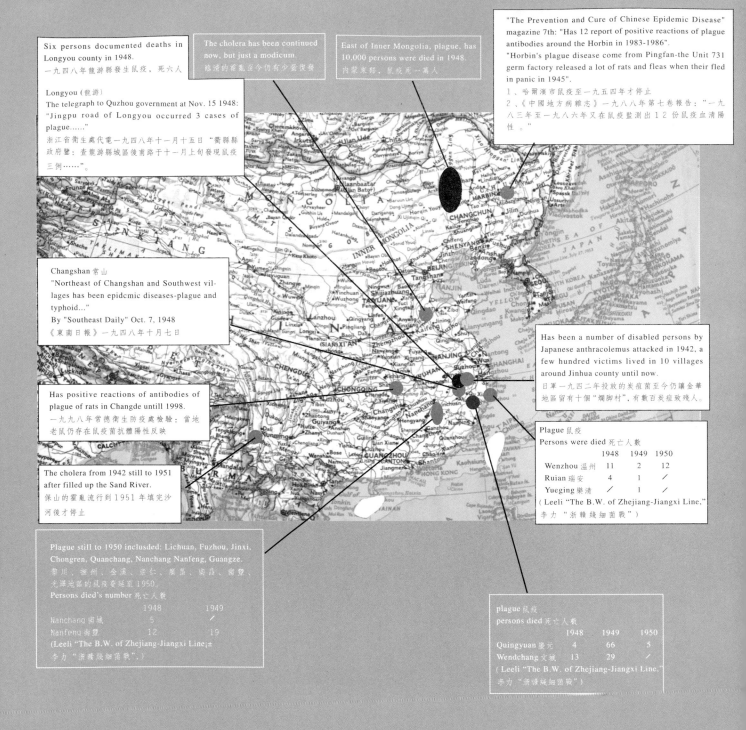

Six persons documented deaths in Longyou county in 1948.
一九四八年龍游縣發生鼠疫，死六人

Longyou（龍游）
The telegraph to Quzhou government at Nov. 15 1948:
"Jingpu road of Longyou occurred 3 cases of plague......"
浙江省衛生處代電一九四八年十一月十五日"衢縣縣政府鑒：查龍游縣城區後甫路于十一月上旬發現鼠疫三例......"。

The cholera has been continued now, but just a modicum.
瘟濟的霍亂至今仍有少量復發

East of Inner Mongolia, plague, has 10,000 persons were died in 1948.
內蒙東部，鼠疫死一萬人

"The Prevention and Cure of Chinese Epidemic Disease" magazine 7th: "Has 12 report of positive reactions of plague antibodies around the Horbin in 1983-1986".
"Horbin's plague disease come from Pingfan-the Unit 731 germ warfare factory released a lot of rats and fleas when their fled in panic in 1945".
1、哈爾濱市鼠疫至一九五四年才停止
2、《中國地方病雜志》一九八八年第七卷報告："一九八三年至一九八六年又在鼠疫監測出12份鼠疫血清陽性。"

Changshan 常山
"Northeast of Changshan and Southwest villages has been epidcmic diseases-plague and typhoid..."
By "Southeast Daily" Oct. 7, 1948
《東南日報》一九四八年十月七日

Has positive reactions of antibodies of plague of rats in Changde untill 1998.
一九九八年常德衛生防疫處檢驗：當地老鼠仍存在鼠疫菌抗體陽性反映

The cholera from 1942 still to 1951 after filled up the Sand River.
保山的霍亂流行到1951年填完沙河後才停止

Has been a number of disabled persons by Japanese anthracolemus attacked in 1942, a few hundred victims lived in 10 villages around Jinhua county until now.
日軍一九四二年投放的炭疽菌至今仍讓金華地區留有十個"爛腳村"，有數百炭疽致殘人。

Plague 鼠疫
Persons were died 死亡人數

	1948	1949	1950
Wenzhou 溫州	11	2	12
Ruian 瑞安	4	1	／
Yueging 樂清	／	1	／

(Leeli "The B.W. of Zhejiang-Jiangxi Line," 李力 "浙贛線細菌戰")

Plague still to 1950 inclusded: Lichuan, Fuzhou, Jinxi, Chongren, Quanchang, Nanchang Nanfeng, Guangze.
黎川、撫州、金溪、崇仁、廣昌、南豐、光澤地區的鼠疫蔓延至1950。
Persons died's number 死亡人數

	1948	1949
Nanchang 南城	5	／
Nanfeng 南豐	12	19

(Leeli "The B.W. of Zhejiang-Jiangxi Line¡± 李力 "浙贛線細菌戰".)

plague 鼠疫
persons died 死亡人數

	1948	1949	1950
Quingyuan 慶元	4	66	5
Wendchang 文城	13	29	／

(Leeli "The B.W. of Zhejiang-Jiangxi Line," 李力 "浙贛線細菌戰")

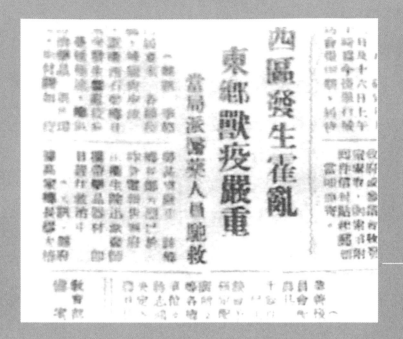

"Da Ming Press", Quzhou, Aug. 4, 1948
"West villages occurred cholera and east villages was covered by anthrax."
衢州《大明報》 （1948，8，4）一版

The Dep. of Southeast Plague Prevention & Treat will set up a branch in Quzhou , "Da Ming Press" Oct. 1, 1948
衢州《大明報》 （1948，1，10）一版

"Southeast Daily", Nov. 4, 1948
"Plague rampant in Longyou spread fast, has been 4 people were death in last two days."
浙江"東南日報"（1948,11,4)四版

The figure of rats quarantine of manchuria (1950–1953)
東北1950–1953老鼠檢疫統計

	檢鼠（疫）	鼠疫	鼠疫率
1950	18,507	169	0.91%
1951	11,077	64	0.57%
1952	14,759	5	0.03%
1953	10,680	0	0

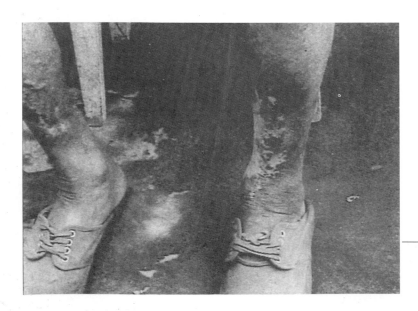

One anthrax case happened in Zhejiang, 1963
一九六三年浙江發生炭疽病例一件

CHAPTER VI
THE JAPAN'S B.W. CRIMNALS AND REPENTERS

第 六 章
日軍細菌戰的罪犯和懺悔人

Shinotsuka Yoshio　篠塚良雄

Section 1

Ishii's Diabolical Plots/Schemes

〈Ishii Shiro's life of lies〉

Ishii Shiro, the founder of "Unit 731 ", head of the Unit and Lt. General, was an extremely clever person. Starting from 1926 when he worked for his doctorate dissertation to 1959 when he died of throat cancer, he lived under disguise and lies for as long as 32 years. hiding his true career all through his life.

When he was at the Kyoto Imperial University in 1926. Ishii worked under the direction of his bacteriology Professor Kimura Ren conducting research on germ positive twin bacteria. Ishii always sneaked into the laboratory to use the supplies and apparatus and left without cleaning up. His professor Kimura remembered this well, and he noted as follows:

"To get to the point, Ishii was very bright. At that time there were 30 to 40 students. They had to be very careful in using the laboratory because of the shortage of supplies. Ishii would do his work at night affer everybody had left, using all the supplies and test tubes cleaned by others. Surely the students were very upset when they returned the next morning to find the equipment and apparatus dirty and used". (1)

In April 1928 Ishii went to Europe and America for two years under the pretense of inspection and study on infectious disease origin, hiding his real purpose in developing biological warfare. After visiting 27 countries, Ishii returned to Japan and reported to his senior officials with deceit that all of the strong countries in the west were conducting secret biological warfare research.(2) His deception was particularly misleading in emphasizing how America was producing voluminous biological.

Already possessed with a proclivity to expansion, Ishii's lies critically influenced the raving mood of the Japanese leadership levels. Japan's research on biological warfare started after Ishii was promoted to Major.

For Ishii, he came to a small fortune with the receipt of a royalty of 50,000 yen from the Imperial Medical Treatment Inc. because of his invention of water filters. This amount was equivalent to 500 times the net income of a young businessman for three months. Living in new affluence, Ishii often lied to his wife, daughter of the President of Kyoto University, flavoring his excuses that he was busy doing research but in reality he was spending his days at the high class brothel, or geisha house. One time he was discovered and arrested by the military police but released after 10 days with the help of the war minister Nagata Tetsuzan.(3)

Ishii's betrayal to his wife and involvement with prostitution were even worse affer 1936. The historian Morimuri Masaichi had pointed out that when Ishii was in the Northeast of China, he took his sleep during the day but sneaked out at night to Harbin and Shenyang to visit first class geisha houses such as "Powder HIll". He could not be found even when the Kwantung Army commander summoned him in an emergency. Thus it could be seen that his lies also eluded his teachers, senior officials and family.

While pursuing his goals for research and developing biological warfare, and in order to keep the "secret amidst secrets" and protect his promotional prospects, Ishii likely could not even keep count of the many lies that he had told and the many deceptions that he had practiced. And among the deceptions, there were three that were directly linked to the top secrets of the Japanese government's central office, which even now had not been made public, and they were related to the Imperial Emperor.

第一節
石井的騙局

Ishii Shiro(1943) 石井四郎

〈 欺騙的一生 〉

石井四郎從一九二六年攻讀博士學位到一九五九年死于喉癌，幾乎都是生活在彌天大謊之中，達三十二年之久。

當他還在京都帝大時（1926），石井在木村連教授指導下從事細菌研究，就常常私下使用實驗室的用具又不予清洗。

木村教授回憶說："石井是很出色的，在當時的三十至四十名學生中，實驗室設備不足，石井就在入夜所有的人離開後使用那裏的用品，而用後又不洗滌，使學生在次日進入時無法立即實驗而惱火。"(1)

一九二八年偽裝赴歐美學習、研究傳染病源而暗藏考察細菌武器的目的，在訪問二十七個國家，之後返回東京，向上級虛報所有強國都在研究細菌武器，(2)謊稱美國在進行龐大的細菌生產，成功地煽動日本開始細菌戰的研究，而石井也晉級為少佐 。

石井隨後在水過濾裝置上幸運獲得一筆五萬元的采購特金，這筆錢相當于當時一個年輕商人三個月收入的五百倍。石井瞞着他的妻子（京都帝大校長的女兒），到豪華的夜總會、高級妓女樓揮霍無度。一次被憲兵逮捕，由軍務局長永田鐵山保釋而出。(3)

一九三六年石井在東北也幹着不忠于他妻子的事。史學家指出石井常常在人們睡後潛入哈爾濱或沈陽的日本歌妓院，甚至發生關東軍司令官緊急找他時找不到人的情況。如此種種祇是指出他的欺騙已經泛及他的老師、上司和妻子。

為了謀求細菌武器的發展并保守"秘密中的秘密"，石井經常是謊話連篇，當然，石井的撒謊，其實就是日本政府的謊騙，其中有三次重大的騙局。這三次騙局是：

1）石井貪污離職事件

2）石井之死

3）"伯力審判"。

Analyzing the three deceptions would help to uncover the sins of the Japanese biological warfare.

Ishii's three big deceptions were:

1. Corruption and transfer from "731" to Taiyuan,

2. Ishii's sudden, or faked, "death", and

3. The Khabarovsk Trial.

Realistically speaking, the three deceptions of Ishii's were actually the deceptions of the Japanese government and Emperor Hirohito. The mastermind of the deceptions was Japanese Cabinet, but it was Ishii and his followers who put them in practice.

⟨ Corruption and transfer ⟩

It was on August 24, 1942 and durinq the Japanese retreat that Ishii arrived at the warfront of Zhejiang. He had a meeting at the army division commanders headquarter and after planning for germ release, he left for Nanking and "disappeared" for a while from the active biological warfare grounds. Ishii was transferred go Taiyuan where he assumed the position of Chief of Medicine Dep. of the First Army. His transfer was clouded in mystery and doubt as to the motive. Whereas the Kwantung Army did not disclose the reason for his departure, the internal rumor for Ishii's "disappearance" from "Unit 731" was that he was relieved of his duties because of his corruption. (4)

But during the U.S. trial in 1946, Ishii's response to the biological warfare investigator Colonel Albert Thomson regarding why he was discharged from commanding "Unit 731" was as follows:

"I was transferred to the First Army because the higher leadership levels did not allow me to continue research on biological warfare. Probably it was related to my promotion to Lt. Gen. For that purpose I needed the field experience and to be the chief of a unit. So if I stayed in the laboratory I would not be able to be promoted to any level, but then if I receive a promotion first, I could use my elevated rank to return to the laboratory." He also said, "The position I held as the Chief of Medical Dep. of the First Army was very important because I was responsible for the entire army and the health of 100,000 people."

Clearly Ishii was lying to Thomson. This is because although the Japanese Chief of Medical Dep. of Army had the highest military rank of Major Gen., the officer could also be a Colonel. For example Kiyoshi Kawashima, Chief of Medical Dep. in 1943 of the 12th Army that was stationed in China, was a Colonel.

Regarding Ishii's departure, the historian Fujii Shitsue believed that the reason for his leaving was to allow him to devote totally to the development and application of biological warfare. There was little success in tracing the status of Ishii for the period starting from when he left "731" in August 1942 to March 1, 1945. It was a total blank in the public domain except for some scarce information from the Shanxi First Army.

But then again, as things happened, often as strange as a fiction, the more one wanted to hide the more the secrets could not be kept. In Chinese proverbs, there is a saying, "Affer walking a long time in the dark, one would inevitably meet a spirit." How could Ishii hide forever and not be discovered?

Since the summer of 1942 have not heard from sb. about Ishii, as if he stayed in 1'st Army to March, 1945. Untill to same month, Tokyo news reported Ishii was promised a lecturer of the Medical School of Army Surgeons. Few days later, appointed Ishii back to Pingfan for reinstated, and promoted to Lt. Gen., be like no corruption happened.

Now, some confessions of the members of B. W. units give new informations that the Tokyo employed the tricks at these

〈 貪污、調職事件 〉

石井在一九四二年八月到浙贛前綫舉行師團長戰地會議後返回南京就沒有消息。後來知道石井調到太原，出任日本第一軍軍醫處長。他的離職，關東軍司令部沒有宣布原因，私下裏人們則"傳言說"石井是犯了貪污罪受懲的。(4)

而石井在一九四六年面對美軍調查員湯姆遜上校時所做的解釋則是：

"我調到第一軍是為了脫離細菌研究機構而獲得升遷的安排，因為我希望升至中將。由于這目的，我需要有一個晉階的職位，而在實驗室裏是沒有的。

我出任的第一軍的軍軍醫處長是一個重要職位，在那裏要對十萬軍人的健康負責。"

石井當然在欺騙湯姆遜，因為日本陸軍一個軍的軍醫處長最高軍階是少將，或是大佐，如川島清在一九四三年出任第十二軍軍醫處長時，即為大佐。

石井在謊言下杜撰的故事不能長期掩蓋真相。正如中國俗話說"走多了夜路，總要碰到鬼"一樣，石井的謊言也是掩蓋不住的。

自一九四二年八月後，石井是烟消塵散了，仿佛他從一九四二年八月到一九四五年三月都呆在山西第一軍。到一九四五年三月東京發布石井擔任陸軍軍醫學校講師的消息，不多久又宣布他調回平房復任"七三一部隊"部隊長，并官升中將，好象石井并沒有貪污醜聞發生。

現在，一些參與細菌特種部隊的日軍戰俘先後供認出石井在一九四二年至一九四五年的行蹤：

一九四二年八月，日軍宣布石井奉調山西第一軍軍醫處長，但未立即到任；

一九四二年十一月二十日，石井出現在"太原防疫給水訓練班"上，但不是第一軍軍醫處長；

一九四二年十二月，石井視察潞安（山西）陸軍醫院，但仍不是以第一軍醫處長身份；

一九四二年十二月止，第一軍軍醫處長是兵頭周吉（少將），不是石井（野田正彰"戰爭罪責"P.20）

至一九四三年，石井才以軍醫處長身份現身山西：三月在潞安、四月在崞縣、七月在太原并講話、九月再到潞安，之後石井就沒有到過山西了。日俘中島三郎一九五四年八月二十六日供稱：一九四四年一月他到山西時，第一軍軍醫處長是近藤少將。

現已知石井一九四三年十月在東京出席了"保號"會議。（一次對美細菌戰的參謀會議）。⑤

石井一九四二年十二月在上海停留，這時上海有五百名美俘在進行活體試驗。到同年年末，石井到東北的海拉爾，并在海拉爾的"入舟飯店"放話說：

"我仍舊領導七三一部隊，而且有權指揮全部防疫給水部隊。"

這時有1485名美英戰俘進入沈陽，并在那裏受到活試。

石井的脚迹與美俘的活試如此相隨，是巧合嗎？

"一八五五部隊"成員、參加一九四三年魯西霍亂攻擊的日俘林茂美的供詞，證明石井在這次攻擊中是主要的領導人之一。

曾任第二任"七三一部隊"部隊長的少將北野政次，在一九四六年對美軍審訊人員說：石井一直領導七三一部隊，就在他離開平房後也沒有失去領導權。

石井在一九四二年至一九四五年多次參加東京參謀本部舉行的細菌戰決策會議。中國長期研究日軍細菌戰的專家韓曉指出：石井在一九四二年至一九四五年間可能出任日軍軍醫總監，他把東京的陸軍經理學校改造為細菌

years. The movement of Ishii from Aug. 1942 to March, 1945 as followings:

Aug. 1942 appointed the position of Chief of Medical Dep.of the 1'st Army (Taiyuan, Shanxi province), but Ishii did not take up an official post;

Nov. 20, 1942, Ishii take a unknown identily appeared in "Taiyuan Epidemic Prevention Train Class" and in Dec. 1942, Ishii inspected the Luan military hospital, and then Ishii were missing again. But Kanisawa has pointed out: G. Maruyoshi Hyotou is the Chief of Medical Dep.of 1'st A., not Ishii (Kanisawa was a surgeon in there from Jan. 1942 to end of the war).

After March, 1943, Ishii take some inspections in Shanxi with the chief of M. of I'st A, March to Luan, Apr. to Chunxian, July to Taiyuan and speaking there, Sep. to Luan, from then on, Ishii never come to Shanxi, Major Gen. Koudou take over Ishii's position (Nakamura Saburo confessed at Aug.21, 1954). In Oct. 1943 Ishii attened "Hou Go conference" of Gen. Chief of Staff in Tokyo.(5)

In the term office, Ishii gone to Shanghai in Dec. 1942, same moment has had 500 prisoners of Amerian live experiments there. At the end of this year, Ishii came to Hailer (Hailongjiang province) and take said out in "Iri Bune Hotal": "I have still lead unit 731, and I have power to command all epidemic prevention and water supply units".

In the same time, 1,485 prisoners of Amercan-Anglo came to Mukden (Shenyang) for experiments.

Ishii's footpoints with prisoners of American have identical, it is coincidence ? It is not most be so.

Shigerni Hayashi, a member of "Unit 1855" with cholera attacked on West Shandong, 1943, he confessed: Ishii was a leader of these germ attacking, has been confirmed Ishii has the power of command to the B .W. units.

The 2'nd Chief of "Unit 731", Major Gen. Masaji Kitano, tolk the U. S. military prosecution tribunal in 1946 that Ishii had never lost his control over "731" even after Ishii left the unit in 1942.

Ishii attened every important conferences of policy decissions of B.W. in Tokyo in 1942 to 1945. Chinese specialist Han Xian after a long course of study for Ishii's tracks, he pointed out: Ishii got the position was the Chief of the B. W. of Japan after he left "Unit 731."

At these years, Ishii made a hard word for supplied spick and new equipments of B.W. for Pingfan and set up new large base in Chinese-Karea area, because Tokyo has determination that the appropriations of "Epidemic Prevention Research Section" did need pass off the Diet. He remodelled the Military Management School to G. chief office for his control.

Following this, Ishii's name appeared numerous times in the records:

In April 1943, the high command held a meeting of the committee to discuss the use of biological warfare in the "south" military zone, which included various countries in South Asia, Southeast Asia and South Pacific. The meeting listed four major proposals submitted for advice from the chief commander.

The fourth proposal was the Ishii protocol, or the committee's confirmation plan which was to use 27 air bombers to conduct dispersion of bacteria in Burma, India, South China, New Guinea and Austria, and to "ignore international opinion" on bacteriologic attack.

戰的總部。

石井在一九四二年五月二十七日參謀本部會議上提出"為進行細菌戰需要編成中央機制（李利"戰爭責任研究"，一九九三年第二號），顯然石井已處在這一位置上。

石井在那些時間，花大力向平房提供了新的生產綫，并開始在中朝邊境建立第二個更大的細菌戰基地，因為東京作出了一個非常有利的決定："傳染病防疫研究室"的預算自一九四二年四月起，其撥款不經過國會審批。

以下是一些有關石井出席重要會議的記錄：

一九四三年四月，出席討論在"南方軍區"（包括南亞、東南亞和太平洋）進行細菌戰，其中第四方案即"石井提案"，要求以飛機 27 架在華南、新幾內亞、印緬和澳大利亞進行細菌撒播，而不用理會"國際輿論"的指責；

一九四三年七月，石井秘密出席參謀本部會議，商討對塞班島和貝克島使用細菌對付美軍；

一九四五年一月八日，石井的名字第三次出現在記錄上：

"石井方案……要求生產 300kg 鼠疫菌。"

除日本陸軍檔案的記錄外，還發現石井曾要求組成 17 人的敢死隊（由七三一隊員中選出），身染鼠疫病源到塞班島污染機場跑道，但由于途中被美國潛艇擊沉，攻擊計劃不成，祇有一人生還。

在一九四五年二月，美軍占領硫磺島時，石井再次提出以細菌攻擊美軍。(6)

顯然，石井貪污和調職是日本政府的一個重大騙局。

〈 石井之死 〉

一九四五年石井在完成炸毀平房之後，慌逃返日。在美軍登陸并占領日本後，報紙即報導石井被射殺至死，石井的家鄉并為其舉行了葬禮。(7)

五個月後，石井被發現并面對美軍的審詢，揭穿了他的假死。但是，石井利用這五個月時間從美蘇的利益衝突中找到一個機會，可以讓他與美軍之間達成合作的協議。

石井在與美軍審詢人員接觸後，很好地了解到盟軍最高當局的意圖，石井的女兒春美直率地說出：盟軍要求有關細菌戰的資料"決不能落到蘇聯手中"。(8)于是石井和他的助手們經過協調與美軍代表周旋，回答湯姆遜的審問。湯姆遜在他的工作報告中說："我相信……從認為獨立來源所獲得的日本細菌戰活動的資料，在一點上是一致的，就是似乎所有的告發者得到了指示，在審詢下他們泄露的資料的數量與性質……"

石井假死，使他贏得了五個月的時間，一方面可以摸清美方企圖，一方面又利用空間與美蘇兩方代表接觸中，制造矛盾，形成美蘇雙方爭搶石井的局勢，從而有利于石井與美方最後的討價還價，保了石井等人自己，也保了日本天皇。

這是繼石井調任第一軍騙局後又一次成功的騙局。

The braveyard of Ishii
石井的墳地

Ishii's second secret appearance was shown in the brief report of the unscheduled meeting of the department heads of the army on July 5 of the same year. The brief report said that the army and the high command planned for the use of biological weapons on Becker Island and Saipan. It also stated that from this plan one could see that the most difficult part was the limited production capacity of the fleas and rodents and the lack of planes. Ishii suggestsd that in order to solve the problem of transportation, they should start to store the plague germ in the lead islands of the Bonin Islands and lwo Jiwa. He predicated that the incubation period for the bubonic plague germ was ten days, but also he stipulated that multiple hits in a human body by fleas could shorten it to four days. Even for the U.S. army, Ishii believed that the U.S. would not initially have effective protective measures in response.

Ishii's third secret appearance was in the record of the army provincial chief of department on January 8, 1945: " ......In the matter of Major General Ishii......The department head requested production of 300 kgs (meaning bubonic plague germ)."

In June 1944, Ishii again appeared when U.S. attacked Saipan. According to the correspondence from Nagasaki University Professor Tsuneishi, dated December 14, 1985 to the British writers Peter Williams and David Wallace, Ishii decided on the plan to conduct biological attack on the U.S. army in Saipan. He selected 17 most capable members of Unit 731 to lead an attacking troop. The plan was to disperse fleas infected with bubonic plague on the airport runway of Saipan so that it would become useless to the U.S. army. However, on its way to Saipan the attack ship was sunk by U.S. submarine, with only one survivor.

In February of 1945 the U.S. occupied lwo Jiwa. Ishii again advocated biological attacks. ¢Ê

⟨ **Ishii's faked death** ⟩

In 1945 Ishii escaped from China after attempts to thoroughly destroy the Pingfan buildings, the huge and complex building built and used by the Japanese for conducting many of the live human experiments.

But when the U.S. troops landed and occupied Japan, the newspaper reported that Ishii was shot to death. Ishii's home-town fellows and relatives Kamo Village even had a funeral for him. This was later found to be a mock funeral. (7)

The whereabouts of Ishii during this period and the mysteries surrounding the issue make it critical to examine the responsibility of the Allies and raise questions regarding their fact-finding efforts about the biological warfare. Information supports that while the Allies proclaimed trials of prisoners of war, Ishii was hiding at Kamo Village.

After Five months of Ishii 's " sudden death" , Ishii got out and face up U.S. military interrogations exposed his lie. But Ishii has been knew that the confict of interests between U. S. with Soviet (8), and give him a new opportunity make a deal with Ameriacan.

⟨ **The Khabarovsk Trial** ⟩

From December 25 to 30, 1949 the public trial of 12 Japanese prisoners of war relating to the biological warfare crime was held in Khabarovsk. The ones on trial included Commander of the Kwangtun Army Yamada and other criminals who had directly participated in the biological war. It was reported that they all admitted "honestly" about their crime on biological warfare.

〈伯力審判〉

一九四九年十二月二十五日至三十日，蘇聯在伯力對十二名涉嫌參與日軍細菌戰的罪犯進行公開審判，被審判対象包括關東軍司令官山田。

這是被蘇聯宣布為成功的正直的審判。

審判結果裁定："前日本陸軍準備和使用細菌武器。"

這個結輪，從現在揭發的證據重新判斷，認為"伯力審判"的十二名日軍戰犯是集體玩弄法庭，進行了一次巨大的欺騙：

1，裁定為"準備與使用"，是完全低估了日軍細菌戰的能量和深度。日軍細菌戰已發展為日軍戰略攻擊的重要組成部分；

2，"伯力審判"所得日俘供認的罪行，在石井向美軍提供的範圍之內，他們同樣沒有交代細菌攻擊緬甸、昆明——保山等重大罪行以及在華作廣泛的細菌撒播等，隱瞞了許多重大的歷史真相。

就日俘和石井等向美蘇承認的寧波、常德、浙贛綫三次細菌攻擊説，也是大為縮水的。常德鼠疫致死人數他們一直未做供認，祇供認了寧波的死亡為106人。而一九四二年浙贛綫攻擊之前的一九四零年，日軍已在浙江上虞、慈溪、臺州、金華、湯溪、溫州、麗水、衢州、龍泉、慶元和江西的玉山進行過以鼠疫為主的攻擊，又在一九四一年對浙江的諸暨、衢州、義烏等地撒播鼠疫，均一字不提。

據調查現在發現的真實攻擊次數超過一百六十一次，致死七十四萬多人。

顯然，石井在"8·10"平房撤毀前後已與關東軍山田司令就日本戰敗後的"口供"底綫達成了某種協議。

注释

（1）、彼得·威廉斯，大衛·瓦雷斯"七三一部隊"，國史館，中譯本P.5.

（2）、同注（1）P.6.

（3）、森村誠一"惡魔的飽食"No.1，1983

（4）、森村誠一"腐蝕的媒介物".

（5）、"井本日記".

（6）、吳天威"日本對美國發動細菌戰的內幕"，"僑報"，1977年9月22日.

（7）、史密斯，1974年4月18日，RG331，MFB，WNA.

（8）、"女兒眼中的魔鬼隊長石井中將"，"日本時報"，1982年8月29日.

As a result of the trial: "the trial materials for the case against the former Japanese army for their preparation and use of biological warfare."

When examined and checked against the materials not uncovered until recently, the testimonies provided by the 12 war criminals, who once were thought by the Soviet Court to have completely and "honestly" reported on the crimes of biological warfare, were found to be only very superficial. The main points of the dishonest reporting, or intentional deception, included the following:

1. The reports from the prisoners of war focused on presenting the picture that the main phase of Japan's biological warfare process was the preparation phase. This led to the misguided use by the Soviets in the announcement of the "Khabarovsk Trial" the terms "preparation and use" as the title, placing the word "preparation" before "use". But now, a lot of reports testimoneid it's an important stratigy of Janpan's Army.

2. The scope of the so-called "honest" acknowledgment of crimes by the war criminals was almost exactly the same as that provided by Ishii to the American military, just covering the matter superficially. For example, they did not mention the biological attack in Burma ,Kunming-Boashan by the Japanese south army. They were from the visits of the Allies' intelligence agents, soon Ishii understood the fears of the highest occupying authority. Ishii's daughter Ishii Samuri had said, "The materials cannot get into the hands of the Soviets." Ishii and his group separately took advantage of the concerns of the Allies, and displayed total response to the Allies' inquiries when answering to Thompson's interrogations. Following that, Thompson wrote in his report, "Regarding Japan's activities in biological warfare, I believe, based on the various independent sources, the materials on Japanese biological warfare were consistent. It seemed like all those who confessed had received instructions on how much and what aspects to reveal of the materials."

Ishii's deception worked. Peter Williams and David Wallace also concluded on the deception in their book "Unit 731: Japanese Secret Biological Warfare in World War II". They noted that based on the reports completed by Sanders and Thompson, the Japanese seemed to have achieved an extraordinary miracle through a continuous series of lies although the war crimes could clearly be seen everywhere. It was true that the Americans did not mean wholeheartedly to obtain materials or testimonies from the Japanese to reveal the hideous Japanese crime of biological warfare. But it is also difficult to believe that the members from Fort Detrick and General MacArthur's intelligence organization had performed so poorly. Silent on the Japanese wide scale use of biological warfare in China after 1942, hiding great historical truth of the Japanese crime in biological warfare.

According a lot of investigations and found to be true, Japanese has 161 times germ attacked on China, and killeded seven hundred fourty thousand people were death.

Notes:
(1). Peter Williams, David Wallace "Unit 731" P.5
(2). Ibid (1) P.6
(3). Siichi Morimura "The burp of monster" No.1, 1983
(4). Siichi Morimura "The intermediarys of corrode"
(5). "Imoto Diary "
(6). Tienwei Wn "The inside informations of Japanese launch B.W. to U.S."
(7). Smith, Arp. 18, 1947, RG 331, MFB, WNA
(8). "Lt.Gen.Ishii, a captain of monster of daughter's eyes", "The Japan Times" Aug. 29, 1982

滿洲第七三一部隊高等官團 [於昭和十八年六月二十五日第八回創立記念日]

Top level officers of "Unit 731" (Photo was taken on June 25,1943--the eighth anniversary of "Unit 731")

Ishii's supporters and assistants

(1). Major Gen. Masaji Kitano　　　北野少將

(2). Major Gen. Syoichi Ootani　　大谷章一（少將）

(3). Dr. Kawashima Yoyaku　　　　川上漸

(4). Major Iwa Tabe　　　　　　　田部井和（少佐）

(5). Major Gen. Hitoshi Kikuchi　　菊地範滿

(6). Colonel Ibusu Ishimitsu　　　　石光熏

(7). Colonel Naga Yama　　　　　　永山太郎

(8). Colonel Kanekura Nakadome　　中留金藏

(9). Colonel Taro Sonoda　　　　　園田太郎

(10). Yoshimura Hisato　　　　　吉村壽人

(11). Ishii Takeo　　　　　　　　石井剛男

(12). Minako Masao　　　　　　　湊正雄

(13). Tetsuo Horikchu　　　　　　堀口鐵夫

(14). 1'st Liutenent Aushke Hikaryama　　景山

各部長支部長出張所所長記念寫眞
昭和拾八年拾二月三日

前排自左至右：	永山太郎	診療部長	Naga Yama
	石光重	調查課長	Ibusu Ishimitsu
	菊地範滿	第一部隊隊長	Hitoshi Kikuchi
	大谷章一	資材部部長	Syoichi Ootani
	北野政次	部隊長	Masaji Kitano
	安東洪次	所長（大連研究所）	Koji Anto
	太田澄	總務部部長	Ota Kiyoshi
	園田太郎	教育部部長	Taro Sonoda
中排，左第一人	田部井和		Iwa Tabe
後排中央	伊地知後雄	經理課長	Sugureo Ichiji

287

eyoshi TAKEDA. 竹田宮恆德親王。

Prince Tsuneyoshi Takeda

「満州516部隊」の本部は、赤レンガ造りだった――写真は
昭和17年、同本部前でのある部隊の軍人、軍属たちの記念撮影

第七三一部隊が建立した「東鄉神社」前での隊員

1943 group photo at Pingfan of General Yoshimi Haruo, Commander
of the Kwantung Army, and his top commanders
梅津美治郎（關東軍司令）視察平房（中座者）１９４３

Ishii and his family in 1938. In the back row, left to right: the brother
Takeo, Mitsuo and Shiro.
1938 年石井一家：後行左起老二剛男，老三三男，及石井四郎

Takeo Ishii, His family at Harbin Station . Man at
the left is Takeo Ishii, an older brother of Shiro Ishii.
He was responsible for the management of specially
constructed prison.

石井剛男和家人在哈爾濱車站前，石井剛男（左
邊）是石井四郎的大哥，負責特設監獄。

1942～44年までの間に撮影されたものと考えられる。前列中央の
軍人が第七三一部隊を "訪問" した際の記念写真であろう。

Officers of Education Dep.
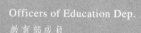
教育部成員

Major Gen. Kitano (sitting in the Middle)

北野正次少將（中坐者）

Ishii with his supporters(1942)
石井及其支持者

This is Sasada Osamu (a Lieutenant Colonel), who had been transferred from "Unit 731" to be the chief of the germ research section of "Unit1855".
從七三一部隊調至"第一八五五部隊"任細菌研究課課長的彼田統（中佐）。

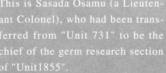

This is Endo Kazuo, (Major General), when he was promoted the vice Chief of Staff of Kwantung Army.
晋升爲關東軍副參謀長的遠藤三郎（少將）。

近野孝男

Okamoto as director of Kinki University, Osaka

大阪近畿大學主任岡本耕造

Gouji Satou

佐藤後二

Magor karasawa Tomio

柄澤十三支

The former members of "Unit 731".

原 "七三一部隊" 隊員

The former members of the Transportation Detachment of "Unit 731".

原 "七三一部隊" 運輸班的隊員

Yoshimura

京都帝大衛生學教授吉村

Tanaka Hideo the flea expert
跳蚤專家田中日夫

Yagisawa, the plant expert
植物學家八木澤行正

Hideki Tojo
東條英機

Naito
石井的親密助手內藤中校成
功的欺騙了美國調查人員

293

Geremony to initiate the Togo
Temple (Togo is the former name
of Unit 731).
731 部隊東鄉神社落成典禮

Yoshiyasa Masuda (center of
front) with his polits
增田美保（前排中立者）和
其他"731 部隊"飛行員

This is the group photo of the performers
after the performance of the stage play "God
of War" which was to worship Ishii Shiro.
七三一部隊拍演崇拜石井四郎話劇《軍
神》後，演員合影。

1939 group photograph of Unit 731's leading scientists taken at a banquet in Harbin.
1939 年在 731 部隊的科學家在哈爾濱留影

Nakatome (Crouching in the middle), Head of Unit 731's G. Affairs Department.
"七三一部隊" 總務部長中留（中間蹲者的）（１９４０）

The member of Investigation Section
調查科成員

Youthful recruits serving in Unit 731.(Y.T.)
731部隊的少年隊員

Section 2
The list of Japanese germ warfare criminals

How many persons take part in Japanese germ warfare ?

No one knows it ,they are too secrets and too many to enumerate, it is a riddle until today.

Japanese famous author Eugu Etsjii Etsuko counted out epidemic prevention and water supply units of Japanese Army system had 10,045 persons, it's not included obviously as following as:

1).Germ research organizations of school, such as The Japanese Medical School of Army Surgeons;

2).Leadship, scheme departments of germ warfare such as The Kwantung Army Command Department, The General Chief of Staff of Japanese Army, The Nobe Research Institute;

3).Manufactorys of biological weapons, as bolloon bombs for American homeland;

4).A lot of medical men and surgeons made human experiments and dissections except the epidemic prevention and water supply units of Japanese Army, such as cuptured Allied U.S.pilots were sent to Kyushu Uni. for live human dissection experiments, the Luan Army Hospital's dotors made in vivisection;

5).Germ weapon research organizations of Japanese Navy;

6).The army units for put in to effect of germ attacking, ad 15th D., 59th D.

7).Supported and transfered "Logs" organizations, for example: Special Military Agency in Harbin;

8).Culture organization of rats for plague and bacterias, for instance: The "Unit 2646" locatid in Manchuria, the Xinhuayan in Jinan, Shandong.

Have collected 1,400 names of criminals of germ warfare in this article.

第二節
日本細菌犯罪者名單

日本從事細菌戰的人員有多少？至今是謎。

日本作家藤井志津枝指出日本陸軍各級防疫給水部隊的人員有10，045人，這顯然未包括：

1） 細菌研究機構，如：陸軍軍醫學院實驗室、東大、京大、慶大、滿州醫大、大陸科學院以及一些研究所；

2） 領導、策劃細菌戰的部門，如：天皇中樞、東京大本營、陸軍參謀本部、關東軍司今部；

3） 制造細菌武器的工廠，如攻擊美國的氣球彈制造廠；

4） 陸軍防疫供水部系統外日本醫務人員中進行活體試驗和活體解剖的醫生，如九州大學解剖美國飛行員，在華各陸軍醫院、醫生解剖中國平民；

5） 為活體試驗和活體解剖服務的單位（憲兵、警察、戰俘所等）；

6） 具體實施細菌戰的陸軍作戰部隊，如十五師團、五十九師團、航空隊；

7） 海軍的細菌戰研究系統；

8） 培養、繁殖老鼠的部門和部隊，如孫吳以北的"二六四六部隊"、"日本養鼠社"、濟南"新華院"。本書共收集到參與犯罪的一千四百名名單。

The list of B.W. Criminals

日本細菌罪犯者名單

"Unit 731" ("七三一部隊")

Japanese name 日文姓名	English Name 英文譯音	Crimes 罪行
中留金藏	Kanakura Nakadome	The second term leader of Gerneral Affairs Department, Colonel.
中山安	Yasushi Nakayama	Member of Y.T.(Youth Team)
中山正	Tatashi Nakayama	Member of Y.T.
中遲	Nakaosore	Member of Y.T.
中山德	Megumi Nakayama	Member of Y.T.
中林	Nakabayashi	Member of Y.T.
山本清	Kiyoshi Yamamoto	Member of Y.T.
山野内佑次郎	Tasukejiro Yamanouchi	Virus research
山下升	Noboru Yamashita	Leader of platoon, sergeant.
山口一孝	Yamaguchi	Germ culturing, Second Lieutenant.
山下健次	Kenji Yamashita	The second leader of Personal Affairs Department, Major.
山本吉郎	Yoshiro Yamamoto	Saff, Lieutenant Colonel
山影	Yamakage	Warehouse member
山川升	Noboru Yamakawa	The 1' st. Department laboratory, technician
山口吾一	Wareichi Yamaguchi	Germ bomb research team leader, Lieutenant Colonel
山形風二	Kazeji Yamagata	Captain
山内中茂	Nakashige Yamauchi	Lieutenant Colonel
山田豊紀	Toyonori Yamada	The 4th Department, high grade officer
山下	Yamashita	Member of Y.T.
山谷	Yamatani	Sergeant, attended Zhejiang germ attack
山田利和	Toshikazu Yamada	Germ research
山中多重	Tatami Yamanaka	Artificer
山本佑	Tasukeru Yamamoto	Member of Y.T.
山崎	Yamasaki	Member of Y.T.
三谷恒夫	Tsuneo Mitsutani	Squad leader of arid germ, Major
三友數夫	Kazuo Mitomo	Anthrax research
三根生太郎	Kyota Minai	Mudanjiang Detach. employee
山田正	Tatashi Yamada	Mudangjiang Detach. leader of the 3rd Department.
中村	Nakamura	Linkou Detach. laboratory control
佐賀井	Sagai	Sunwu Detach. leader of mouse team
細禾	Hosoama	Linkou Detach. leader of the 1st Office, Major
小山	Koyama	Linkou Detach. sergeant
田中村	Tanakamura	Sunwu Decach. control laboratory director
加藤恒則	Tsunenori Katou	Hailar Detach. leader major
神尾	Kano	Linkou Detach. member
細尾	Hosoo	Linkou Detach. Lieutenant Colonel
官澧	Miyayutaka	Linkou Dctach.,sergeant
山口省一	Syoichi Yamaguchi	Linkou Deta. leader, Colonel
小島三郎	Saburo Kojima	Dysentery bacterium research
小上正男	Tatao Okami	Bacterium culturing
小林信	Yuki Kobayashi	The 4th Department artificer
小上	Okami	Head of Personal Affairs Office Major
小畑	Kokemori	Education assistant
小林榮三	Ensan Kobayashi	Member, Second Lieutenant
小松	Komatsu	Garrison team, squad leader
小林松藏	Matsukura Kobayashi	Material squad, Second Lieutenant
小林智	Chie Kobayashi	The 4th Department, "mitsutani" germ squad
小原直	Naoru Ohara	Linkou Detach, director
小川透	Sukushi Kogawa	Linkou Detach, germ research

Japanese name 日文姓名	English Name 英文譯音	Crimes 罪行
小林喜作	Yoshisaku Kobayashi	Ishii's adjutant
小出	Ode	Maggot bomb, Lieutenant Colonel
小野武次	Takeji Ono	Member
小幡石雄	Ishio Ohata	The team of "cherry blossom night" attack plan for U.S
山下	Yamashita	Photographer
大山	Oyama	Plague attack of Longan
石田	Ishida	Plague attack of Longan
杉木	Sugimoto	Plague attack of Longan
小林	Kobayashi	Instructor
小倉勇治	Youji Okura	General affairs
小山	Koyama	Jail garrison
小川	Kogawa	Member of Y.T.
小口	Okuchi	Member of Y.T.
小板	Koita	Member of Y.T.
小林茂	Tadashi kobayashi	Member of Y.T.
小林勇	Isamu kobayashi	Member of Y.T.
小池	Koike	Member of Y.T.
小田	Koda	Member of Y.T.
小林	Kobayashi	Corporal.
西山	Nishiyama	Mudanjiang Detach, first class private
西俊英	Toshihide Nishi	Leader of Education Department, Col.
西郡	Hikotsugu Nishigori	Director of treatment, Major
西尾	Nishio	Overseer
西尾數正行	Shikitatayuki Nishio	Linkou Detach, director
西原	Nishihara	Member of Y.T.
太田澄	Kiyoshi Ota	Head of General Affairs Department, Col
太谷	Futotani	Head of Treatment Department, Major General
太田正夫	Tatao Futoda	The 4th Department, artificer
生田	Namada	Member of Y.T.
手塚	Tetsuka	Member of Y.T.
西澤	Nishizawa	Squad leader of Y.T.
白臼	Shirausu	Member, first Lieutenant
長谷川	Nagasegawa	Instructor
長房	Nagabusa	Instructor
北野政次	Masaji kitano	Second unit leader, Lieutenant General
北野丹了	Niwaru Kitano	Member
北川	Kitakawa	Leader of Specialty Department, Col.
長治	Nagaji	Member of Y.T.
長野昭	Akashi Nagano	Member of Y.T.
安藤小三	Koji Antou	Dalian vaccine Farm, leader
安東清	Kiyoshi Ando	Member, 2'nd Lieutenant
安藤山	Yama Antou	Employee
吉田政	Matsuri Yoshida	Member of Y.T.
吉田太	Yama antou Futoru Yoshida	Member of Y.T.
吉田博	Hiroshi Yoshida	Member of Y.T.
古川	Yoshikawa	Member of Y.T.
吉本	Yoshimoto	Member of Y.T.
今野信次	Imano	Member of the fourth Dep.
無野勇	Shinji Amano	Member, first Lieutenant
天辰良道	Yoshimichi Amatatsu	Pathology section, Lieutenant Col.
立川	Tachikawa	Member of Y.T.
笠松	Kasamatsu	Member of Y.T.
	Yoshihiro Unada	Member of Y.T.
田文男	Fumio Michi	Director, leader of vivisection section
田部數	Kazoe Tabe	Typhoid bacillus research

Japanese name 日文姓名	English Name 英文譯音	Crimes 罪行
田中秀夫	Hideo Tanaka	Lieutenant Colonel
田部井和	Kazu Tabei	Head of the first Department, Lieutenant Col.
久島	Hisatome,jima	Linkou, I'st. part of germ room
田宮糾夫	Tokeo Tamiya	Special agent
田中	Tanaka	Overseer
臺田嘉廣	Yoshihiro Tamichi	Linkon, detach. sergeant
吉田	Yoshide	I'st. Lt., attended Changchum's plague
田邊邦男	Kunio Tabe	Education Department team leader, Lieutenant Colonel
	Michi Toyohiro	4th Department, germ study
田野	Tano	Member of Y.T.
石井虎雄	Torao Ishii	Special task class, squad leader
石鳥	Sekitor	Member
石川立尾丸	Tachiomaru Ishikawa	Germ study prof.
石田直孝	Naotsuka Ishida	Starving experiment program leader.
石丸高夫	Takao Ishimaru	Germ dare-to -die corps member
石光熏	Ibusu Ishimitsu	The Second Survey Department leader, Colonel
石井剛男	Takao Ishii	Jail header
吉都良雄	Yoshio kotou	Medical worker
石井三男	Mitsuo Ishii	Animal team squad leader
石井恒久	Tsunehisa Ishii	The fourth Department employee
石川昭	Akashi Ishikawa	Member of Y.T.
石原	Ishihara	Member of Y.T.
砂場	Sunaba	Member of Y.T.
砂田	Sunamichi	Member of Y.T.
石井正雄	Tadaro Ishii	Boiler room
井上	Inoue	Squad leader of Y.T.
正山勝	Katsu Masayama	Member
千葉	Chiba	Engineer
岡本耕造	Kozo Okamoto	Dr. make live vivisection (99 persons) in Hailar
岡本光三	Mitsusan Okamoto	Member
岡田秋夫	Akio Okada	Engineer
久留美澤球	Kwrumizawa	Vivisection assistant
久野寧	Yasuraka Hisano	Member
久保田	Kuboda	Instructor
官田井部	Heyai Tsukada	Vivisection assistant 1'st D.
官本光一	Kouichi Miyamoto	2'nd D.
官崎淳臣	Junsei Miyasaki	1'st D. experiment leader, 1'st lieutenant
官一	Miyaichi	Member of Y.T.
官島	Miyashima	Member of Y.T.
官崎	Miyasaki	Member of Y.T.
宇津美	Utsumi	Special of bacteriologist
宇野誠	Makoto Uno	1'st D. engineer
宇佐見	Usami	Member of Y.T.
富塚	Tomitsuka	Anda expriment safekeeping
大熊	Ookuma	Suanwu detach, boiler management
大滝	Ootake	Instructor
大屋	Ooya	Instructor
大馬	Ooba	Member of Y.T.
市川	Ichikawa	Member of Y.T.
平林	Hirabayashi	Member of Y.T.
平山官一	Miyaichi Hirayama	General affairs
平山廣三	Hirosabu Hirayama	General affairs
平山源山	Gensan Hirayama	General affairs

Japanese name 日文姓名	English Name 英文譯音	Crimes 罪行
衝山	Okiyama	Mudanjiang Detach. squad leader
衝崎	Okisaki	Mudanjiang Detach. flea culturing
片岡澧潔	Kataoka	Member of Y.T.
江島信平	Shinpei Ejima	Dysentery germ team, squad leader
江口江	Toyoketsu Eguchi	Third Department, Lieutenant Col.
江村寬二	Hiroji Emura	Sergeant, Linkou
江田武一	Takeichi Eda	Statistician, squad leader
從以内海	Uchimi Shitai	Specialist, reseach about white race's immunity in 1943 on Inner Mogolia
河合美人	Miuto kawaai	4th Dep, mitsutani team. employee
江崎	Ezaki	Member of Y.T.
須永	Sunaga	Member of Y.T.
濃野	Koino	Member of Y.T.
瀬戸口	Sedoguchi	Member of Y.T.
河山善	Yoshiki Kawayama	Pathologist
河島三德	Kawashima	Drug department, Lt. Col.
河野	Kawano	Animal team squad leader
海内	Umichi	Specilist of plague prof.
浦山	Urayama	Member of Y.T.
渡邊道	Michiru Wadanabe	Specialist, Major
渡邊誠	Makoto Wadanabe	Linkou Detach. first lieutenant
渡喜一	Yoshiichi Wadaru	The fourth Department
渡邊榮	Sakae Wadanabe	The fourth Department, "Arida" team
渡邊龍三	Ryusan Wadanabe	The fourth Department, medical survey room, Lt.
渡邊照	Terashi Wadanabe	Member of Y.T.
油利	Yuri	Member of special task team
須田明	Akashi Suda	Mudanjiang Detach. member
津山義文	Tatafumi Suyama	Disinfection
津野謙次	Kemji Kyono	Specialist, professor of Kyoto University
	Naiji Waku	Germ warfare liaison man of shanghai
湊正雄	Tatao Minato	Specialist
淺沼清	Kiyoshi Asanao	Specialist
濱田豐博	Toyohiro Hamada	Specialist
濱崎水雄	Mizuo Hamasaki	Sergeant
池田齋	Monoimi Ikeda	Leader of specialized profession, Major General
池田	Ikeda	Imployee
溝淵	Misofuchi	Linkou, Squad leader
酒井三千助	Michisuke Sakai	Military Police, squad leader
酒井亭三	Yadomi Sakai	Head of general affairs, Captain
金城五郎	Itsuro Kiniyo	Specialist
金子澤一	Junichi Kameko	Specialist, Major
金田康志	Yasushi kanada	Member of Y.T.
金澤謙一	Kenichi Kanazawa	Germ research
金子	Kanako	Shengwu Detach. labour manager
金澤一久	Hitomasa kanazawa	Shengwu Detach. the second department leader captain
金田	Kanada	Leader of Education Department, first Lieutenant
金田	Kanada	Member of Y.T.
金尾	Kanao	Member of Y.T.
金谷	Kanatani	Member of Y.T.
金井章次	Syoji Kanai	Dalian laboratory, first chief
鈴木啓之	Herayuki Suzuki	The second production Droup, Major
鈴木重夫	Shigeo Suzuki	The third Department, sintering team
鈴柱	Suzukashira	Member
鈴木	Suzuki	Flea culture
鈴木春善	Harufusa Suzuki	Copyist
鈴江	Suzue	Member of Y.T.

Japanese name 日文姓名	English Name 英文譯音	Crimes 罪行
鈴木鬱	Kaguwashi Suzuki	Member of Y.T.
鈴木保	Mamoru Suzuki	Member of Y.T.
増田美保	Yoshiyasu Masuda	Air second class squad leader, Major
増田	Masuda	Transportation team truck, driver
鈴木春一	Shunichi Niizuma	Member
岩崎	Iwasaki	The first Department member
岩澤	Iwazawa	Member of Y.T.
堀田正夫	Masao Horikuchi	Germ missile, engineer
堀田錬一郎	Ryoichiro Horida	Hailar Detach.
堀口鐵夫	Tetsuo Horikuchi	Member
堀内	Horiuchi	Instractor
坂井金	Kane Sakai	Squad leader of transportation, first Lieutenant
崎藤	Sakifuji	Member of Y.T.
碇常重	Tsuneshige Ikari	Colonel, Mukden American POW, experiment manager
島田精	Kuwashii Shimada	Member of Y.T.
島田岩	Iwashi Shimada	Member of Y.T.
野合文彦	Fumihiko Noai	Member
野口圭一	Kadoichi Noguchi	The fourth Department
野澤	Nozawa	Member of Y.T.
野澤幸雄	Yoshio Nosaki	Ishii's assistant
辰已	Tokimi	Ishii's assistant
木村	Kimura	Warrant officer
木村	Kimura	Member of Y.T.
松木	Matsuki	Member of Y.T.
松岡	Matsuoka	Member of Y.T.
松井寛治	Hiroji Matsui	"Shinoda" team, second-class private
松平	Matsuhira	Sunwu Detach. leader
植樹肇	Hajime Uemura	The fourth Department researcher
橋本一男	Ichiro Hashimoto	Attended Zhejiang germ attack
桜井三	San Sakuri	Member of Y.T.
桜井富	Tomishi Sakurai	Member of Y.T.
桜山辰	Tatsu Sakurayama	Member of Y.T.
根津尚元	Takamoto Netsu	The second Department member
村尾	Murao	Attended Zhejiang germ attack
村上隆	Takashi Murakami	The second Department leader, Lieutenant Colonel
村上勇夫	Tatao Murakami	Member of the first Department, first Lieutenant, attended Zhejiang
村上仁勇	Hitosamu Murakami	First Lieutenant
杉原	Sugihara	Squad leader of Y.T.
柳澤謙	Herikuda Yanagizawa	Specialist
柳澤富男	Tomio Yanagizawa	Leader of specialized profession, Captain
柳澤吉政	Yoshinori Yanagizawa	Specialist
柳瀬	Yanagise	Pilot, Captain
桂島長次郎	Nagajiro Katsurashima	Member of Zhejiang germ attack team, employee
桂重喜	Shigeyoshi Katsura	Organizer
相馬	Aiba	Sergeant
森岡	Morioka	Medical worker
森川	Morikawa	Member of special attack team
森大清	Kiyoshi Morishita	The fourth Department, germ research
森下幹	Miki Morishita	Member of Y.T.
森田	Morida	Member of Y.T.
森下正	Masashi Morishita	Member of Y.T.
楊廬木	Ioriki Yanagi	Member of Y.T.
樋渡森	Mori Hiwada	Military office
柏熊富三	Tomisan Kashiwakuma	Gerneral affairs

Japanese name 日文姓名	English Name 英文譯音	Crimes 罪行
森	Mori	Linkou Detach.sergeant
作山之治	Motonao Tsukuyama	Major, leader of Nomanhan
依地治俊雄	Nochio Ijinao	Gerneral Affirs Department, business part leader
七夕利則	Toshinori Hatataba	Linkou Detach, sergeant
飯田奈良	Nara iida	Attended Zhejiang-Jiangxi Line germ attack, Major
佐藤	Satou	Head of military supplies branch, Major
佐久三	Motoharu Sakugama	Specialist, Lt-Col.
佐藤俊二	Gouji Satou	Major general, manager in vivisection
佐藤實	Minoru Satou	Instructor, Captain
佐田	Sada	Military Police, warrant officer
佐佐木孝義	Yoshitaka Sasaki	Leader of Shengwu Detach. Lt-Col.
佐川	Sagawa	Artificer
佐藤儀	Nori Satou	Member of Y.T.
佐佐木	Sasaki	Member of Y.T.
佐藤義	Tadashi Satou	Member of Y.T.
佐藤秀	Hideshi Satou	Member of Y.T.
佐久間	Sakuma	Gerneral affairs
伊東新平	Niikira Itou	Probation engineer
伊藤	Itou	Engineer
伊澤	Izawa	Member of the second warehouse
條原	Sujihara	Leader of Gerneral Affirs Department, Captain
保坂	Tamosaka	Member of Y.T.
後藤	Goutou	Member of Y.T.
固井田登	Michinobory Katai	Member
園田太郎	Taro Sonoda	Specalist Col.
園田忠男	Tatao Sonoda	The 2'nd Department, Lieutenant, Zhejiang attacking
政邦	Matsurikuni	The fourth department, attended Nomanhan attacking
粟原	Awahara	Medicine worker
奥村	Okumura	The 3'nd Department Ll . Col.
奥富克二	Katsuji Okutomi	4th D., Nomanhan attacking
前川	Maekawa	Member of Y.T.
前川富治	Tomiji Maekawa	4th Dep., sergeant
賴戸川	Sedokawa	Specialist, Major
降旗	Orihata	Specialist, Major
影山	Kageyama	Mudanjiang Deta. G. Affairs Dep. Leader
速中	Hayanaka	Education assistant
近兼	Chikakane	Member of Y.T.
近倉	Chikakura	The first Department, Major
蓬田三平	Yomogimichi Mihira	Garrison commander, Captain
闕德間	Tokuma kaku	Member
間所登	Noboru Madokoro	Linkou Detach. leader
內藤	Naitou	Member of Y.T.
瓜生榮二	Eiji Urii	Attended vivisection
瓜生貞子	Tatako Urii	Telephone operator
管	Kuda	Linkou, Sergeant
青柳雄	Otoko Aoyanagi	Cook team
尾上正男	Tatao Onoue	Mudanjiang Detach, leader, Major
成田飯治	Iinao Narida	Member
肥野藤	Fuji Koeno	Specialist of pathology, Major
筧	Kasai	Specialist of pathology
君島	Kimishima	Specialist of pathology, Lieutenant Col.
內藤良雄	Ryoichi Naito	Ishii's assistant
	Okutani Tani	Member of Y.T.
谷澤	Tanizawa	Member of Y.T.

Japanese name 日文姓名	English Name 英文譯音	Crimes 罪行
并木	Kasaki	Instraction
乾	Kawaku	Squad leader of Y.T.
朝日向	Mukai Asahi	Insect research
朝比奈正三郎	Asahina Syojiro	Squad leader of eruptive-typhoid bacillus geam
福森	Fukumori	Ishii's Supporter
福富秀夫	Hideo Futaki	Specialist
福利覺藏	Kakukura Fukutoshi	Member of the first warehouse
福田	Fukuda	Member of the second warehouse
福井	Fukui	Member of Y.T.
福松	Fukumatsu	Member of Y.T.
秋元壽惠夫	Sueo Akimoto	Artificer
秋葉	Akiba	Artificer, Captain
秋本未夫	Sueo Akimoto	Specialist
秋元熏	Ibusu Ogihara	Cook team
秋原三雄	Mitsuo Ogihara	Pesticide team
羽振一良	Hitoyoshi Haneburi	Member
高木	Takagi	Instractor
高階	Takahashi	Squad leader
高橋正彦	Masahiko Takahashi	Gerneral Affairs Department, Major
高橋正廣	Masahiro Takahashi	First Lieutenant
高木	Takagi	Member of Y.T.
高味	Takaaji	Member of Y.T.
細谷省吾	Syogo Hosotani	Specialist of gas carbuncle
細昭清一	Seiichi Hosoaki	The fourth Department "shower" team
細田剛男	Takao Hosoda	Special team
細夭	Hosoya	Squad leader, member of Y.T.
細夭博	Hiroshi Hosoya	The fourth Department, first Lieutenant
細川	Hosokawa	Member of Y.T.
細井	Hosoi	Employer
有木	Ariki	Instractor
有田正義	Seigi Arida	Specialist, Major
廣田	Hiroda	Member of Y.T.
越川	Koshikawa	Member of Y.T.
常世田	Michi Tokiyo	Member of Y.T.
和田	Wada	Member of Y.T.
鵜飼	Ukai	Member of Y.T.
武田	Takeda	Member of Y.T. squad leader
兒島	Kojima	Member of Y.T.
荒瀬清一	Seiichi Arase	Linkou Deta. leader, Major
芳金	Kanbakana	Member of Y.T.
藤原	Fujihara	Head of Gerneral Affairs Department
藤井信	Nobura Fujii	Member of Y.T.
齋藤正輝	Masahikari Saitou	Specialist
齋藤	Saitou	Member of Y.T.
齋藤春吉	Haruyoshi Saitou	Gerneral affairs
早川清	Kiyoshi Hayakawa	Specialist
外間所	Tokoro Hazuma	Vivisection place, Second Lieutenant
齋藤通	Tsujiru Saitou	Gerneral affairs
春日中一	Nakaichi Hasuka	Military Police team, Translater officer
卧慶千守	Sensyu Fusuyuka	Military Police team leader
倉原一吾	Ichiware kurahara	Special transportation, Military Police squad leader
倉内喜久雄	Uchikisaro Kurauchi	Dalian laboratory second air department
林一郎	Ichiro Hayashi	Artificer

Japanese name 日文姓名	English Name 英文譯音	Crimes 罪行
居池	Sumiike	Overseer
德水	Tokumizu	Overseer
倉上正博	Masahiro Kurakami	The fourth Department, attended Nomanhan attacking
熊尾	Kumao	Mudanjiang Detach.leader of supply department
熊谷	Kumatani	Squad leader of Y.T.
熊本一男	Ichiro Kumamoto	Corporal
黑澤	Kurizawa	Specialist, Major
黑川	Kurokawa	First Lieutenant
神日重啓	Niiyoshi Kami	Member of Y.T.
神崎知	Satoru Kamisaki	The fourth Department, non-germ room, Captain
神谷	Kamitani	Member of Y.T.
春日忠善	Takayoshi Hasuka	Dalian laboratory specialist of bronchocephalitis
出倉	Dekura	Member of Y.T.
東城政雄	Norio Toujyo	Member
鶴田兼敏	Kasatoshi Tsuruda	Member of Y.T.(flea)
群司陽子	Youko Gunji	Raiser
美馬孝義	Kougi Miba	The fourth Department, attended Nomanhan attacking
愛智	Aichi	Mudanjiang Detach. medical worker
真子憲治	Kenji Majime	Dalian laboratory, specialist of blood serum
屋上	Yanoue	Mudanjiang Detach. eader, Major
貞政	Matsuri Tadashi	Member of Y.T.
關根隆	Takashi Sekine	Ceramics team
關取	Sekitori	Assassination skill
關岡	Sekioka	Labour affairs team director
多井	Ooi	Likou Detach garage
磯村	Isomura	Member of Y.T.
永野	Nagano	Member of Y.T.
日好	Michiyoshi	Member of Y.T.
設樂	Moukeraku	Member of Y.T.
妹尾左知丸	Sachimaru Imoo	Member
所安夫	Yasuro tokoro	Specialist
翼司	Tsubaji	The first Department
雨海惠	Meguru Futaumi	The first Department
國行昌瀨	Sakase Kuniyuki	The first Department
賓亮户	Akido Maroi	The first Department
德久知正	Noritada Tokuhisa	Member
重富廣一	Hiroichi Shigetomi	Member
肥田中信	Nakanobu koeda	The fourth Department, attended Nomanhan attacking
肥之藤俊二	Nobusan Koenofuji	Specialist of bacillus, Major
竹田宮	Miya Takeda	As Prince Tsuneyoshi Takeda was the representative of kwantung Army in "Unit 731"
久留島	Shima Kurumi	Linkou Detach. the first germ room
確恒成	Tsunenari Tashika	Nomanhan germ attacking commander, Major
日野富士	Nobakazu Hinofuji	Lt-Col.
草味正夫	Masao kusami	Pharmacology squad
古市	Yoshimura	Hisato Yoshimura's assistant
倉門	Satoru Kurakazu	M.P.
新妻誠一	Seiichi Suzuki	Ishii's helper
濱武正喜	Masayoshi Hamatake	Biological Dep.
小館美實	Mura Ogi	General Affaies Dep.
白井竹次郎	Takejiro Usui	General Affaies Dep.
新井	Niii	General Affaies Dep.
永松橋	Hashi Nagamatsu	General Affaies Dep.
小山博	Hiroshi Komichi	General Affaies Dep.

Japanese name 日文姓名	English Name 英文譯音	Crimes 罪行
在田勉	Tsutome Arida	General Affaies Dep.
吉田源二	Genji Yoshida	I'st. Dep.
官川正	Tadashi Miyagawa	I'st. Dep.
粟秋要	Kaname Awuaki	I'st. Dep.
石井利夫	Toshio Ishii	I'st. Dep.
松尾光	Hikari Matsuo	2'nd Dep.
山田二郎	Jiro Yamada	2'nd Dep.
小原定夫	Sameo Kohara	2'nd Dep.
河上清久	Kiyohisa Kawakami	Mudanjiang Detach.
竹田源藏	Genzo Takeuchi	Mudanjiang Detach.
神久賴久	Tayohisa Kamio	Mudanjiang Detach.
浦部倉次	Kuraji Urabe	Hailar Detach.
伊藤嘉明	Yoshiaki Itow	Hailar Detach.
松浦茂輝	Shigeak Matuura	Hailar Detach.
瀨越健一	Keuichi Sekoshi	Hailar Detach.
岡本良三	Yoshisan Okamoto	Dalian laboratory
池井貞夫	Norio Ikei	Mudanjiang Detack.
清水富士夫	Fujio Shimezu	Hailar Detach.
小關重雄	Shigeo Koseki	4th Dep, employee
表已	Omateore	Captain, Nomanhan attacking
宇田	Uda	member
項藤良雄	Yoshio Sufuji	Plague team
青柳	Aoyanagi	Constructor
井上	Inoue	Animal room
增田義惠	Yoshiichiro Hashigi	Major, airpilot
利本	Norimoto	Employee
今津綱幹	Tsunamiki Imatsu	Genesal Affairs Dep. chief
早川正敏	Tatatoshi Hayakawa	2'nd Dep. chief
今瀨一夫	Ichiro Imase	3'rd Dep. chief
柴野金吾	Kanaware shibano	Logistics Dep. chief
乙津一彦	Hitohiko Utsu	M.P. I'st leader
田坂千晴	Chiyhare Tazaka	M.P. 2'nd leader
青木廣市	Hiroichi Aogi	Adjutant
田野口	Tanaguchi	Attended experiment for P.O.Ws in Mukden
滌原岩助	Iwasuke sujihara	Attended experiment for P.O.Ws in Mukden
鈴木竜男	Akio Suzuhi	Attended experiment for P.O.Ws in Mukden
中村留八	Tomeya Nakamura	Management section
小滵秀雄	Ibusu Uchimi	I'st Dep.
樋渡喜	Akio takarain	I'st Dep.
阿部德光	Isamu Yobumoto	Education Dep.
西田重衛	Akiichi Nakada	Education Dep.
中田秋市	Hajime Vemura3'rd	3'rd Dep.
藪本勇	Kazukachi Saitou	3'rd Dep.
齊藤和勝	Hironao Ogihara	3'rd Dep.
秋原博治	Sueo	Logistics Dep.
藤井英太郎	Hidetaro Fujii	Hailar Detach, 1'st leader
藤田正二	Syoji Fujimiche	Hailar Detachb 2'nd leader
木佐貫木雄	Tsurukio Kisa	1'st Dep. sergeant
平澤正欣	Shigee Nishida	2'nd Dep. airpilot, Major
景山杏佑	Ausuke Hikariyama	Adjutant room
高橋賈	Takashi Takahashi	Logiatics Dep.
柄澤十三夫	Akeyuki Suzuki	4'th Dep.
蓮見	Hasumi	"Unit Togo"
關島	Sekitori	Prof.

Japanese name 日文姓名	English Name 英文譯音	Crimes 罪行
村上高士	Takashi Murakami	Lt. Col.
安東洪次	Kouji Anto	Dalian Laboratory leader, Major Gen.
藤野恒三郎	Tsunesaburo Kanazawa	Prof.
池田苗夫	Naeo Ikeda	Prof.
北條遠良	Enryo Hoji	Stayed in shanghai 1937
安藤浩二	Koji Ardo	Member
柄澤富男	Tomio Karasawa	Member
島崎	Shimasaki	Hailar
松村	Mat Sumura	Member
越貞夫	Koshi Norio	Ishii's car driver
戸口	Toguchi	Employee
奥寺	Okutera	Employee
玉井	Tamai	Zhejiang Jiangx Line germ attacking
金井	Kanei	Member
島田	Shimada	Personal section
大木啓吾	Akeware Ooge	Major
細島	Hososhima	I'st Lt.
島田恒二	Tsumji Shimada	Prof. made experimentr for U.S. POWs of Mukden
吉村壽人	Yoshimura Hisato	Ishii's helper
安達	Anta	Inspected Beiyinhe in 1933, Colonel
立花	Tachibana	Inspected Beiyinhe in 1933, Lieutenant Colonel
濱田豐博	Toyohiro Hamada	Assistant of G. kitano
柏村	Kashimura	Changchun plague
天野昭二	Syoji Amano	
坂口弘	Hiroski Sakiguchi	
桜山裕曉	Hiroaki Urayama	
澆井	Asai	
野崎	Nosaki	
野田正彰	Noda Yoshiaki	The attacking of Zhejiang-Jiangxi(1942)
内藤良一	Naito Yoshichi	Ishii's helper
菊地範満	Hitoshi kikuchi	Ishii's assistant, Major Gen.
來鳩有次一	Yuji Koihata	Srevicer
永山太郎	Taro Nagayama	Leader of treatment, Col.
飯田堅	Katai Iida	General affairs department, director, Captain
佐佐木	Sasaki	Instructor, second Lieutenant
大谷章一	Syoichi Ootani	Equipment supplying department leader, Major General
田中兵枝	Tsuwanoeda Tanaka	A specialist of flea, Lieutenant Colonel
加藤加之	Kuwaeyuki Katou	First group material class, employee
内海薫	Utsumi Yoshiki	A specialist of bacteriology
四部	Yotsube	A specialist of bacteriology
近野壽男	Toshio Chikano	Colonel
一條	Hitosuji	Water pump control
二木秀夫	Hideo Futaki	The second leader of business. Col.
二木日出雄	Hideo Futagi	Member
八木澤正行	Yukimasa yagisawa	Plant study
三浦久	Hisashi Miura	Member of Y.T.
三浦昌	Sakan Miura	Member of Y.T.
三角	Mitsuno	Member of Y.T.
川島清	Kiyoshi Kawashima	Major Gerneral
川上漸	Yoyaku Kawakami	Head of survey department, pathological anatomy dissect,
川島三德	Zen Kawashima	Pathology, Captain
島正敏軍	Sebiku Kawashima	Nomanhan germ attacking team commander, Major
川名	Kawana	Artificer

Japanese name 日文姓名	English Name 英文譯音	Crimes 罪行
上田彌太郎	Watataro Kamida	The 4th dep. assistant
上田正村	Tataki Kamida	Germ research
上田正明	Tataaki Kamida	Germ research
上野	Ueno	Employee
工藤忠雄	Tataro Takumifuji	
工藤與四郎	Yoshiro Takumifuji	Labour service leader
中黑秀外之	Hidesodoyuki Nakakuro	"The self-defence forces satellite school", principal
中村道夫	Michio Nakamura	"shower class", employee
中入恒	Tsune Nakairi	Germ spreading
中野 Nakano	Captain	
中前秋雄	Akio Nakamae	The 4th dep. sergeant, Zhijiang germ attacking team
中村	Nakamura	Mudanjiang Detach. head of the first Dep.
凌	Shinoku	Take experiment in mukden P.O.W. camp
秋村	Ogimara	Logistics dep.
秋原博治	Hironuo ogionara	Logistics dep.
三根生清太	Kyota minei	Hailin deta. emplyee

"Unit 1855" ("一八五五部隊")

Japanese name 日文姓名	English Name 英文譯音	Crimes 罪行
野武夫	Takeo Yomano	Head of business department
三浦安一	Yasuichi Miura	The first germ production
小森源一	Genichi Komori	Head of medical quarantine department
小川吉榮	Yoshien Kogawa	First germ production room, assistant.
小田切政則	Seisoku kodakiri	First germ production room, assislant
小林太重	Yasushige kobayashi	3rd department
小林保	Yasushige Okubo	3rd department
小山清次郎	Kyojiro Koyama	Member
小添三郎	Saburo Kozoe	Germ room
西川兵長	Tsuwanage nishikawa	Member
西村祥三	Kyosan Nishimura	Treatment department, assistant
西原不二雄	Fujio Nishihara	Germ culture room
西村英二	Hideji Nishimura	Team leader
長瀬信行	Nobuyuki nagase	Special research dep.
長田龜磨	Kamegaki Nagada	Assistant
長崎七郎	Nanaro Nagasaki	Assistant
長島武治	Takeji Nagashima	The first germ production room, assistant
長田友吉	Tomoyoshi Nagada	Leader of medical worker
長木大三	Daisan Nagaki	Germ room
安藤	Antou	Jinan Detach. sergeant
吉村	Yoshimura	Jinan detach. director of manage room, first Lieutenant
吉田道雄	Michio yoshida	The first germ room, assistant
占田長之	Nagayuki yoshida	BCG vaccine room
吉種繁次郎	Shigejiro yoshitane	Germ room assistant
吉村博	Hirishi yoshimura	Antiepidemic class, Second Lieutenant
吉野文雄	Fumio Yoshino	The third department
吉村英二	Hideji Yoshimura	Colonel
吉野太郎	Taro yoshino	The third dep.
田口正治	Syoji Taguchi	The first germ production room, assistant
田治良一	Yoshiichi Michiji	Study assistant
田口義雄	Tadao Taguchi	Member
田友吉	Michi Tomoyoshi	Member
石渡秀男	Hideo Ishiwada	Pathology anatomy room
石塚義	Tadashi Ishitsuka	Personal affairs-achievement department leader, Captain

Japanese name 日文姓名	English Name 英文譯音	Crimes 罪行
石井正雄	Tadao ishi	Third department
石田和夫	Kazuo Ishida	Member
岡田和夫	Kazuo okada	Engineer
岡健	Sugoyada Oka	The first germ production room, assistant
岡孝元	Kougen Oka	Squad leader
岡田玉	Tamashi Okada	Leader of Jinan Detach, Captain
阿部磨	Migaki Abe	The second germ production room, first Lieutenant
馬場貞美	Tadami Baba	Blood serum room, assistant
定貴治	Naoru Sametaka	Antiepidemic & water offering room, first Lieutenant
宮崎佐市	Saji Miyasaki	Germ room
宮田宏	Hiroshi Miyada	Second germ production romm, assistant
寶田平八	Hiraya Michi	Epidemic disease room, assistant
大橋義雄	Tadashimakoto Oobashi	Blood serum room, Captain
大野高	Takashi Oono	First germ production room, assistant
大森清位	Seii Oomori	First germ production room, assistant
平野晟	Jyo Hirano	Germ department leader, Major
平川喜一	Kiichi Hirakawa	The third department
門多魁	Sakigake Tota	Germ room, Captain
片桐辛喜	Yoshiki Katakiri	Production room
河合誥	Tsugeru Kawaai	Third leader of the second department
河本一俊	Hitosugure Kawamoto	Medical examine dep, first Lieutenant
柳瀨	Yanaginose	Pilot of "unit 731", died on kunming when spreading bacteria in 1942
渡邊中重	Nakashige wadanabe	Head of general affairs department, Lieutenant Colone
油石愷生	Kai Aburamichi	Assistant
澤渡壽夫	Toshio Sawawada	Physico-chemical examination, 1'st Lt.
瀬越	Sekoshi	Germ production, Second Lieutenant
瀬戸川武	Takeshi Sedogawa	Leader of Nomanhan germ attack team, Major
清原龍	Tatsu Kiyohara	Antiepidemic & water offering room, Captain
淺川喜榮	Yoshie Asakawa	1'st germ production room
淺井願一	Genichi Asai	Blood serum room, assistant
池田重武	Shigetake Ikeda	The first germ production room, assistant
波邊鼎	Kanae Wadanabe	The first germ production room, assistant
金久保	Kubo kane	Jinan Detach. the second leader of the team, major
鈴木東吾	Toware Suzuki	The first germ production room, assistant
鈴木一	Hajime Suzuki	Jinan detach. medical team
鈴木	Suzuki	Jinan detach, director of accounting department, first Lieutenant
土田政治	Seiji Tsuchida	The first germ production room, assistant
岩瀬滋	Shigeshi Iwase	The second germ production room, assistant
岩瀬	Iwase	Jinan Detach. director of sterilization, first Lieutenant
寺田道雄	Terada Michio	The first germ production room, assistant
寺島升	Noboru Terashima	The first germ production room, assistant
野澤安太郎	Yasutaro Nozawa	Anatomy dissect room
木村稔	Mitsuru Kimura	Jinan platoon, Captain
林克巳	Katsuonore Hayashi	Ther first germ production room, assistant
村田英太郎	Hidetaro Murada	Leader of education team, Captain
村本壽夫	Toshio Muramoto	File department, assistant
柳田純孝	Junko Yanagida	File department, assistant
柳田	Yanagida	Jinan detach. the first leader of detach, Majoy
森登	Morinoboru	Production room
横田豊次	Toyoji Yokoda	The second germ production room, assistant
佐藤恒信	Naganobu Satou	Germ culture room, second Lieutenant
佐藤俊選	Gosen Satou	The first germ production room, warrant officer
伊田登	Ida Noboru	The third department
伊島正太郎	Syotaro Ishima	Physico-chemical examination room

Japanese name 日文姓名	English Name 英文譯音	Crimes 罪行
後藤正彦	Masahiko Goutou	Plan department leader, Major
儀右衛六	Ueroku Nori	The third department
近木英哉	Hidekana Chikaki	Flea production
遷井春雄	Haruo Sujii	Production room
間山哲男	Tetsuo Iyama	Anatomy dissect room
内田長松	Nagamatsu Uchida	Thr third department, flea culture
尾崎繁雄	Shigeo Osaki	Artificer
節杉茂次	Shigeji Fushisugi	Blood serum room
勝谷達三	Tatsumi Katsutani	Physico-chemical room, second Lieutenant
谷山直記	Naonori Taniyama	Examination room, assistant
谷藤直雄	Fujio Tanifuji	Member
稿木泰雄	Yasuo waragi	Head of treatment department
羽根由清谷	Yukiyoshi Hanene	The first germ production room, assistant
那須毅	Tsuyoi Hasu	Anatomy dissect room, Captain
男澤安太郎	Yasutaro Otokozawa	Anatomy dissect room
星清入	Kyoiri Hoshi	Medical survey room
飯森勤	Tsutome Limori	Department of treatment, assistant
飯田義治	Tatanao Iida	Department of treatment
飯塚茂	Shigemi Iitsuka	The second department
高橋平之助	Hiranotsuke Takahashi	The third department
高岡満	Michiro Takaoka	Special study room, Captain
高橋重治	Jyuji Takahashi	The third department
上田正臣	Masaomi Kamida	Leader of file department, Major
上杉	Kamisugi	Member, first Lieutenant
中山春吉	Haruyoshi Nakayama	Germ room
中溝保三	Tamomi Nakamiso	Tuberculosis room, first Lieutenant
中村長吉	Nagayoshi Nakamura	The 3rd department
中村三郎	Saburo Nakamura	Member
三郎	Saburo Yamazoe	Germ room
山崎長太郎	Nagataro Yamasaki	The 3rd dep.
川島實	Minoru Kawashima	The first germ production room, assistant
告見亨	Towaru Tsugemi	Leader of gerneral affairs department, Major
有島小誠	Arishima	Carbuncle room, assistant
時岡孝元	Tsukaemoto Tokioka	Squad leader
喜陽宗永	Munenaga Yoshihi	Cowpox virus room, assistant
兒玉寛	Hiroshi Odama	Education teamb assistant
荒木乾	Kawaku Araki	Tuberculosis room, first Lieutenant
荒井貞	Tadashi Aria	The second germ production room, assistant
藤代渡助	Wadasuke fujiyo	Examination room, assistant
齋藤力	Chikara Saitou	Jinan Detach, second team leader, Captain
倉内常太郎	Jyotaro Kurauchi	The first germ production room, assistant
黑江	Kuroe	The first leader of the army squad
黑岩	Kuroiwa	Antiepidemic team, first Lieutenant
黑川然	Shikari Kurogawa	Jinan Detach, director of laboratory, Captain
鹽谷雲	Kumori shiotani	Medical survey room
香川正雪	Masayuki Kaorigawa	Protozoosis room, first lieutenant
名取邦雄	Natori Kunio	The first germ room, assistant
神新吉	Niiyoshi Kami	The second germ room, assistant
志賀一雄	Ichiro Shiga	The first germ room, assistant
喂園國夫	Kunio Kaizono	Jiujiang branch
赤誠茂三	Shigemi Akasei	Head of the army, major
關荘	Sekimura	Thought measure team, sergeant
關崎繁夫	Shigeo Sekisaki	Office, Captain
關根健見	Kenmi Sekine	Treatment department, assistant

310

Japanese name 日文姓名	English Name 英文譯音	Crimes 罪行
良田邦治	Kuninao Yoshida	The first leader of the first department
夏林	Natsubayashi	The second leader of the first department
篠甲統	Suberu Shinoda	Leader of germ research department
矢野真澄	Masumi Yano	Protozoosis room, first Lieutenant
加藤一	Hajime Katou	Examine department, first Lieutenant
杉田壽年	Toshihira Sugida	Tiantang epidimec prevention office
杉田昭子	Fikiko Sugida	Tiantang epidimec prevention office
杉田奉子	Sasako Sugida	Tiantang epidimec prevention office
永淵勝子	Katsuko Nagafuji	Tiantang epidimec prevention office
岩谷義宏	Tatahiro Iwatani	Tiantang epidimec prevention office
三宮	Mitsunomiya	Tiantang epidimec prevention office, I'st Lt.

"Unit 1644" ("一六四四部隊")

Japanese name 日文姓名	English Name 英文譯音	Crimes 罪行
瀬戸	Sedo	Photography department, sergeant
中前秋夫	Akio Nakamae	"Nara army", sergeant
山崎新	Arata yamasaki	6th leader
山下	Yamashita	The first department, Major
山中	Yamanaka	Artificer, instructor
山之内忠	Takashi Yamanouchi	Head of materials department
小野寺秀雄	Hideo Onotera	Head of first department
土屋吉博	Yoshi Tsuchiya	
小官義孝	Gikou Omiya	Research assistant
小松	Komatsu	Water offer department, emproyee
立澤忠夫	Tataro Tachizawa	Leader of medical worker
立澤多太雄	Totao Tachizawa	Attaned germ attack by air
岡本啓	Hiraku Okamoto	Supporter
大河内稚末	Masami Ookawauchi	Head of antiepidemic department, Captain
大隈	Uokuma	Major
岩崎	Iwasaki	Leader of the first department, Major
島田横二	Yokoji Shimada	Specialist of dysentery
島田	Shimada	Experiment room, warrant officer
野壽雄	No Toshio	The fifth leader of the army, Captain
村上	Murakami	Germ geam, Lieutenant Colonel
粟屋一步	Hatsuyuki Awaya	Head of gerneral affairs department, Major
近藤肇	Chikafuji Hajime	Attended Zhejiang germ attack
秋元	Akimoto	Sergeant
奉馬冶	Osame Hataba	Member
高山緑郎	Rikuro Takayama	Attended Zhejiang germ assault
齋藤七部	Nanaro Saitou	Jiujiang branch leader of antiepidemic part, first Lieutenant
矢野	Yano	Employee
増田知貞	Tomosada Masuda	Chief of aircrift unit of "Unit 731"
大川清	Toru Ogawa	Prof.
山中多望若	Taboku Yamanake	Member

"Unit 8604" ("八六〇四部隊")

Japanese name 日文姓名	English Name 英文譯音	Crimes 罪行
山口雅	Masashi Yamaguchi	Member
山内義夫	Tadashio Yamanouchi	Member
小口	Okuchi	The 3rd department leader, Major
小田記信	Shirunobu Konishi	Member
白木春市	Haruichi Shiraki	The second leader, Colonel

Japanese name 日文姓名	English Name 英文譯音	Crimes 罪行
田中嚴	Kibishi Tanaka	Member
石田中夫	Kazuo Ishida	Member
井上疆	Sakai Inoue	Member
岡村正雄	Tadao Okamura	Member
久保田選	Tatsumi Kuboda	Member
馬群弘	Hiroshi Bagun	Member
大森一二三	Ichinisan Oomori	Member
北野静男	Shizuo Kitano	Member
市川太郎	Taro Ichikawa	Member
平法友	Tomoe Hiranori	Member
江頭勇次	Yuji Enokashira	Member
渡邊健一	Kenichi Wadanabe	Head of the fourth department, Lieutenant Colonel
澤井正治	Tatanao Sawai	Member
清水清	Kiyoshi Shimizu	Member germ research team, squad leader, head of The Refugee Camp
鴻江勇	Hiroe Esamu	Member
溝口	Misokuchi	Head of the first department, Major
淹瀬勇	Isamu Midase	Member
窪田久	Hisashi Waida	Member
地場守喜	Mamoyoshi Chiba	The first department examine team, squad leader
島嚴	Shimagake	Member
木吴邦夫	Kunio Kigo	Member
鬆浦吉次	Yoshiji Matsuura	Member
橋木敬佑	Keiu Hashimoto	Squad leader of pathology team
村鬆直治	Naoji Muramatsu	Member dissect assistant
佐藤	Satou	The first department examine director, Major
佐藤吉已	Yoshisude Satou	Member
佐藤亮男	Akiro Satou	Member
佐口木高行	Takayuki Sasaki	Colonel
伊熊忠雄	Takao Ikuma	Member
伊佐茂太郎	Shigero Isa	Member
粟林敏秀	Satohide Awahayashi	Member
内山正通	Masadori Uchiyama	The fourth department leader, Captain
内山武彦	Takehiko Uchiyama	Member
穂坂八部	Hachiro Hozaka	Member
高橋聖治	Seiji Takahashi	Member
若山豊市	Toyoichi Wakayama	The fifth leader of the unit, Major
蘆塚 定壽	Sametoshi Ashitsuka	Member
熊倉	Kumakura	Head of gerneral affairs department, Major
元山	Motoyama	Member
關莊太郎	Taro Sekigoso	Member
糟川長谷	Yoshotani Kasukawa	Member
彌吉光雄	Mitsuo Michiyoshi	Member
的野千佐	Sensa Yano	Member
鷹野志郎	Tataro Takano	Member
龜次六郎	Mutsuro Kamesawa	The 4th leader of the unit, Major
磯貝	Isokai	Major
松本弘道	Hiromichi Matsumoto	
井上睦雄	Mutsuo Inoue	
島義雄	Shima Yoshio	The chief of inspection of Quangzhou harbor
岩瀬佑一	Iwase Uichi	Inspector
江口	Eguchi	The chief of 1'st section
龜澤鹿郎	Kanezawa Shikao	The chief a "Unit 8604"
山内正道	Yamauchi Tatamichi	The chilf of 4rth section
寺師勇	Tera Shie	The head of Malaria section

Japanese name 日文姓名	English Name 英文譯音	Crimes 罪行
金光克巳	Kanamifsu Norio	The 1'st section
馬場	Baba	Warrant officer
橋一	Hashiichi	Viviscction room
高杉	Takasugi	Assistant of vivisection room

"Unit 100" ("一〇〇部隊")

Japanese name 日文姓名	English Name 英文譯音	Crimes 罪行
三友數夫	Toshio Mitomo	Made bacillus anthracis for germ attack
三友	Kazuo Mitomo	Senior surgeon
山口文二	Yamaguchi Fumiji	The 2nd depattment laboratory, second Lieutenant
三友勝雄	Katsuo Mitomo	The 2nd department, 6th part, attended vivisection
三友一男	Masao Mitomo	Member
山田重治	Jyuji Yamada	Germ researching room, director
山野紀道	Norimichi Ono	Lieutenant Colonel
立河才三	Zaisan Tachikawa	Major General
田水章	Akiraka Michi	Employee
井田清	Kiyoshi Ida	Engineer
平櫻全作	Zensaku Hirazakura	First Lieutenant
市川	Ichikawa	Captain
淺尾	Asao	Leader of hailar expedition team, Captain
滿田	Michida	Member
橋勇	Hashiisamu	Specialist
櫻下清	Kiyoshi Sakurashita	Employee
村田良介	Yoshisuke Murada	Major
村木	Muraki	Major
佐藤秀之	Hideyuki Satou	Instructor
保坂斯道	Sonomichi Tamosaka	Veterinarian, Lieutenant Colonel
遷	Suji	Veterinarian, Lieutenant Colonel
逆瀨川	Scgawa Sakarau	Captain
若松侑次郎	Yujiro Wakamatus	Leader of unit
福住光田	Mitsuda Fukusumi	Second Lieutenant
高島一雄	Ichiro Takashima	The second leader of the unit
高橋義夫	Tatao Takahashi	Researcher
高秋	Takaaki	Second department, Captain
北坂惟道	Koremichi Hosaka	Yuji's assistant
桑原明	Akiraka Kuwahara	Employee
雄坂	Toshisaka	The second department leader, Lieutenant Colonel
林本	Hayashimoto	Major
中村吉二	Nakamura	Biological prof. Lt.-Col.
灌田	Sosomichi	Anthrax germ discharging
池田	Ikeda	Anthrax germ discharging
石井	Ishii	Anthrax germ discharging
長谷川	Nagasegawa	Anthrax germ discharging
木村	Kimura	Anthrax germ discharging
中島	Nakashima	M.P. 1'st. Lt.
松井	Matsui	Technician Megunizuka M.P.
惠坂	Noboru Mitsuki	2'nd Chief of "Unit 100"
下河邊	Shitakawabe	Detach. 141 leader
鈴人	Suzuuto	Detach. 141 leader assistance
橫山	Yokoyama	Detach. 141 leader assistance
吉田	Yoshida	Detach. 141 leader assistance
山上	Bunji Yamaguchi	Engineer
細香	Hozaka	Vivissction attended

"Other parts" (其他部門)

Japanese name 日文姓名	English Name 英文譯音	Crimes 罪行
湯面竹三	Takemi Sawao	The 39th division 233th united group, sergeant, attended vivisection
原見權一	Kenichi Harami	Hebei mixture 3rd brigade, head of military surgeon office, attended vivisection
荻尾	Ogio	The 59th D. 113th united group, attened China-Burma germ attacking
荻野	Ogino	Hebei Mixture 3'rd B., attened vivisection
高橋	Takahashi	The 53th D., office, sergeant, attened vivisection
高黎文雄	Fumio Takanashi	The 108th D., 108th united G. of Field Gun, attened viviscction
米田壽春	Toshiharu Komeda	The 11th D., 1'st. class private, attened viviscction
牧野毅	Tsuyoi Makino	The 39th D., 233th U. G, leader, Captain, attened vivisection
和田	Wada	The 35th D., 2'nd Lt., attened vivisection
武田	Takeda	The 56th D., 113 U.G., Major G., attened China--Burma germ attacking
譽野	Sugino	The 11th D., Captain, attened vivisection
藤田	Fujida	Baoding 66 Brigade, attened vivisection
德久知正	Shisei Norihisa	The office of 35th D, attened vivisection
木村兵太郎	Heitaro Kimura	Burme battle commander of infantry (1944)
松山佑三	Tasukemi Matsuyama	The leader of 56th D., attened germ spreading in Burma
松井秀治	Hidenao Matsui	The 56th D.,113th U.G., leader, attened germ spreading in Burma
松尾元治	Motonao Matsuo	The Hebei Indepdent infantry 16th G., 1'st Lt. vivisection
林吾夫	Wareo Hayashi	The 63th D., high grade adjutant, vivisection, Col.
杉野俊三郎	Suguresaro Sugino	Taiyuan Tel. 9th U.G., leader, Col., vivisection
柳田之三	Yukisan Yanagida	The 33th D. leader, attened Burma germ attacking
柳川	Yanagigawa	The 39th D., 233th U.G., adjutant, vivisection
相樂圭三	Kadosan Airaku	Shanxi 3'rd B., 1'st Lt.,vivisection
森木捨三	Sutesan Morigi	Hebei Railuray U.G., major, vivisection
森野溝明	Sonoaki Morino	37th D, 225 U.G., sergeant, vivisection
佐久間盛一	Moriichi Sakuma	Boading 16th B. leader, Major G., vivisection
佐佐木	Sasaki	Hebei mixture 8th brigade Sano platoon, sergeant, attended vivisection
佐藤	Satou	Hebei mixture 8th brigade Sano platoon, sergeant, attended vivisection
古閑健	Sugoyaka Furuhima	The 54th D. U.G. 2'nd Lt. (1944), China-Burma aera germ assault participator.
原田	Harada	The 56th D. 113 U.G. 2'nd Lt. China-Burma aera germ assault participator
黑江	Kuroe	Hebei mixture 3rd B. office, fiest Lt., attended vivisection
篠田	Shinoda	Shanxi mixture 3rd B., medical sergeant, attended vivisection
築館熊雄	Kumao tsukutate	The 108th D., 108 field gun U.G., military surgeon, attended vivisection
兵頭周	Maruyoshi Hyotou	The 1' st. Army Military Surgeon Department laeder, Major G.
矢野太郎	Taro Yano	The 59th D., 110 G., first Lt. Attended vivisection
葛成	Kusunari	The 1' st. Army, epidemic prevention & water supplying department, instructor, attended vivisection
中村三夫	Mitsuo Nakamura	Mixture 3rd B.(Shanxi), 7th group, military surgeon, first Lt. Attended vivisection
長鹽	Nagashio	The 12th A., military surgeon, Lt. Col. Attended germ warfare
安部	Anbe	Hebei mixture 8th B., company commander, attended vivisection
草羽		Commander of transpartation for germ attaced on Zhejiang in 1940
大道文男	Fumio Oomichi	Henna, 35th D., 204th G., military surgeon, first Lt. attended vivisection
平野孝次	Koji Hirano	Vivisection, Luan Army Hospital, dissector
小竹		The chief of medical department of Japanese army division, Luan, vivisection
工藤	Takumifuji	Beijing, 4th independent garrison team, 21st G., medical squad leader attended vivisection
山恒内	Tsuneuchi Yama	Chengchun military police team, translator, attended vivisection
小林藤平治	Fujihiraji Kobayashi	Chengchun military police team, second Lieutenant, attended vivisection
安達千代吉	Chiyoyoshi Anda	Hebei 6th garrison team, 21' st. G., warrant officer, attended vivisection
小笠原武	Harafuji Okasa	Chengchun military police team, first Lieutenant, attended vivisection
小田	Koda	Chifeng military police team, sergeant leader, attended vivisection
大田同原	Onahara Ooda	Chengchun military police team, sergeant, attended vivisection
山本升	Noboru Yamamoto	Tongliao hospital leader, attened vivisections, Lt.-Col.
山下龜久	Kamehisa Shitayama	Liaoyuan charcoal and mineral hospital, president assistance, vivisection
高野寅之助	Toranosuke Takuno	Liaoyuan charcoal and mineral hospital, president, vivisection
岡田	Okada	Dr., Fuming hospital, shanghai

Japanese name 日文姓名	English Name 英文譯音	Crimes 罪行
坂本	Sakamoto	President of Taiji hospital, attaned vivisection
石山	Ishiyama	Professor of Tokyo Imperial University, attended vivisection
川村義明	Tataaki Kawamura	Tokyo Imperial University Infections Disease Institute, assistant
小澤市三郎	Ichisaburo Ozawa	Saitama Japan, mouse offer
小林廣造	Koybayashi Mutsutsuku	Keiou University professor, germ war supporter
桃井直幹		The Chief of the Japanese Medical School of Army Surgeons
高橋義夫	Yoshio Takahashi	The Sanitalion Material Factory, plague research.
山本原一	Haroichi Yamamoto	The stuff officer of Kwantung Army, plague attacking
船田仁禮	Jinrei Funeda	The Unit of Yangtz river special agent, bacteria sprrading by aircraft, Lt. Col.
北條圍了	Enlyo Kitasuji	Ishii assistant, military attaché officer
朝枝繁春	Shigeharu Asaeda	The dirctor of Japanese G. Staff
新美倌太	Talefuto Niimi	The chief of The Hourse Epidemic Disease Section
佐藤秀三	Hidesabu Satou	The chief of the Shanghai Natural Science Insti.
野田正彰	Tataaki Nomechi	Special transfer
桔武夫	Tachibana Takeo	Jiamus military police team, leader
玉井	Tamai	Hebei independent garrison force 16th group, sergeant, attened vivisection
重戶廣--	Shigedo Hiroichi	Hebei Miyun garrison force, attended vivisection
戶上	Tonoue	Chengchun military police, sergeant leader, attendee vivisection
毛利	Mori	Tongzhou Garrison force team, sergeant, attended vivisection
白井定夫	Sadao Shirai	Tieling police office, attended vivisection
安藤久男	Hisao Antou	Chengchun military police team, squad leader, warrant officer, attended vivisection
宮本道友	Miyamoto Michitomo	Shengyang Shanfudi military police leader, "logs"carrying, man of germ spreading
平野	Hirano	Shanxi Datong military police team, leader, Captain
渡邊	Wadanabe	Chifeng military police team, sergeant, "logs" carrying
渡邊輝雄	Wadanabe	Shengyang Shanfudi military police team, platoon leader, attended germ spreading
鈴木	Suzuki	Chifeng military police team, sergeant leader, attended vivisection
野副	Nozoe	Linjiang military police commander, Major G., "logs" carrying
谷川	Tanikawa	Chengde military police team leader, Major, attended vivisection
米木	Komegi	Chifeng military police team, sergeant, attended vivisection
深野時之助	Tokinosuke Fukano	Hebei independent garrison force, leader of 16th G., Colonel, attended vivisection
丸尾勇三	Yuosan Maruo	Hebei 4th independent garrison team, 21st G., Captain, attended vivisection
廣瀬	Hirose	Tieling police office, sergeant, attended vivisection
荒谷定藏	Sadakura Aratani	Shanxi Painkguan garrison team, squad leader, second Lt., attended vivisection
荒木純戒	Junkai Araki	Tongzhou military police, platoon leader, firat Lt., attended vivisection
蒔田	Makida	Shanxi Datong military police team, first-class private, attended vivisection
菊堤修	Syuichi Kikuji	Shanxi Painkguan garrison team leader, attended vivisection
松百光穗	Mitsuho Matsuyu	Shanxi Datong military police team, first-class private, attended vivisection
森澤	Morizawa	Chifeng military police team, "logs" carrying, attended vivisection
榎本	Fnokimoto	Chifeng military police team, sergeant, "maruda" carrying
近藤新入	Niihachi Kindou	Chengchun military police team leader, Colonel, "maruda" carrying
逢見谷正夫	Tsurio Aimitani	Tongzhou military police team, squad leader, "logs" carrying
風間	Kazema	Hebei 4th independent garrison team, 21st G, medical worker, attended vivisection
竹三德壽	Noritoshi Takesan	Shanxi Ensure Dublic Security Care School president, attended vivisection
賀甚五郎	Kangoro Iwai	Yehe military police, platoon leader, "maruda" carrying
田村政夫	Tatao Tamura	North chengchun military police team, squad leader, attended vivisection
河原佐三	Tasukemi Kawahara	Shanxi, Painkguan county garrison team. military surgeon. attended vivisection
木村	Kimura	Harbin military police team, adjutant, "logs" carrying
三浦卓	Takaku Miura	Laoheishan military police platoon, general affairs, director
三田正夫	Tatao Mitsuda	Xinfu military police platoon,
三宅	Miyake	Baoqing military police platoon leader
三品彥八	Hikoya Mishina	Chengchun Heasun aera police office, director
三島	Mishima	Dalian military police team, sergeant
川口保	Mamoru Kawaguchi	Independent garrison force, 6th group, leader of platoon
上坪鐵一	Tetsuichi Uetsuno	Andong military police team leader, Major, attended vivisection

Japanese name 日文姓名	English Name 英文譯音	Crimes 罪行
上野	Ueno Boli	Military police team
工藤	Takumifuji	Harbin military police team, Daowai platoon, squad leader, vivisection objects offer
山岸研二	Kenji Yamakishi	Xiangfang protect-garden, director, imformation survey department leader, vivisection,materials offer
三宅秀	Hideru Miyake	Manchukuo Security Department, haed of police department, Nongan pestis germ spreader
山口	Yamaguchi	Fujin military police platoon
山本	Yamamoto	Hegang military police platoon, sergeant
山本	Yamamoto	Independent garrison force 25th group, squad leader
小越	Okoshi	Fujin military police platoon
小野武次	Takeshi Ono	Fujin military police platoon
小林喜一	Kiichi Kobayashi	Fentian military police platoon
小林正口	Tatakuchi Kobayashi	Dongan province Bureau of Public Defence Department internal
小美野戰利	Tadatoshi Komino	Chengchun military police team, squad leader
小野寺留寺	Ryuji Onotera	Dalian military police team, sergeant
小笠原	Okasahara	Shansengfu military police team, squad leader
小川伍男	Kumio Kogawa	Laoheishan military police platoon leader
小林	Kobayashi	Tumen military police team, sergeant
小池	Koike	Independent garrison force 6th group, first class private
小川政夫	Tatao Kogawa	Independent garrison force 2nd group, sergeant
西尾昭行	Akayuki Nishio	Shansengfu military police team, first class private
太田秀清	Hidekiyo Ooda	Chengde military police platoon, first class private
白濱重夫	Shigeo Shirahama	Dalian military police team leader
白井	Shirai	Hegang military police platoon, sergeant
北川明	Akashi Kitakawa	Andong military police platoon, sergeant
長望月政吉	Tatayoshi Nagamitsuki	Mudanjiang military police team, assistant leader, Colonel
長島玉次郎	Gyojiro Nagashima	Andong military police team, first lieutenant
吉田	Yoshida	Baoqing military police team, sergeant
吉房虎雄	Torao Yoshitsubu	Kwantung Army Military Police Commander Office, leader of third department
吉川勇一	Yuichi Yoshikawa	Jiamusi military police team, sepecial department, squad leader
安藤次郎	Jiro Antou	Gongzhuling military police platoon leader, Major
今島山	Shimayama Ima	Laoheishan military police team, squad leader
今關喜太郎	Yoshitaro Imaseki	Kwantung Army Pilitary Dolice Commander Office, Garrison Department
今中俊雄	Sugureo Imanaka	Dalian military police team, special task department
立元喜太郎	Yoshitaro Tachimoto	Head of Tailai county
田附常鱗	Tsunenari Tazuke	Beian military police team, first Lieutenant
田昌雄	Michi Sakaro	Beian military police team, Lieutenant Colonel
田上惟敏	Omosato Tanoue	Dumen military police team leader
田上半藏	Suekura Tanoue	Fujin military police platoon, general affairs squad leader
岡野令吾	Imaware Okano	Chengchun military police platoon, sergeant, Nongan germ spreader
岡户和三郎	Kazusanro Okado	Bamiantong military police platoon, second Lieutenant
宫崎	Miyasaki	Leader of Jilin military police platoon, first Lieutenant
宫崎行	Yuki Miyasaki	Beian military police platoon, squad leader
宇津木孟雄	Hajimeo Utsugi	Chengchun military police platoon
富田	Tomida	Hegang military police platoon, first class private
守屋秀雄	Hideo Mamoya	Andong military police team, squad leader
大須賀	Iwal Uosu	Mudanjiang military police team, first Lieutenant
大窪武夫	Takeo Ookuba	Fentian military police team, squad leader
大藪武雄	Takeo Ookage	Harbin police department
平野	Hirano	Kwantung Army Military Police Teach Team, Lieutenant Colonel
平木武	Takeshi Hiragi	Dongan military police team leader
平中清一	Seiichi Hiranaka	Anshang military police platoon leader
平田	Hirada	Dalian military police team, sergeant
本田貞曉	Tatashiaki Honda	Kwantung Military Commander Office, general affairs department, first part, Captain
平林茂樹	Shigeki Hirabayashi	Jiamusi military police team
臧	Yodo	Shanshenmiao military police platoon, squad leader

Japanese name 日文姓名	English Name 英文譯音	Crimes 罪行
渡邊卯一郎	Uichiro Wadanabe	Harbin garrison force department leader
渡邊長太夫	Nagataro Wadanabe	Fentian military police team
渡邊一雄	Ichiro Wadanabe	Fentian military police team, squad leader
清香	Seikou	Leader of Fentian military police team, Major
渥美	AtSumi	Beian military police team, second Lieutenant
淺井仙一	Senichi Asai	Gongzhuling military police team, first class private
浜端三郎	Saburo Hamataba	Chengchun military police team, special task team, squad leader, warrant officer
池山清	Kiyoshi Ikeyama	Harbin military police platoon leader, major
潮海辰亥	Tokii Shioumi	Kwandong police department leader
游佐卓平	Takahira Ogisa	Manchukuo head of the vil service
鈴木勇	Isamu Suzuki	Harbin military police team, sergeant
土屋	Tsuchiya	Fujin military police platoon, squad leader
堀口正雄	Masao Horikuchi	Jinzhou military police team, team leader, Lieutenant Colonel, vivisection object offer
磯	Iso	Fentian military police team leader, Colonel
坂口直蔵	Naokura Sakakuchi	Shengwu military police platoon, sergeant
坂根覺次郎	Kakujiro Sakane	Fentian military police team, general affairs director
城戸哲朗	Tetsuro Shirodo	Nahe military police platoon leader, warrant officer
寺尾格太郎	Kakushiro Terao	Aihui frontier police team
島田	Shimada	Head of Tongan province Ensure Public Security Department, spy office, Lieutenant Col.
木村光明	Koumei Kimura	Boli military police platoon
松本英雄	Matsumoto	Harbin military police department, judgement department
松岡	Matsuoka	Jiamusi military police team squad leader
松島	Matsushima	Chengchun military police team ,judgement department
	Takeo Tachibana	Jiamusi military team leader
森三吾	Mitsuware Mori	Dongning military police team
柴尾	龍卧虎 Shibao	Chengde military police team, Captain
佐澤	Sazawa	Harbin military police team, head of the special task department, Major, vivisection object offer
佐藤信雄	Nobuo Satou	Fujing military police platoon
佐藤福次	Fukuji Satou	Shuangchong police branch department, tour of inspection
伊藤孝仁	Tsukaeuto Itou	Dongan province Public Security Department, affairs officer
貝治一郎	Ichiro Kaiji	Baoqing military police team, garrison worker
鹿毛繁太	Shigefuto Shigake	Harbin police department, leader of judgement department
劉憲補	Shironori Ogina	Hegang military police platoon
内海未十郎	Mijyuro Uchimi	Shanshemfu military police platoon leader, first Lieutenant
同林次郎	Jiro Tomobayashi	Chengchun military police team, sergeant
風間	Kazema	Aihui frontier police team leader
成國升	Noboru Narikuni	Fujin military police platoon, gerneral affairs assistant
成錦升	Noboru Narinishiki	Kwantung Army Military Dolice Commander Office, the first department, assistant
成倉義衛	Tadamachi Shimokura	Kwantung Army Military Police Commander Office, gerneral affairs department commander,Major Gerneral.
原口一八	Ichiya Harakuchi	Xinanbei province garrison department, agent leader
原田左中	Sanaka Harada	Nenjiang military police platoon, special task team
原	Hara	first Lieutenant, kwantung Army Independent Garrison, 6th G.
想路	Omoji	Kwantung army independent garrison 6th group, leader of company
福谷	Fukutani	Dalian military police team, sergeant
稻田定一	Teiichi Ineda	Boli Military Police Platoon leader, first Lieutenat
稻恒征夫	Yukio Inatsune	Manchukuo Agricultureal Development Department, adjutant
羽田盡	Tsukushi Haneda	Harbin Xiangfang Rossian Captive Department, warrant officer
星敏實	Satomi Hoshi	Qiqihar military police team leader
加藤圭二	Kiji Katou	Harbin military police team leader
飯島良雄	Yoshio Lishima	Xiangfang protection garden, Major, "logs" offer
飯原軍司	Genji Lihara	Beian military police team, sergeant
東一兵	Hitotsuwa Higashi	Laoheishan military police platoon, squad leader
米倉憲一	Kenichi Akakura	Leader of laoheishan military police platoon
高木貞和郎	Shinchiro Takagi	Boli military police platoon, director of gerneral affairs department

Japanese name 日文姓名	English Name 英文譯音	Crimes 罪行
高木忠夫	Tanoue Tatao	Harbin military police team, first class private
高場	Takaba	Jingchang military police platoon
高橋正鋭	Seietsu Takahashi	Independent Garrison Infantry 25th group, squad leader
和田	Wada	Harbin military police team leader, Colonel
鵜野晋太郎	Ashintaro Uno	Hubei Anyuan county captive camp, leader of the camp
來鳩有次	Yuji Koihata	Hubei Anyuan county captive camp, assistant
武田恒義	Tsunegi Takeda	Hubei Anyuan county captive camp, overseer of imperial
武下虎市	Toraichi Takeshita	Beian military police platoon, Captain
新澤	Niizawa	Jiamusi military police team, squad leader
兒島正範	Tatakata Kojima	Mudanjiang military police team leader, Lieutenant Colonel
藤本吉一	Yoshiichi Fujimoto	Kwantung Army Military Police Commander Office, garrison department, the second part
藤田正	Tadashi Fujida	Dalian military police team, special task department leader Major
藤原廣之進	Hironoyuki Fujihara	Chengchun military police platoon leader Major
菱治相沼	Souji Hishinao	Bamiantong military police platoon
苗憲補	Enoriogina Na	Jingchang military police platoon, sergeant
陰地茂一	Shigeichi Nenji	Fujing military police platoon, gerneral affairs, assistant
阪本喜三郎	Yoshisanro sakamoto	Mudanjiang Linfu military branch, team leader, warrant officer
老村行雄	Yukio Shimura	Hailar military police team
齊藤美夫	Mio Saitou	Kwantung army garrison department leader
齊藤翌	Asahi Saitou	Nenjiang military police platoon, first Lieutenant
齊藤美夫	Mio Saitou	Chengchun military police team
春日馨	Kaoru Hasuka	Harbin military police team leader, Lieutenant Colonel
奥田勝	Kachi Okuda	Beian military police team, translater
唐木田博	Michihiro Karagi	Harbin Guanwangmiao Protection House professor Captain, "logs"offer
莊治常二	Tokiji Syoji	Fujin military police platoon leader, second Lieutenant
日野需口	Notomeguchi hino	Dongan public security department
關孝	Sekitaka	Chengchun medical material factory, vaccinum research
關山	Sekiyama	Aihui frontier police team, officer
篠田重稔	Shigeminoru shinoda	Munitions factory military police team leader
篠原隆雄	Takao shinohara	Dongan military police team
毛利幸三	Yoshisan Mori	Shengwu military police platoon leader, Captain
弘田利光	Toshimitsu Hiroda	Nenjiang military police team, assistant
書店一義	Hatsugi Kakumise	Harbin military police team platoon leader, first Lieutenant
莊司	Syoji	Harbin military police team, Daowai branch dispatch team, sergeant
曽場	Soba	Pinyuang military police platoon leader, first Lieutenant
永井	Nagai	Fujin military police platoon, squad leader
笹誠户哲	Tetsu Sasasedo	Kwantung Army Military Police Commander Office, gerneral affairs department, sergeant
笹鳩松夫	Matsuo Sasahata	Shengwu military police platoon, gerneral affairs, director
二宮正三	Tatami Futsunomiya	Mixture 15th brigade, leader of squad, attended vivisection
川吉春	Yoshiharu Kawa	Mixture 15th brigade 79th group, leader of the group, Major, attended vivisection
中井	Nakai	The 109 division, medical team, sergeant, attended vivisection
中野	Nakano	The 37 Division 225 united group, medical worker, attended vivisection
山部	Yamabe	Mixture 3rd Drigade, probation officer, attended vivisection
永浜健雄	Kenyu Nagahama	The 59th Division 110th group, attended vivisection
石本正男	Tatao Ishimoto	The 39 Division 233 united team 1' st. class private attended vivisection
岡野廣	Kuwashi Ookubo	Shanxi province Fighting Commander Office, first Lieutenant, attended vivisection
河邊正三	Tatami Kawabe	Burma war zone, commander, General(1944)
河村州美男	Sanjumio Kawamura	The 39th Division 233 united group, first class private, attended vivisection
水上原藏	Harakura mizukami	The 56th Division infantry commander, leaded China-Burma area germ assault
渡邊	Wadanabe	Hebei mixture 8th Brigade, sergeant, attended vivisectionc
水谷	Mizutani	The 117th Division, military surgeon center, probation officer. Attended vivisection
高橋高厚	Takaatsu takahashi	Leader of kwantung Army Military Surgeon Office
和泉	Kazuizumi	Shanxi mixture 3rd Brigade, military surgeon. Attended vivisection.
松下兼藏	Kanekura sugishita	The 109th Division medical unit leader, sergeant. Attended vivisection.

Japanese name 日文姓名	English Name 英文譯音	Crimes 罪行
尾塚隆隆三	Ryuiji kajitsuka	Kwantung Army Medicine Department leader, a specialist of bacteriology.
進藤升	Noboru Shindou	The 11' st. Army, medical department leader, Major General, Changed germ attack leader
三輪幸敏	Yoshisato Mitsuwa	The 39th Division, 232 united group, military surgeon, second Lieutenant, attended vivisection
田村	Tamura	Kwantung Army Commander Office, Colonel, had inspected the "unit 731"(1945)
植田謙吉	Rikudayoshi Ueda	Kwantung Army Commander(1937).
草場	Kusaba	Kwantung army Field Fighting Railroad Commander, Lieutenant General
川上	Kawakami	Thailand "the death railroad" army group, Colonel.
川口	Kawaguchi	Jinan medical materials room, first Lieutenant.
下定村	Samemura Shita	The first Army, commander.
中村俊二	Kouji Nakamura	The 116 Division leader, attended Zhejiang Jiangxi germ attack
中馬	Nakauma	Leader of Beiyinghe germ experiment farm Captain
中山源夫	Motoo Nakayama	Kwantung Army Staff Office
中村二郎	Jiro Nakamura	Taizuan epidemics prevention and water supply dep.
山田乙三	Otozo Yamada	Kwantung Army Commander
山下守邦	Mamokuni Yamashita	The 59th Division, engineering corps team. Attended Shandong cholera attack.
三品隆三	Takami mishina	The 13rd Army, imformation diretor. Attended Zhejiang Jiangxi germ attack
山下	Yamashita	Mixture 131 Brigade, high grade adjutant, Captain
山田浩造	Hirotsuku Yamada	The 39th Division, 232 united roup, second Lieutenant.
小松原道太郎	Michitaro Komatsuhara	Nomanhan attack, Kwantung Army front commander
島高夫	Takao Kojima	The 59th Division, 44 group, second Lieutenant. Attended Shandong cholera attack
小四島多多志	Tatashi Odashima	Epidemics Prevention and water sapply manager, Colonel.
小四春一	Haruichi Koda	The 39 Division, 233 uniteed group, first class private.
西浦進	Susumi Nishiura	Leader of staff department.
長島勤	Tsutome Nagashima	The 59th Division, 54th Brigade, head of the brigade. Shandong cholera attack leader.
長田友吉	Tomoyoshi Nagada	The 59th Division, attended shandong cholera attack
長谷川	Nagasegawa	The 39th Division 233 united group, military surgeon.
長尾正夫	Tatao Nagao	Changde germ attacking, staff officer
吉武秀雄	Ilideo yoshitake	The 117 Division leader of Brigade.
安藤爲一	Yariichi Antou	The 39 Division, 232 united group, leader of the second group, Major.
吉信雅之	Masayuki Yoshinobu	The 59th Division, information squad leader, first Lieutenant. Shandong cholera attack attender
田坂八十八	Yajiya Tasaka	The 59th Division, head of Brigade. Attended Shandong cholera attack
田謙吉	Herikudayoshi Michi	Nomanhan attacking, kwantung Army Commander.
石井	Ishii	Mixture 131' st. Brigade, impediment group, Captain
石原	Ishihara	Mixture 131' st. Brigade, engineering corps group leader.
井上	Inoue	The 21' st. army Apidemics Prevention $ water supply department, team leader, Major.
千田謙太郎	Kensanro Senta	Mixture 131' st. Brigade group, first Lieutenant
少野寺	Sugunodera	Zhejiang Jiangxi germ attack, organizer.
阿部	Abe	Head of Chengchun medical materials factory.
大久保精	Kuwashi Ookubo	Shanxi province Fight. Commander Office, first Lieutenant
宮布升	Noboru Miyanuno	The 59th Division, attended Shandong cholera attack.
宇部	Ube	Head of mixture 131st Brigade, Major General.
宮崎弘	Hiroshi Miyasaki	The 39the Division, 233 united group,adjutant, second Lieutenant.
寄國一夫	Kazuo Yorikuni	The 39the Division 232 united group, sergeant
江田稔	Minoru Eda	The 39th Division, leader of staff officer, Colonel. Attended Shandong cholera attack
河野毅	Tsuyoi Kawano	Head of the 13' rd Army Zhejiang Jiangxi germ warfare
河村	Kawamura	Squad leader, Shanxi Linfen germ spreader.
河樹	Kawaki	Shanxi epidemics prevention and water supply, squad leader
水野春陽	Haruhi Mizuno	The 39th Division, 232 united group, military surgeon.
津田玄郎	Kenro Tsuda	Shanhaiguan united foreign affairs team specialist task leader
酒井次郎	Jiro Sakai	The 39th Division, 233 united group, probation officer.
鈴木敏夫	Satoo Suzuki	The 59th Division, leader of military surgeon department. Attended Shandong cholera attack.
鈴木元之	Motoyuki Suzuki	Taiyuan independent impedimenta first united group, second Lieutenant.
鈴木啓久	Hirahisa Suzuki	Leader of the 117th Division.
増田孝	Tsukae Fueda	The 59th Division, military surgeon, Captain. Attended Shandong cholera attack.

Japanese name 日文姓名	English Name 英文譯音	Crimes 罪行
坂本嘉四	Yoshiyo Sakamoto	The 59th Division, 11st group leader, Lieutenant Colonel. Attended Shandong cholera attack
坂垣征四郎	Seishiro Sakakaki	Kwantung Army leader, germ warfare early stage supporter.
島崎貫一	Tsuneichi Shimasaki	Monchukou agriculture department, adjutant
島村	Shimamura	Staff, attended Changde germ attack
野口	Noguchi	Army Geology Measure Department single-storey houses prospecter.
木村平多郎	Hirataro Kimura	In Burma Commander of 1944, the leader of Western Yunnan attack.
松島監	Kagami Matsushima	Agricultureal Development, chief director.
板倉	Itakura	Attended germ warfare plans make of 1941.
林田實	Tamitsu Hayashi	Tailai county, the adjutant county leader
林鐵雄	Tetsuo Hayashi	Kwantung Army Jail military surgeon, Captain
林正	Tadashi Hayashi	The 39th Division, 233 united group, firstclass private.
椎名	Shiina	Mixture the 131st Brigade, group leader of artillery group, Captain.
村田一夫	Ichiro Murada	The 39th Division, 233 united group, instractor.
柳澤	Yanagizawa	Hebei Tachibana Army, first class private.
梅崎次郎	Jiro Umetsuki	The 39th Division 232 united group, squad leader.
森田	Morida	Nanjing Captive Accommodation, first Lieutenant. Vivisection object offer.
佐藤武章	Takeaki Satou	The 39th Division, 232 united group, squad leader, attended vivisection.
佐久間爲人	Nariuto Sakuma	The 11st Army, division leader, head of the Zhejiang Jiangxi germ attack
佐藤貞人	Tatauto Satou	The 39th Division 232 united Group.
住岡儀一	Noriichi Sumioka	Shangxi, Independent Mixture fourth Brigade.
前川	Maekawa	Shangxi, independent mixture fourth brigade, 12th group, leader of company, first Lieutenant.
遠藤三郎	Endo Kazuo	Kwantung Army, Lieutenant Gerneral, inspection and support Ishii's army in 1933.
間庭	Iniwa	Kwantung Army veterinarian, Lieutenant Colonel.
原	Hara	The 39th Division, 233 united roup, military surgeon.
谷正五郎	Itsuro Tanimura	Mixture 131'st. brigade, staff, lieutenant Colonel
町田次郎	Jiro Machida	Kwantung army treatment department leader.
福田武志	Takeshi Fukuda	The 59th division, head of company, attended shandong cholera attack
荻原	Ogihara	Hebei tachibana army, sergeant.
秦彦三郎	Saburo Hatahiko	Kwantung Army, second leader
飯友田祥三郎	Kyojiro Iida	Burma, Japaness army commander, leader of Kunming, Baoshan cholera attack
飯村穰	Yuzuru Iimura	Kwantung army leader
細川忠康	Takayasu Hosokawa	The 59th division head of the division, Shandong cholera attack
山川速水	Hayamizn Yamakawa	The 39th division 232 united group military surgeon, second Lieutenant, attended vivisection
山之内	Yamanouchi	The 59th divison field hospital squad leader, attended viviseetion
有未次	Miji Ari	Kwantung army staff officer.
廣本	Hiromoto	Middle china dispatching army commander office, the third department, captain.
芳信雅	Nobumasa Kanba	The 59th division, director of imformation, first lieutenant.
藤田	Fujida	Gongzhuling air force army, Major.
萱内芳次郎	Houjiro Kayauchi	Hebei tachibana army, second-class private.
荒木貞夫	Asaki Sada	Army minister assestant
降旗武臣	Takeomi Orihata	The 125th division military surgeon department agent leader.
老田衛一郎	Sudeichiro Shida	Jiamusi chemistry laboratory.
多田駿	Sumiyaka Oomichi	Kwantung Army commander
梅津美治郎	Mijiro Umezu	Kwantung Army commander(1943)
龜三衛	Kanichiro Kami	Developed germ army
曾田	Soda	Mixture 131'st. brigade communication group leader, first Lieutenant.
曾根	Sone	Shanxi independent mixture 4th brigade, 12th GROUP, military surgeon, Captain.
泰彦	Yasuhiko	Middle China dispatch army commander office, attended zhejiang germ attack
長野	Nagano	Agricultureal development department Livestock products department, artificer.
山本	Yamanoto	Kwantung Army vaterinariovn, Captain
山田	Yamada	Jinan "Xinhua compound", leader
鈴木一郎	Ichiro Yamamoto	
伊藤	Itou	Germ attacked on Wengyoung (zhejiang province)

Japanese name 日文姓名	English Name 英文譯音	Crimes 罪行
金林	Kanabayashi	The chirf of Military Medical Bureau of Japanese Army (1943)
矢崎賢三	Kensan yasaki	59th D. cholera attacked werstern Shandong
厚守	Haramori	Kwantung Army M.P. commander Lt.Gen. (1941)
黑田	Kuroda	Beipiao police Bureau chief
平林	Hirabayashi	The leader of Japanese army in Xuzhou(1942)
板田	Itamichi	Subordinate of Hirabayashi, Lt. Major
元泉	Motoizumi	The chief of staff under Hisabayashi, Major Gen.
牧野亞一	Tsukuichi Makino	The chief of Police Bureau of South Market, Shengyang
望月升	Yoshio Sasahara	Sanilation dep. Of Jilin province leader
笠原幸雄	Tatae Fueda	The chirf of staff of Kwantung Army (1938)
橋木喜一郎	Totakuma Satou	Security Dep. of Shanjiang province, special task killed some Chinese in Sandao physics and chemistry research instituLe in "Aug. 15"
佐藤正熊	Otoko Inomitsu	Same as Tatakama Satou
井光男	Yoshisan Tanikuchi	Same as Tatakama Satou
谷口傳三	Taro Takabashi	Same as Tatakama Satou
高橋太郎	Kitahara Yamamoto	Same as Tatakama Satou
北原	Tatakama Satou	
上谷内	Uchi Uetani	Shanxi province Linfen 114th military depot hospital, squad leader. Attended vivisection
小笠原	Okasahara	Shanxi Siangxian army hospital, sergeant. Attended vivisection.
山崎	Yamasaki	President of So.M.T.corp. Chifeng hospital. Attended vivisection.
西	Mishi	President of Shanxi Xiangxian army hospital, Colonel. Attended vivisection.
西村慶次	Keiji Nishimura	Shanxi Luan army hospital, military surgeon. Attended vivisection.
西村	Nanman Nishimura	Medicine uni. Attended vivisection.
長田文男	Fumio Nagada	Baoding army hospital, director of military surgeon, first Lieutenant. Attended vivisection
白石	Shiraishi	An expert in medical, was stay and working in Jiangsu 11th division. Attended vivisection.
木原原壽人	Toshiuto Hara	Shanxi Linfen 114th military hospital, greneral affairs office. Attended viviaection
井績	Itsumi	Jinan army hospital, second Lieutenant. Attended vivisection.
岡野弘	Hiroshi Okano	The 59th division field fighting hospital, leader of detention center, first Lieutenant. Attended vivisecLion.
岡本	Okamoto	Shanxi Linfen 114th military depot hospital, president, colonel. Attended vivisection.
大橋莊吉	Okosoyoshi Oobashi	Linfen 114th military depot hospital, sergeant. Attended vivisection.
大津三好	Yoshisabu Ootsu	So. M.T.corp. Medicien university, murse. Attended vivisection.
酒井滿	Michiru Sakai	Shanxi Luan army hospital, president, Major General (1943). Qttended vivisection.
窪田	Kuboda	Baoding army hospital, head of nurse. Attended vivisection.
鈴木	Suzuki	Jiana army hospital, drector of education, military surgeon, Captain. Attended vivisection
飯岡	Iioka	Jinan army hospital, sergeant. Attended vivisection.
高岩	Takaiwa	The 117th division field fighting hospital, military surgeon, second lieutenant. Attended vivisection.
高木千年	Senhen Takagi	Jinan army hospital, president, lieutenant colonel. Attended viviaection.
柴田長七	Naganana Shibada	Baoding army hospital, president, lieutenant colonel. Attended vivisection.
丹保司平	Tsukasahira Enhou	The 117th division field hospital, president, Major, attended vivisection.
廣田	Hiroda	Shanxi linfen 114th army hospital, head of general affairs office, Captain attended vivisection.
新谷	Niitani	Shanxi Pingyuan army hospital, probation officer, attended vivisection.
德久知正	Shisei Norihisa	Tianjin army hospital first-class private. Attended vivisection.
赤誠茂三	Shigemi Akajero	Dongan public security dep., Major
關喜太郎	Taro Sekigoshi	M.P. commander office, garrison dep.
關慶	Sekiiwa	Hrsbin M.P. sergeant
菊野廣	Hiroshi Kikuno	Changchun M.P. sergeant
岩田茂	Shigemi Iwamichi	Continantal academy of sciences, germ rasearch room
木木	Hayashi	25th D. epidemic prevention & water supply unit leader, Major
尾上	Shiokami	11th D. epidemic prevention & water supply unit leader, Major
野原	Nohara	12th D. epidemic prevention & water supply unit leader, Major
磯外蓮助	Hasunosuke Isohare	Kwangtun Army's G. Staff (1938)
板東	Itahigashi	Nanman medicine university, vivisecfion attened
松田	Matsuda	Shanxi, Luan army hospital, leader of surgery. Attended vivisection.
	Mamori Kamisan	The 39th D., 232 U.G., post officer

Naoji Uezono
植園直寺

Shigemi Mekro 目黑正彦

Niata Ishibashi 石橋直方

Cui Heng Zhen
崔亨振

Takeo Kozawa 小澤武雄

Mr. Maruyama, a former member of the Japanese Army Unit 8604, shaved his head, offered flowers as well as incense and knelt down to repent before the memorial of the victims in Guangzhou.

前華南第 8604 部隊成員丸山茂剃成光頭作為罪人，向廣州受害者墓碑燒香、念經、跪拜

Naeo Ikeda
池田苗雄

Kojima Takao
小島隆男

前華北支甲第 1855 部隊，第三課（細菌武器研究所）鼠疫跳蚤飼養員伊藤影明（左）于 1995 年 3 月來華請罪。右屬作者
Kageaki Itou

田中信一（中）、鈴木進（左）
Shuichi Tanaka, Susumi Suzuki

The record of autopeis in vivisections

Date	Location	Died	of autopy	Evidence
(1) Sep .1935	Mudanjiang, Yehe army hospital	1	Confessed by amenoumi meguru	June 18 1956
(2) June 1936	Harbin, Harbin army hospital	1	Confessed by katakisi sumisowro	Aug 17 1954
(3) Aug. 1937	Mishan ,Mishan army hospital	1	Confessed byamenownu megusu	June 18 1956
(4) Jan .1938	Hulin ,Hulin army hospital	1	Confessed by takeuchi yutaka	Nov 1954
(5) Oct. 1940	Fujin ,Fujin army hospital	1	Confessed byono takaji	July 11 1954
(6) Dec. 1940	Buyan ,So district of Buyan city	1	Confessed by takahashi seiestu	Aug 13 1954
(7) March 1943	Sihui ,Xigangyi army hospital	1	Confessed bynakajima muneichi	July 1954
(8) Sep .1934	Hailong, 6th independent garrison force	1	Confessed bykawakuchi mamoru	Aug 15 1954
(9) Sep. 1935	Donghua 3' rd independent garrison force	1	Confessed by kogawa norio	Oct 9 1954
(10) Nov .1937	Chengchun Xingjing arnry hospital	3	Confessed by utsugi hajimes	Sep 10 1954
(11) Dec. 1937	Shenyang Nanman medical university	10	Confessed by nagataro wadanabe	Sep 12 1954
(12) Dec.1939~1937	Chengchun Nanlin 10	1	Confessed bynagajima gyojiro	June 10 1954
(13) Sep .1940	Chengchun Nanlin	1	Confessed by ornino giri	Sep 8 1954
(14) Sep 1936	Chifeng, Chifeng haspital of so.M.R.Inc	1	Confessed by kobayashi yoshichi	June 10 1954
(15) 1942~1943	Shenyang, Nanman medical university	25	Accuser changpiging	June 29 1954
(16) July 1936	Shenyang ,Nanman medical university	1	Sep 22 1954	
(17) Dec. 1943	Shenyang ,Nanman medical university	1	Confessed by tamura yashio	Oct 10 1954
(18) 1940~1945	Linkou ,Linkou detachment of unit	731		
(19) 1940~1945	Mudanjiang, Mudanjiang detachment of unit	731		
(20) 1940~1945	Shenwu, Shengwu detachment of unit	731		
(21) 1940~1945	Hailar, Hailar detachmunt of unit	731		
(22) 1932~1945	Wuchang, unit togo			
(24) 1940~1945	Harbin ,pmzfan unit	731		
(25) 1938~1945	Harbin, mengjiadun unit	100		
(26) 1939~1945	Nanjing ,unit	1644		
(27) 1939~1945	Guanzhou ,unit	8604		
(28) 1936~1945	Harbin, Bakuanzi city unit	100		
(29) Dec. 1939	Chengde ,Chengde army hospital	1	Confessed by futoda hideyoshi	Aug 15 1954
(30) Dec. 1939	Shahe, 8th composite beigade	1	Accuser makida	feb 7 1944
(31) May 1944	Tongxian Tongzhou M.P. corp'	1	Confessed by aimitani totao	Nov 20 1954
(32) July 1940	Miyun, 16th Independent garrison force	1	Shigetomi hiroichi	Aug 1954
(33) Oct .1942	Baoding ,Baoding army hospital	1	Nada minorn	Aug 1954
(34) 1942~1945	Anda, Anda experiment place	1		
(35) Nov .1943	Fuping , 3' rd composite brigade	1	Yoshizawa yukio	Nov 15 1954
(36) 1943				
(37) May 1944	Baoding, Baoding army hospital	2	Hayashi wareo	Apr 20 1954
(38) Sep.1936				
(39) July 1944	Pinggu, 15th composite brigade	1	Confessed by futsunorniya totami	July 31 1954
(40) Sep. 1939	Yangwu ,15th division	1	Confessed by Tokuhisa chisei	Aug 25 1954
(41) Sep. 1944	Xinxiang, 204th regiment	1	Confessed by Nagada totao	Aug 18 1954
(42) Oct. 1944	Zhengzhou ,hospital directly und 12th mihlary station	1	Confessed by Noda minoru	July 31 1954
(43) Apr. 1945	Jaiozuo ,fild hospital of 117th diviscon	1	Confessed by Noda minoru	July 31 1954
(44) Apr~june 1942	Jinan, Jinan army hospital	1	Confessed by Nagada tomoyoshi	Aug 4 1954
(45) Sep. 1942	Jinan Jinan army hospital	2	Confessed by Nagada tomoyoshi	Jan 11 1954
(46) June 1944	Chaocheng 53th composite brigade of 59th division	1	Confessed by Nagada tomoyoshi	Nov 3 1954
(47) July 1943	Linging ficld hospital of 59th divission	2	Confessed by ishida matsuo	Aug 20 1954
(48) Aug.~Sep. 1943	Chanygiu, 54th composit brigade of 59th division	1	Confessed by nagahama kenyu	Oct 8 1954
(49) Oct .1944	Yanzhou, Yanzhou army hospital	1	Confessed by tanemusa fumisan	Aug 21 1954
(50) Apr. 1938	Luan Xikum village, 108th division	1	Confessed by takanashi fumio	Nov 24 1954
(51) June 1938	Changzhi Xiyangshi, industry school	1	Confessed by sugishita kanzo	Aug 13 1954
(52) March 1940	Chunxian 3' rd composite brigade	1	Confessed by yoshizawa yukio	Nov 15 1954
(53) March 1940	Unit Xi hospital	2	Confessed by changzhuanfu	Apr 3 1954
(54) Autumn 1940	Linwu, 3' rd composite brigade	1	Confessed by airaku kamaji	Nov 22 1954
(55) June 1941	Datong, Datong army hospital	1	Confessed bymatsunaga mitsue	Nov 7 1954
(56) Sep .1941	Painkguan county garrison	2	Confessed bykikuchi syuichi	Mmarch 12 1955
(57) March 1942	Luan, Luan hospital	2	Confessed by kanisawa	Nov 20 1954
(58) Apr. 1942	Luan, Luan hospital	4	Confessed by kanisawa	Nov 20 1954
(59) Aug. 1942	Luan, Luan hospital	1	Confessed by kanisawa	Nov 20 1954
(60) March 1943	Luan, Luan hospital	2	Confessed by kanisawa	Nov 20 1954
(61) Apr .1944	Luan, Luan hospital	2	Confessed by kanisawa	Nov 20 1954
(62) Sep .1941	Luan, Luan hospital	1	Confessed by kanisawa	Nov 20 1954
(63) Jan. 1945	Luan, Luan hospital		Confessed by kanisawa	Nov 20 1954
(64) March 1945	Luan, Luan hospital	2	Confessed by kanisawa	Nov 20 1954
(65) June 1943	Jishan, 225th regiment of 37th division	1	Confessed by morino hiroaki	Nov 1954
(66) Jan .1944	Linfen, Linfen army hospital	10	Confessed by touyama tetsuo	Nov 18 1954
(67) Jan. 1944	Taiyuan , epidemic prevention and water supply uni .	8	Confessed by nakamusa sabwro	Aug 21 1954
(68) July 1944	Xianxian, Xianxian army hospital	2	Confessed by yoshizqwa yukio	Nov 15 1954
(69) July 1944	Xianxian, Xianxian army hospital	1	Confessed by zhang shanduo	Dec 25 1954
(70) Sep .1944	Xianxian, Xianxian army hospital	3	Confessed by duan xinkuan	Sug 11 1952
(71) Oct. 1944	Linfen, Linfen army hospital	1	Confessed by touyama tetsuo	Nov 18 1952
(72) Nov. 1944	Linfen, Linfen army hospital	3	Confessed by touyama tetsuo	Nov 18 1952
(73) June 1945	Xiangxian, Xiangxian army hospital	1	Confessed by kikuchi syuichi	March 12 1955
(74) July 1945	Xiangxian, Xiangxian army hospital	1	Confessed by nakamusa sabuso	Aug 21 1954

附錄:

日軍進行活體解剖記錄

發生時間	發生地	被活體解剖人數	證 據	
(1) 一九三五年九月	牡丹江披河陸軍醫院	1	雨海惠供認	一九五六年六月十八日
(2) 一九三六年六月	哈爾濱陸軍醫院	1	片桐濟三郎供	一九五四年八月十七日
(3) 一九三七年八月	密山陸軍醫院	1	雨海惠供	一九五六年六月十八日
(4) 一九三八年一月	虎林陸軍醫院	1	竹内豐供	一九五四年十一月
一九四二年	1855部隊濟南部隊	11	竹内豐供	一九五四年十一月
(5) 一九四0年十月	富錦陸軍醫院	1	小野武次供,	一九五四年七月十一日
(6) 一九四0年十二月	巴彥縣城南	1	高橋正銳供	一九五四年八月十三日
(7) 一九四三年三月	瓊琿西崗子陸軍醫院	1	中島崇一供	一九五四年七月
(8) 一九三四年九月	海龍縣,獨立守備第六大隊	1	川口保供	一九五四年八月十五日
(9) 一九三五年九月	敦化獨立守備第二隊	1	小川政夫供	一九五四年十月九日
(10) 一九三七年十一月	長春,新京陸軍醫院	3	宇津木孟雄供	一九五四年九月十日
(11) 一九三七年十二月	長春,新京陸軍醫院	1	渡邊長太夫供	一九五四年九月二十二日
(12) 一九三九年十一月至一九四0年二月	沈陽,南滿醫科大學	10	長島玉次郎供	一九五四年六月二十日
(13) 一九四0年九月	長春、南嶺	1	小美野義利供	一九五四年九月八日
(14) 一九三六年九月	赤峰、滿鐵赤峰醫院	1	小林喜一供	一九五四年六月十日
(15) 一九四二年至一九四三年	沈陽,南滿醫科大學	25	張丕卿(原醫大活體解剖助手)控 一九五四年六月二十九日	
(16) 一九三六年七月	沈陽,南滿醫科大學	1	渡邊長太夫供	一九五四年九月二十二日
(17) 一九四三年十二月	沈陽,南滿醫科大學	1	田村良雄供	一九五四年十月十日
(18) 一九四0年至一九四五年	林口,"七三一部隊"林口支隊			
(19) 一九四0年至一九四五年	牡丹江,"七三一部隊"牡丹江支隊			
(20) 一九四0年至一九四五年	孫吳,"七三一部隊"孫吳支隊			
(21) 一九四0年至一九四五年	海拉爾"七三一部隊"海拉爾支隊			
(22) 一九三二年至一九四五年	五常,背蔭河"東鄉部隊"			
(23) 一九四0年至一九四五年	哈爾濱,平房"七三一部隊"			
(24) 一九四0年至一九四五年	哈爾濱,孟家屯"一00部隊"			
(25) 一九三八年至一九四五年	北京"一八五五部隊"			
(26) 一九三九年至一九四五年	南京,"一六四四部隊"			
(27) 一九三九至一九四五年	廣州,"八六0四部隊"			
(28) 一九三六年至一九四五年	八寬子城			
(29) 一九三八年十二月	承德,陸軍醫院	1	太田秀清供	一九五四年八月十五日
(30) 一九三九年十二月	沙河,混成第八旅團	1	木田供	一九四四年二月七日
(31) 一九四0年五月	通縣,通州憲兵分隊	1	逢見谷正夫供	一九五四年十一月二十日
(32) 一九四0年七月	密雲,獨立守備第十六大隊	1	重富廣一供	一九五四年八月
(33) 一九四二年十月	保定,陸軍醫院	1	野田實供	一九五四年八月
(34) 一九四二年至一九四五年	安達試驗場	1		
(35) 一九四三年十一月	阜平,混成第三旅團	1	吉澤行熊供	一九五四年十一月十五日
(36) 一九四三年秋	阜平,混成第三旅團	1	吉澤行熊供	一九五四年十一月十五日
(37) 一九四四年五月	保定,陸軍醫院	2	林吾夫供	一九五四年四月二十日
(38) 一九三六年九月	鐵嶺,警察署	1	白井憲夫供	一九五四年七月二十六日
(39) 一九四四年七月	平谷,混成第十五旅團	1	三宮正三供	一九五四年七月三十日
(40) 一九三九年九月	陽武,第三十五師團	1	德久知正供	一九五四年八月十八日
(41) 一九三九年九月	新鄉,第二0四大隊	1	長田政雄供	一九五四年八月十八日
(42) 一九四四年十月	鄭州,第十二直轄兵站醫院	1	野田實供	一九五四年七月三十一日
(43) 一九四五年四月	焦作,第一一七師團野戰醫院	1	野田實供	一九五四年七月三十一日
(44) 一九四二年四至六月	濟南,陸軍醫院	2	長田友吉供	一九五四年八月四日
(45) 一九四二年九月	濟南,陸軍醫院	2	長田友吉供	一九五四年一月十一日
(46) 一九四四年六月	朝城,第五十九師團五十三旅團	1	小島隆男供	一九五四年十一月三日
(47) 一九四三年七月	臨清,第五十九師團野戰醫院	1	石田松雄供	一九五四年九月二十一日
(48) 一九四三年八九月	章丘,第五十九師團第五十四旅團	1	永濱健勇供	一九五四年十月八日
(49) 一九四四年十月	兗州,陸軍醫院	1	種村文三供	一九五四年八月二十一日
(50) 一九三八年四月	潞安,西關村第一0八師團	1	高梨文雄供	一九五四年十一月二十日
(51) 一九三八年六月	長治,西羊市工業學校	1	松下兼藏供	一九五四年八月十三日
(52) 一九四0年三月	崞縣,混成第三旅團	1	吉貝引雄供	一九五四年八月十三日
(53) 一九四0年秋	崞縣,西部隊醫院	2	張存福控	一九五四年十一月十五日
(54) 一九四0年七月	寧武,混成第三旅團	1	相樂圭三供	一九五四年十一月二十二日
(55) 一九四一年六月	大同,陸軍醫院	1	松永光穗供	一九五四年十一月七日
(56) 一九四一年九月	偏關,縣警備隊	1	菊池修一供	一九五五年三月十二日
(57) 一九四二年三月	潞安,陸軍醫院	2	湯淺謙供	一九五四年十一月二十日
(58) 一九四二年四月	潞安,陸軍醫院	4	湯淺謙供	一九五四年十一月二十日
(59) 一九四二年八月	潞安,陸軍醫院	1	湯淺謙供	一九五四年十一月二十日
(60) 一九四三年三月	潞安,陸軍醫院	2	湯淺謙供	一九五四年十一月二十日
(61) 一九四四年三月	潞安,陸軍醫院	2	湯淺謙供	一九五四年十一月二十日
(62) 一九四四年九月	潞安,陸軍醫院	1	湯淺謙供	一九五四年十一月二十日
(63) 一九四五年一月	潞安,陸軍醫院	1	湯淺謙供	一九五四年十一月二十日
(64) 一九四五年三月	潞安,陸軍醫院	2	湯淺謙供	一九五四年十一月二十日
(65) 一九四三年六月	稷山,第三十七師團,二二五聯隊	1	森野博明供	一九五四年十一月
(66) 一九四四年一月十五日	臨汾,陸軍醫院	10	遠山哲夫供	一九五四年十一月十八日
(67) 一九四四年一月	太原,第一軍防疫給水部	8	中村三郎供	一九五四年八月二十一日
(68) 一九四四年二月	崞縣,陸軍醫院	2	吉澤行雄供	一九五四年十一月十五日
(69) 一九四四年七月	崞縣,陸軍醫院	1	張三多控	一九五四年十二月二十五日

Sam Chen 陳憲中

Richard Y D Chen 朱永德

Y H Tam 譚汝謙

Sulia Chan 林翠玉

Jack Meng 孟憲章

C C Tien 田長焯

Mr. & Mrs. Thomas Keng Lu 陸鏗夫婦

Bak May Wong 黃碧瑂

Johnson Chiang 姜俊生

Paul Chang 張博明

程懷澄

陳裕如

Norman Yang 楊海平

Kai Ping Liu 劉開平

Shao Dan 邵丹

Barry Chang 陸錫恩

S Y Luk 張紹富

Quan Chen Pang 潘觀成

Wang Xing Chu 王性初

Mr. & Mrs. Seng Z. B. 沈珍寶夫婦

Mr. & Mrs. Ding L C 丁立中夫婦

Lisa Yang 楊華莎

Henry Lun Wong 汪倫

Dai Ming Kang 戴明康

Wang Xuan 王選

Tsuin Ho Kwoh 郭俊鍒

Mr. & Mrs. Adrew H K Tu 杜學魁夫婦

Kan Siu Ping 簡兆平

Albert Ho 何俊仁

Mr. & Mrs. T C Wang 王天循夫婦

Wang Kenneth & Jessia 王樹治夫婦

Trank Tao 陶繼臺

Marry Wu 吳尊白

Linda Pei 牛飛月

L J Luo 羅珞嘉

Lee Chao Qun 李超群

C Q Yin 尹集群

N Y Yin 尹立勇

Qu Xiao L 顏小荔

Wu S M 吳師孟

Geng K H 耿寬宏

Zhou K Y 周開業

張思萍

夏寶珍

陶耀宇

吳宗獄

楊子

陶孝忠

陳玉芳

劉體雲

何英珍

葉榮開

丁德望

劉述文

張禮忠

李明庭

王躍來

孫克福

李本福